AF247541

THE FORGING OF A PROPHET

TOM & MARIANNE KAPINOS

Anvil Publishing

The Forging of a Prophet

Copyright© 2018 by Tom and Marianne Kapinos

Cover Design by end2end books.co

All rights reserved. This book or any portion thereof may not be reproduced or used in any manner whatsoever without the express written permission of the author except for the use of brief quotations in a book review.

TABLE OF CONTENTS

INTRODUCTION

Join us on a riveting supernatural sojourn of visions revealing snippets of evidence connected to five murdered co-eds from Gainesville, Florida, in 1990.   A subsequent airplane ride to Florida with a television producer, film crew and a parapsychologist followed in an attempt to locate the murder weapon.

Law enforcement, a judge, the FBI, a newspaper reporter and others, both friend and foe, contribute to all the disappointments, clarity and small victories along the way.

From the wrong side of the supernatural realm to the incalculable spiritual and prophetic learning acquired at the feet of prophetic giants at MorningStar Ministries. Numbered among the humorous, serious, heartbreaking and some downright scary anecdotes include the first prophetic word received detailing the writing of this book, trances and even an experience of spiritual translocation, allowing our readers a glimpse into who we are and what we are about.

Our pilgrimage navigates the treacherous waters prophets struggle to swim and survive within the church today. Shining a light on the ignorance, unnecessary fear and envy, and in some cases abuse, will be recognized by all those with prophetic gifting endeavoring to find their place within the political church.

Tom recounts a ministry-time modern day Ananias and Sapphira episode that will have all God's servants paying close attention; and when God placed our little Fellowship in the shadow of one of Catholicism's greatest treasures it was definitely not for the purpose we assumed.

Finally, it is no coincidence the earth is experiencing an uptick in both the number and magnitude of earthquakes. Tom shares a timely prodigious prophetic message from the Lord for the church today exemplifying His absolute Love for His bride and all of humanity. It is written "judgment comes first to the house of God" speaking directly to current events plaguing the Christian Church today.

PROLOGUE

From Wikipedia

Danny Rolling

On August 28, 1990, the last 2 victims of serial killer Danny Rolling were discovered in Gainesville, Florida. He murdered five students in a four day span. One was a student at Santa Fe College and four attended the University of Florida. The murders received much media attention, and the unknown killer at the time was referred to as the Gainesville Ripper.

Photo from The Gainesville Sun

The first attack occurred early on August 24, 1990. Rolling broke into an apartment shared by Sonja Larson and Christina Powell. He found Powell asleep on a downstairs couch where he stood over her shortly but did not wake her up. Rolling then went upstairs and discovered Larsen sleeping in her bedroom. He then went back downstairs and taped Powell's mouth shut and stabbed her to death as she tried to fight for her life. Rolling then went upstairs and taped Larson's mouth shut and her wrists together behind her back. He then cut her clothes off and raped her, then forced her face down on the floor and stabbed her five times in the back. Rolling posed the bodies before leaving.

On August 25, 1990, a day later, Rolling broke into the apartment of Christa Hoyt. Hoyt was not home at the time, so he waited in the living room for her to return. At 11 a.m. Hoyt entered her apartment and was attacked from behind and was placed in a choke hold. After Rolling subdued Hoyt he taped her mouth shut and her wrists together and took her into the bedroom where he raped her. He then forced Hoyt to lay face down on the floor and stabbed her in the back. Rolling then decapitated the corpse and posed the head facing the corpse, to add to the shock value of whoever discovered her.

On August 27, 1990 Rolling broke into the apartment of Manny Taboada and Tracy Paules. Rolling encountered Taboada, a burly 200 lb man, in his bedroom as he awoke, and after a struggle, Rolling eventually killed him.

Upon hearing the commotion Paules went down the hall to Taboada's bedroom and encountered Rolling, Paules ran an attempted to barricade herself in her bedroom but Rolling broke down the door. He taped her mouth and wrists, cut off her clothing and raped her before rolling her on her stomach and stabbing her three times in the back. Paules' body was posed but Taboada's was left as it was.

All of the victim's, except Taboada, were petite Caucasian brunettes with brown eyes. Rolling was arrested on a burglary charge in Ocala, Florida. During that investigation his tools were matched to marks left at the Gainesville murder scenes. He was living in a small one man camp in a wooded area near the apartment complexes of those of the victim's. Investigators found recordings of Rolling singing songs alluding to the crimes. He was charged with several counts of murder in June 1992.

It took four years, after the murders, to bring Rolling to trial, and in 1994 just before it began, Rolling pled guilty to all charges. Rolling said his motive was to become a "superstar" like Ted Bundy. Rolling was sentenced to the death penalty on each count.

After Rolling was arrested, police in Louisiana contacted Florida authorities about an unsolved triple murder in Shreveport, Louisiana that occurred on November4, 1989. 55-year-old William Grissom, his 24-year-old daughter Julie and eight-year-old grandson Sean had been attacked in their home while preparing for dinner. Julie Grissom's body had been mutilated and posed.

Daniel Harold Rolling was executed by lethal injection at the Florida State Prison on October 25, 2006, after a last ditch appeal to the U.S. Supreme Court was denied. In a written statement shortly before his execution, Rolling confessed to the murders of the Grissom family in Shreveport.

.

PREFACE

During the late 1990's, at a prophetic conference, my wife and I were given a joint prophetic word. Jane, the middle-aged woman who was on the prophetic ministry team, informed us that together we would write a book. I was charged with narrating the text, while my wife was to be its wordsmith. During that meeting Jane appeared awestruck as she shared the Lord's revelation to her for us. She went on to say that He has shown us not even a third of what He has in store for us.

To be clear, my wife and I have never before written a book, nor are we teachers or scholars, or pastors, nor have we been accorded the accolades of men. The credentials we possess are our experiences with God and being fully known by Him. These experiences, more valuable than anything the world has to offer, are the reason we share them with you throughout this narrative.

For those of you with this book in hand, God has prepared you, as well, for the message contained herein. May God grant you the courage to put aside your preconceived understandings, and the wisdom to be open to the unveiling of the knowledge of Truth.

I thank God He has given me my wife, otherwise this book could never have been written, at least not in an English that could be understood. I have failed in school, business and ministry. My wife and I reside in the family homestead built by my mother and father which has been passed down to me.

So, I said, "Lord, there are many men more successful and smarter than I, men with degrees in theology, men that have a large ministry platform capable of reaching thousands, and men that speak more eloquently than I. Why would you choose me to deliver a message of this magnitude so denied by most of Christendom? I'll be shunned, labeled a heretic or worse."

The Lord replied, *"I groomed you for this time. The other men you speak of are afraid of losing their prized worldly possessions. They do not know Me."*

The message the Lord has given me will rock your religious foundation, just as it has mine.

Some of the names of the characters written about herein have been changed.

Those, whose names that have not been changed do not, in any way, endorse this narrative.

Note Preface: Many of the words written within this book include truths, as we understood and experienced them, and as they unfolded in real time. However, even as the knowledge of Truth was being revealed, later in time, is in some cases written in tandem within this narrative.

FOREWORD

Confined within the borders of this narrative is an incomplete compilation of a series of supernatural events experienced by me (Tom) beginning in August, 1991. I say an incomplete compilation because even though I have notes, journals and a certain chronology, per se, it is not important or possible to describe every jot and tittle.

The events began centered around the 1990 murders of 5 co-eds in Gainesville, Florida and have continued beyond Gainesville for 28 years, journeying into the realm of the Spirit farther than I ever could have imagined.

If you are a Christian and have ears to hear, it will culminate in the very shaking of your foundation. Perhaps, you will weep ashamed and sorrowful. If you are not a Christian, it will bring to you the ultimate Hope.

Join us as we share the most incredible spiritual adventure of a lifetime!

1

MY INTRODUCTION INTO THE SPIRIT REALM

Excerpted from my wife, Marianne's, 1995 college English thesis, the following paragraphs somewhat paraphrased, are included to illustrate where we were spiritually and in what manner our journey began.

Visions. The psychic realm. The paranormal. The spiritual realm. Do you love it or hate it? Do you embrace it or shun it? Is it fact or fallacy? Whatever your opinion, experience, or misinformation, I cannot deny my own initiation into this realm.

For those of us who believe in God, He works in mysterious ways. For those of us who do not believe in God, science has a long way to go to unlock the intricacies of the mind. For those of us who believe in neither, be cognizant of the fact that the anatomy and physiology of one's eye and brain can explain circumstances only so far.

Now don't get me wrong here. It's not that I eschewed psychics and their mumbo jumbo....er, rather their third eye revelations. I just didn't go for those things. However, in July, 1991, here we were, once again, my wife and her cousin both badgering....er, I mean, intensely persuading me to accompany them to Lily Dale, NY. You know the place. A medium's Shangri-La, a highway to heaven or hell. A community dedicated to metaphysical education. To me it was a total waste of time, not to mention money. I mean, c'mon, I am a businessman, an entrepreneur, a connoisseur of all things bottom line and tangible. Miracles and psychic phenomena garnered neither my interest nor concern. Nevertheless, being my wife can be as plucky as a banty rooster protecting his barnyard, on to Lily Dale we journeyed.

Upon arriving at our destination, I had a private reading with Reverend Gary Kane. This was my first meeting with him or any other psychic, for that matter. The reading was pleasant, but the heavens did not open up nor was I struck by lightning. All the same, he did mention a problem we were having with our driveway and he told me to fix my brakes. Hmmm... both were issues I was having. Maybe there was something to this psychic thing....or not. I was not a convert.

<u>Late Aug 1991</u>-During those dog days of summer, approximately three weeks after my reading at Lily Dale, I was walking down to the barn to tend to our horses. It was around 9:30-10:00 pm when I saw what appeared to be a window in the sky. This window had a silhouette of a person. Although a silhouette is black with no dimension, I had the distinct impression that this person was facing toward me. The vision lasted but 2-3 seconds. Quite stunned, my first

thought was what the heck is going on here? Could it be a sign of sorts? A sign? A sign of what? Oh man, I thought, I'm really losing it! Ok, with my eyes closed I silently implored, if this is a sign of something, send me another and give me a clue. As I slowly opened my eyes, I saw a falling star. Again, in disbelief, I asked for another sign. Upon opening my eyes, I witnessed the tail end of another falling star. Being a skeptic, I perceived this to be just a coincidence. Prove it I challenged what I could not see. Show me another. For the third time my challenge was met and a third star fell in the exact place where the other two stars had just fallen. I find it quite astonishing that God had me in that very spot with those very thoughts challenging Him to show me that He is God and He is omniscient.

Now, as even little children are aware, when one sees a falling star, we are to wish upon it. I wish I may, I wish I might have someone explain to me just what the heck is going on here!

When I returned to the house, contemplating the events at the barn and allowing it all to settle into my mind, I had to revisit my whole attitude concerning the supernatural. I was quite negative in my thinking and fought against the validity of such foolishness for years. Perplexed, I shared the events which had just unfolded with my wife.

Unable to sleep and long into the night, we shared our feelings and thoughts regarding the incident. My wife offered that long ago she had read or heard that a window with a silhouette referred to an opening, an awakening, something to be evidenced. In an attempt to make me feel that I wasn't alone in experiencing something like this, Marianne shared an incident that happened to her when she was a teenager.

One windy summer night she and her girlfriends walked over to the nearby creek, located within the golf course, in order for her friend, Higgy, to savor a smoke, as in cigarette. This was a place the friends frequently gathered to girl-talk. Being they were not golfing, not to mention the fact it was after hours, they really should not have been there. As the three friends were sitting on the retaining wall by the creek, chitchatting and gossiping, with Higgy smoking her cigarette, Marianne said she heard her name being called on the wind. She said she jumped and the little neck hairs stood on end. "Hey, did anyone else hear that?" she asked.

"Hear what?" they chorused. Marianne didn't answer but continued to strain her ears for the sound.

Again, she heard her name called and with her voice an octave higher and louder inquired, "Can't you guys hear my name on the wind?"

"What? What are you yapping about?" Higgy retorted. You see, Higgy wasn't quite ready to leave as she was fighting against the wind finagling to keep her lighter lit, hoping for another smoke before the friends had to leave.

"C'mon, you guys, let's get outta here now! I'm serious," the young teenaged Marianne yelled. In those days virtually nothing gave my wife the heebie-jeebies. So, the girls didn't ask twice; they just all ran from the golf course, splashing their way down the puddle pocked dark road.

My wife also reminded of the time in 1979 when we lived in the city. I was at work, the kids were at an overnight at my parents' home, and Marianne was mowing the back lawn with a push mower. It was hot and muggy and she was sweaty and tired and longed to finish mowing the weeds masquerading as a grass. Just at that moment she heard her grandmother call her from the house. Her first reaction was to finish the lawn and then she would go in the house to see what her grandmother's need was. She heard her Gram call again. Exasperated, she stomped into the back hall to find out what was so terribly important that couldn't wait another few minutes. "What, Gram, what?" she yelled from the kitchen door. No answer. With a heavy sigh she began to untie her grass-stained sneakers before entering the kitchen. It was then it hit her. Marianne began to weep as she realized her Gram wasn't there because she had passed away the week prior.

Being this was my first supernatural encounter, her sharing was a comforting reminder that these things do happen.

September 1991 - My wife and I own and operate a retail drapery and floor covering business. The pace is often hectic and fraught with minor frustrations and time delays, leading to potentially explosive situations. Needless to say, little time was available to ponder white lights and windows in the sky.

However, one day in September, 1991, as I was travelling from job to another, fretting over the fact that I was behind schedule, I faced a bad feeling of huge proportions. Out of the blue, I had a spontaneous thought that I was to meet someone placed in the college town of Gainesville, Florida, where in August, 1990, five college students were slain. Now keep in mind, this gruesome crime took place a full year prior to my forewarning and 1500 miles away. I did read about it in the Buffalo newspaper, but it was a rather small article relegated to one of the back pages. I remember feeling very remorseful, while reading the article, at the loss of such young and vibrant life, especially in light of the fact that we had two young adult children of about the same age. But beyond that I did not dwell upon it to the extent that it would suddenly manifest itself in my thoughts during a very busy time for me. My brain was feverishly attempting to process this revelation as I arrived at my customer's home. Inopportunely, there was no time for contemplation as I completed my installation and received a nice tip for a job well done. Besides, tomorrow's installation needed my total focus.

This particular window treatment installation was a commercial job of mammoth scope. The blueprints did not show the hollow walls or steel beams lurking behind the drywall. Nonetheless, after 12 hours, 3 cut fingers, 7 broken drill bits, and one cranky assistant, it was time to go home. Ah, yes, but first, we must exchange pleasantries with the tenant whose vertical blinds we had just installed. "Yes, they are practical. Oh yes, please rotate the vanes before they are traversed. Call me if any problems. Yes, the economy is in a shambles. The politicians are, indeed, greedy. Oh yes, I do agree." So on and so forth.

The electrician on the site had by this time joined our conversation and was going on about the retirees in the south and sharing how they will pay just about anything to have work done. He continued his monologue with, "About 1-1/2 years ago I moved up from Gainesville and…." Excuse me, my tired mush of a brain attempted to comprehend. Gainesville…as in Florida…a couple of years ago did he say? With my mind reeling attempting to do the math, a couple of years ago in Gainesville would put the electrician squarely in the timeline of the coed murders. With my knees a knockin', I rode the elevator with this chap chitchatting about his new home, as the blood pounded in my ears! Is this the connection to the Gainesville murders that I'm supposed to encounter? Omigod, what in the heck was I supposed to do now? I needed to confide in someone, but who would believe it? If these events were occurring to me and I bore skepticism how, in the world, would anyone in authority believe me? The thought of contacting law enforcement left me feeling shaky and ridiculous.

Ok, I thought, I'll just pass this information onto the authorities and that will be the end of it. They'll all get a good chortle out of it and my responsibility is fulfilled. I'll contact the FBI, I rationalized. They're secretive, confidential, and competent. And besides, I reasoned, our company did an installation for both the FBI and one of their senior agents. Surely, they remembered me as stable, well balanced and lucid.....right?

My strategy fell flat on it's, or perhaps, my face. Mr. FBI's phone number was unlisted and our business record of his personal information was nowhere to be found. I was feeling pretty conflicted. On one hand, I was anxious to pass this thing, whatever it was, off to bigger shoulders, while at the same time, I felt a complete fool. Maybe that was a sign my plan was ludicrous. Maybe Mr. FBI would think I was just another kook.

Serendipitously, several days later Mr. FBI, to my surprise, was on the evening sports news being interviewed, as a sports fan, exiting a professional football game. He was not identified by name, but I sure recognized him! Please keep in mind that I had not had any contact with Mr. FBI in better than a year, and while agonizing over whether or not to contact him, he shows up on live television. This definitely was NO coincidence! This prompted a more intensive search of our customer records to ferret out his phone number.

Of all the impossible places to find our customer's sales record was puzzling. Tearing apart the stored boxes and files of past customers finally paid off. Somehow, the invoice had slid behind a file cabinet drawer and was wedged tightly into a corner. How in the world did it end up there? I had no idea. Armed with his phone number I made the call.

Mr. FBI agent was very cordial and helpful as he advised that I contact another agent in a different department, who in turn asked that I write everything down and submit it to him. This I endeavored to do however, not for nearly a year later. At this juncture, I had used up my reserve courage of contacting the authorities. There was a battle of major proportions between intellect and rational thinking vs things of the murky spiritual realm; because spiritual things are foolishness to the carnal mind! And carnal I was!

As for the electrician on the elevator who had my knees knocking and heart pounding, was all for naught, as I would later come to understand. He had no part in the actual crime, but was simply a conduit of affirmation of the open vision of the silhouette in the window, experienced back in August, 1991. What I was to be shown, in the future, all pertained to the Gainesville murders.

<u>October 1991</u>- One fall night, after retiring for the evening, I fell into a peaceful sleep. Suddenly, I awoke and sat up. Approximately four feet from the foot of the bed I saw what appeared to be a hologram of sorts. The illumination was a three inch square. As I attempted to reach for this holographic light, my wife awoke with the testy exclamation of "Tom, what are you doing?!" With no reply, as she related to me the following morning, I promptly lay down and was once again fast asleep.

Over morning coffee we discussed the previous night's adventure. I shared that I felt neither threatened nor fearful of the peculiar brilliance; the truth of the matter being that I was unwillingly being drawn into the realism of the spiritual realm.

<u>November 1991</u>- What is to follow is a series of occurrences that happened over a period of months.

Yet again, I just completed my evening routine of filling the water buckets for the horses, filling their feed pails, supplying their hay and throwing down fresh straw for bedding. I turned out the lights to the barn and was heading up to the house. After a long day, I was tired and looking forward to nothing more than having some supper, watching the news report and some of my favorite TV programs when I was compelled to look upward and behind me. As I did so, what I perceived was a face I did not recognize. Startled, I stopped short, gazing up at the manifestation. My distinct impression was that this face, in the sky, belonged to one of the victims of the Gainesville slayings. Oh boy, here we go again I thought. This was not going to go away! It was a constant reminder of a tragic crime. As a consequence, I was inspired to record the events in a journal. Perhaps, I thought, this is what I should have been doing all along. This was attested to by the advent of ongoing occurrences.

Sure enough, sometime days later, I started to take notice to a cloud formation in the black velvet, otherwise cloudless, starry sky. The letters G-A-I-N-E-S, in white, and then the letter T appeared. Next, what looked to be an astrological sign unfolded. (Unlike today with the instant gratification of knowledge via the internet, it was different back then. I was not readily able to ascertain the significance of this astrological sign until about 6 month later.) Following that sign the letters C-A-L-L came into view. Finally, a heavenly hand began to pen my name above me as if printing on glass. I could see the letters appear as one would witness the lettering from the opposite side of the glass. I challenged the tangibility of the phenomenon. Did I form those letters myself, in my own mind, like one does when one conceives images in the clouds? (Well, I suppose if a heavenly hand could write a message on a wall to Belshazzar, Nebuchadnezzar's son (Daniel 5:5), I guess He could write in the sky or however else He wanted to communicate!) Was I to contact the authorities?

My anxiety to achieve clarity started to ramp up as I continued to make my way up to the house. The night was unseasonably mild for late fall in Boston, NY. I stopped at the babbling brook by the meadow which in summer is filled with fireflies lighting the night. It is a very peaceful and serene setting, perfect for prayer and contemplation. Appealing to God, I inquired as to whether I was on the right track to clarity and understanding. I, again, was compelled to look up; a misty circle, at about a 45 degree angle formed approximately 75 feet above me. The circle was approximately 50 feet in circumference. As I gazed upon the circle with bewilderment and awe for what seemed to be forever was probably only 10 seconds. Then to my astonishment letters began to form within the circle. With a pounding heart I witnessed a Y-E-S, again in white lettering. The letters spelled out my answer which was YES! Then the mist of the word YES vaporized and slowly taking its place was what appeared to be the image of a long haired man cloaked in white raiment. With his arms extended down to me, rays of light emanated from each hand. In the presence of this image I felt a peace which dispelled my anxiety. At the same time, I was totally weakened to the point where I struggled to keep myself standing upright. Time was suspended and I have no sense of how long I stood there. The figure disappeared and I continued up to the house in a state of rubber-kneed astoundment.

As I entered the house, my wife greeted me with, "What happened? Are you alright?" I couldn't reply. "Tom," she implored. "You're white as a sheet! What's going on? Tell me. Please, tell me what happened to you", she urged, placing her hand on my forehead as though feeling for a fever and escorting me to a kitchen chair.

"You will not believe what just happened to me, again," I replied.

As I continued to seek understanding into this realm I was experiencing, I contacted a woman who billed herself as a transpersonal counselor. At this meeting I told her nothing, at first, of the occurrences. She did my astrological chart and told me that there was psychic activity opening up to me. After the discussion of the meaning of my chart, toward the end of our session, I related the events that happened thus far. The counselor encouraged me to seek out a spiritualist and to contact the authorities. My confidence was still shaky, and I was too mortified to approach the authorities, continuing to operate with my rational thinking reality.

Nevertheless, even though I was thinking with a rational mind, the irrational manifestations continued to occupy my logical reasoning! Shortly thereafter, I continued to have manifestations, if you will, all pertaining to Gainesville, Florida.

<u>Dec 1991</u>-In the winter of 1991, I sought advice from Reverend Gary Kane, whom I previously met in Lily Dale, NY, in July, 1991. Reverend Gary Kane resides in Lily Dale only during the summer months. Being December, I called him and made an appointment to make the four hour trek to meet with him at his home in Ohio. As Reverend Gary greeted me at his office, he remarked, "There certainly is an awful lot of psychic activity happening around you!"

Bewilderment and relief fought for dominance, so I said nothing in response.

As I described my encounters, thus far, Reverend Gary first clarified the window with a silhouette vision. "Being the window was opened and the silhouette facing forward", he expounded, "you are to be shown something. Conversely, had the window been closed and the figure facing away, death would be indicated", he concluded.

Secondly, Reverend Gary confirmed my desire to approach the authorities.

"But they'll think I'm looney", I lamented.

"Yes, probably", countered Gary. "But, what's there to lose?"

"Easy for him to say", I thought.

Gary, in turn, shared his murder investigation experience, and also, his intense zeal to avoid said encounters. Indignantly, he admitted, insulting skepticism was ill-fitting.

On the return trip home, my perplexity magnified. On one hand, Gary had corroborated my conviction of approaching the authorities; on the other, facing possible ridicule hindered that disclosure.

2

THE DOOR

No time to ponder the issue as supernatural information hailed fast and furious. Images of an astrological sign, a deer, a curved knife, a set of goal posts, a group of unusual trees and the state of Florida which housed the numbers 6, 10, and 90, the images of a guy and a girl, and another girl walking her dog, decided to introduce themselves to me over the course of the next 8 months. What?! Are you kidding me?! Who sees this kind of stuff? Who else does this happen to?

 One by one, in silent affirmation, each conspicuous image, resembling the negative of a photograph, commenced to metamorphose upon a wooden door within the confines of our home. Trepidation and relief fought for control. Relief reigned victorious. Yes, stuff like this does happen! This was really real! The images were proportioned and recognized by friends and family. I had my tangible evidence and my sanity justified!

Intellectually deducing the facts from these graphic likenesses lent sway to the following ramifications. 1) A set of goal posts indicated a school or athletic field. 2) The state of Florida, being self-explanatory, reinforced an earlier discernment. The number 90 related to the year in which the murders occurred. 3) A group of unusual trees suggested a wooded area. 4) The deer posed a mystifying query. Although woods define their habitat in this area, would these cud-chewing, hoofed mammals roam in Florida? 5) Lastly, the curved knife denoted an obvious weapon.

A sense of profound certainty was that the girl with a dog was Christa Hoyt. My perception of her anguish and despair would cause a wrenching of my heart more than any other. Literally reduced to tears, an utter and deep sorrow engulfed me as murky black water claims a drowning man. It's important to understand that I am not an emotional type of guy. But, somehow, this moved me. The feelings I had while reading the account of the murders was amplified ten-fold because the manifestations made it all the more palpable.

In addition to being a chemistry honor student at Santa Fe College, Christa Hoyt also worked for the Alachua County Sheriff's Office as a records clerk. She planned to attend the University of Florida.

Shaken to my very foundation, closure was needed. At this juncture, this was an unsolved murder with an ongoing investigation. The police had no suspects. This was a three million dollar manhunt with hundreds of law enforcement personnel on the case, including the FBI.

In order to interpret my strangely procured affliction, I enrolled in a paranormal course at a local community college. Although I ascertained a great deal concerning the paranormal, little light was shed with regard to my situation amid the duration of this course. However, the instructor graciously accepted my invitation to visit my home to view the manifestations on the door and offer insight into my experiences. Acknowledged by the clairvoyant/teacher were, indeed, manifestations upon the wooden door, as well as, spiritual activity in our home. One very important revelation that came from this meeting centered on the astrological symbol which appeared to me in the November, 1991 sky and now appeared on the door. At that time, I had no understanding of its meaning. The instructor explained to me that this was the sign for Pluto, which is the sign for transformation.

Metamorphosis is a synonym for transformation and is defined in the dictionary as to change from one form to another. The astrological meaning of Pluto is the metamorphosis of circumstance, drastic change out of nowhere, leaving nothing as it used to be. It brings revelations of the unforeseen and of the mind and the way to look at the world! Little did I understand then the degree to which change had commenced!

In return for attending this course, my instructor shared with me the name of a psychic from Pennsylvania.

Jake Zane has assisted in a myriad of police investigations, in addition to lecturing in respect to the topic. A lengthy and earnest telephone conversation ensued, whereby Jake enlightened me of the enormous responsibility correlating to psychic ability. Jake cautioned a reputable witness and an escort accompany any foolhardy, solo pursuit, lest the acrimonious finger of accusation be pointed solely toward the innocent. This profound advice resulted from Jake's own pathetic and unfortunate incriminations, in lieu of his novice exuberance in sustaining law enforcement queries.

In the interim, I continued to pray for guidance. His response was a cloak of loving protection. The Almighty granted me peace of mind, allayed my fears and promised closure. As entangling uncertainties persisted, this trust in faith was a most welcomed assurance, for the moment.

3

GAINESVILLE

Entreating the support of an incorrectly assumed parapsychology group listed among the credits of a television network program, the segment producer replied in kind. After much soul searching, I acquiesced to film an episode in Florida with the anticipation of uncovering the murder weapon associated with the horrific crime. This experience became part of a valuable learning process.

With Dr. Karson Hargrove, a parapsychologist called in at the behest of this group, our entourage made the pilgrimage to the deceased students' prior residences. The Gatorwood apartments, where Manuel Toboada and Tracy Paules, both age twenty-three years were slain, and the Williamburg complex, where Sonya Larsen, age eighteen years, and Christina Powell, age seventeen years were found, held mute testimony to the grisly crimes committed nearly two years ago. In sharp contrast, the ill-lit grounds of the lonely bungalow, surrounded by wild and overgrown foliage, where

Christa Hoyt, age eighteen years, was found decapitated, screamed the inequity of the horror!

As Dr. Hargrove, the film crew, my wife and I silently inspected the property my previous heart-felt emotions for this young woman overcame the group. Unabashed tears filled the eyes of the producer, film crew, doctor and initiator. In turn, each witness expressed dumbfounded shock at the depth of overwhelming melancholy for this stranger. An indescribable ocean of depression and desperation saddened my soul.

Introspection was curbed as the irate landlord with car wheels spinning, churning up stones and dust, fishtailed into the driveway. Unceremoniously, and without regard for deportment, this lord of the manor quite vocally ordered the premises vacated. Later, revelations exposed the mind-numbing lawsuit with which this man was embroiled. It was later learned that Christa had complained numerous times concerning slipshod safety measures around her abode. Further evidence indicated that Christa Hoyt's murderer gained access to her room through an improperly installed sliding glass door.

We were given an itinerary by the show's producer of possible sites to visit as fit the criteria of the visions including the goal posts, deer and wooded area. After our encounter with the landlord at Christa Hoyt's residence, everyone was on edge due to the fact that we had no permission to enter any of the properties that we did except for the Santa Fe Community College. The show's producer stated that we would be "running and gunning" and did not want to make contact with anyone, including the Gainesville Police

Department, unless anything remotely approaching a clue appear. The fear was that we would not be allowed to do anything or go anywhere.

Sitting in a vehicle behind the University of Florida, everyone exited the car. Walking through the convenient store parking lot, we made our way to the overgrown brush and hundreds of sapling area that lay beyond the campus. As we attempted to enter the area, Susan Fargo, segment producer, shouted out, "You'll be trespassing on private property!" I was insistent about walking into that overgrowth, so powerful was my draw to that area.   However, Susan, after being traumatized by the outraged landlord, was fearful and reiterated that we had no permission to be there and we would be trespassing. Back and forth, back and forth we volleyed. No amount of pleading convinced Susan to acquiesce. Dr. Hargrove agreed with her. As we had no control and little say in where we went or what we could do, Marianne and I were outvoted. They decided that we would visit Santa Fe Community College, instead, where we did have permission to film.

 Santa Fe Community College was our concluding sojourn where Christa Hoyt and Manny Toboada attended classes. Unique to this particular college is a teaching zoo on campus. Within this zoo are deer (vison one). We later learned the teaching zoo was moved from the University of Florida to Santa Fe Community College. Also on this campus, workmen were erecting a nursery school on the grounds of the former athletic field (vision three). Last, but not least, amongst a group of beautiful green, exotic trees, stood the tallest tree, dead and deformed (vison four). Contrary to the fact this site appeared to fit the criteria, I was not beckoned to explore here in equal manner to the overgrowth at the University.

The crew scrambled for shovels and the rented metal detector to locate vision two (the curved knife). However, as he was proving to be the quintessential impediment to all things discoverable, Dr. Hargrove cautioned the folly. He admonished the police be present, for the weapon may be uncovered. Adding insult to injury, in order to satisfy a "deadline", the show's producer, Andy Roth, allotted all of ten minutes to film us "digging" to conclude that week's television episode. He needed the film to be overnighted to the production studio for editing in time for the next show's airing.

To have traveled this far to be thwarted was a major disappointment. The naive realization for us was that they were not there to help us, but to sensationalize a show segment.

We weren't looking for recognition. In fact, at our request, our faces were blocked out and my voice was altered. For us, it was bringing to conclusion months of uncertainty delving into the spirit realm, experiencing things way outside my understanding, knowledge and moxie.

However, the point was moot. On June 10, 1992, while my wife and I were filming this episode for the network's weekly show, Danny Rolling, a thirty-six year old drifter, was charged with the 1990 murders. Serving time for an unrelated string of burglaries, he pleaded not guilty to five counts of first degree murder, three counts of rape and three counts of robbery. The District Attorney issued a "gag" order on any information and the police declined their support. However, all indications suggested that the police still had no murder weapon. The investigation would continue for almost 2 more years. It was the largest, most expensive manhunt in Florida's history at a cost of three million dollars! (Los Angeles Times)

When I read the article in the Los Angeles Times, it brought to mind a conversation I had had with a NY State Trooper friend of mine. Ralph was head of the Blood Hound Division and spent 35 years in service, as well as, serving as a small town judge. As we discussed my situation he gave me his take on it. "What are you looking for?" he asked. "Are you looking for credit? Tell your story. But, if you're looking for credit, even if you find the murder weapon, forget it. You're not going to get the credit because every agency and police officer involved in this thing is going to want to claim that glory. This is how they receive their promotions, son. Don't think for one minute they'll give credit to some "delusional" guy in Buffalo who sees visions and things in the sky!"

My friend, Ralph, was a cop. Cops deal in facts. I took his counsel to heart, which would soon bear out interacting with the Gainesville police.

Previously cited, the number 6 and the number 10 were both metamorphosed over the state of Florida, along with the number 90, which was the year of the murders. The coincidental thing about this is the fact that our flight was delayed by one day. We were supposed to fly down to Florida on June 9. Nonetheless, as we landed in Florida on June 10, the breaking news was that Danny Rolling was charged with the murders! Before this I had no idea of the significance of the numbers 6 and 10. It was astonishing and encouraging to have this affirmation!

Upon returning to the hotel, from our brief, limited and restricted opportunity to explore my revelations, spirits were uplifted. The Gainesville police granted the coveted interview. On arriving at the police station, a young and extremely rude officer disclosed that we were not welcomed. Conversely and appreciatively, a lieutenant, in charge of public relations, was a receptive and generous hostess. While the cameras rolled, the lieutenant delivered a generic speech observing the "gag" order, noting the hundreds of tips received, thus far, and expressing sympathy for the families. When the official interview concluded, I had a private conversation with the police representative. I tentatively offered my vision data, unsure of her acceptance.

Much to my surprise, the lieutenant shared my belief in the unexplained as related to a personal incident regarding a family member. However, the official response indicated that police investigators were veterans and quite reluctant to accept intangible information. She assured me that the data, I had so generously shared, would find its way to the one detective who may take the initiative. However, the lieutenant promised nothing.

Patiently waiting in a hotel room, all that evening and most of the following day, for the phone call from the detective, proved fruitless. Crestfallen, it was time to return home. Although these efforts culminated in a dead-end, there were other avenues to travel.

4

VALIDATED

Upon arriving home, in New York, a videotape of the wooden door manifestations was posted to the Director of Research at The Institute for Parapsychology and telephone calls placed to the Assistant District Attorney, Gainesville, Florida and a certain reporter of the Miami Herald.

The Institute for Parapsychology catalogued the information, which is basically their function. As interest was expressed the Director clarified, at this point, not enough data was present. However, he offered those with psychic ability tandemly have the same ability to project images. To me, this made little sense as others were able to view my "projections".

An account of events was posted to the Gainesville Assistant District Attorney. However, this elicited no response. The Miami Herald reporter avowed polite appeal, albeit, his demeanor indicated more important stories to investigate. That is, until sometime in February, 1993.

On that date, the Miami Herald reported that Danny Rolling had confessed and was cooperating with the authorities. Rolling informed investigators that he had buried three things: the murder weapon, which was a large knife, bloody gloves, and a baggie with body parts. The site, which Rolling denoted, is located approaching the University of Florida. To arrive there, you must follow a dirt road between two fences. The road narrows into a little used path, which splits a meadow and an area thick with bushes. The excavation is fifty feet down the path, which is surrounded by woods, swamp and a grassy area. The old wooden building on the property has about a dozen open stables.

Although we were within the perimeter of this area of the University of Florida, in spite of my insistence, this noteworthy site was denied access. As noted prior, the producer did not have permission to explore the grounds. Precious little time was spent at this location as we were ordered back to the car before we could venture any farther.

In a phone conversation, John Donnelly, from The Miami Herald, stated the area of the search is known locally as "The Old Deer Pen", where deer were housed for an extended period of time. Did you catch that? "The Old Deer Pen"! What a significant discovery! All these months of trepidation, uncertainty, ridicule, thwarted searching and attempts to understand were finally being validated. My portent involving deer proved factual. Had I been given the lead way back in June, 1992, to explore the area that was of my choosing, the turn of events would have been so different. Perhaps, what I had to offer would have been received with more plausibility and integrity. Not only were we in the area of the three items proffered by Rolling, we were in the area where his campsite was situated. At his campsite, investigators found incriminating tapes, tools, his guitar and other personal items. The police did not conduct an excavation of the deer pen or find his campsite for some eight months, thereafter.

Police investigators had indicated that "something" was recovered at this site. Inopportunely, to reiterate, the "gag" order prevented concession.

From the Miami Herald newspaper dated February 10, 1993:

GAINESVILLE-In unusual jailhouse meetings with investigators probing the 1990 Gainesville student murders, suspect Danny Harold Rolling provided information that – if it checks out – implicates him in the five homicides, two knowledgeable sources outside the task force said Tuesday.

For nearly a week, a dozen investigators have been digging with shovels and three bulldozers in and around an abandoned University of Florida open-air stable. When a Miami Herald reporter approached the site Tuesday, surprised authorities escorted him away from the digging and then strung up yellow crime scene tape across a dirt path, blocking access.

The sources, who have talked with task force members, said Rolling informed investigators that he buried three things: the murder weapon, which was a large knife; bloody gloves; and a baggie with body parts.

At 4 p.m., police stopped the excavation for the day. Detectives photographed and video-taped the scores of two-feet-deep holes in and around the building, but declined to say whether they had found any evidence.

"Just doing a little digging," added Gainesville police Detective Steve Kramig, one of the lead investigators in the case.

"We're about halfway through," said Alachua County Sheriff Steve Oelrich.

Rolling (pronounced ROLE-ing), 38, has maintained his innocence in the killings of five college students in August 1990. He is serving five consecutive life terms for a series of unrelated robberies and break-ins and is being held at Florida State Prison in Starke. His trial for the Gainesville slayings isn't set until fall.

His lawyer, Public Defender Richard Parker, did not return telephone messages left at his Gainesville office.

Will Irby, task force spokesman, would only confirm that digging was under way: "We're in search of some evidence and beyond that I'm not able to respond."

The digging started last Wednesday or Thursday, according to Matt Robinson, a Jiffy Lube employee. The site is about 100 yards north of the Jiffy Lube, a Sprint Food Store and three other buildings on Southwest Archer Road and across the street from Gatorwood Apartments – the site of the third murder scene.

Investigators started the search after discussions with Rolling and Bobby Lewis, another inmate. Lewis, a convicted killer, is best known as the only person ever to escape from Florida's Death Row. After he was recaptured, his sentence was commuted to life.

In the unusual meetings last week, which the sources said were requested by Rolling through Lewis, the task force investigators asked Lewis about the murders.

Lewis, who was locked up at the time of the killings and is not a suspect in the case, answered the questions based on information Rolling had given him. The sources said that at times Rolling interjected.

It was not known who told investigators about where to find the murder weapon and two other pieces of evidence. It also was not known whether Rolling had confessed or why he had Lewis relaying information for him. Lewis and Rolling are being held in the high security "V wing" at the Starke prison.

Also still in question is whether the statements made by Lewis and Rolling will be admissible in court. The key point is whether Rolling initiated the contact with authorities.

In the case Massiah vs. United States, the U.S. Supreme Court ruled in 1964 that authorities cannot initiate contact with a defendant after indictment without informing the defendant's lawyer.

If Rolling initiated the contact, authorities appear to be on safe legal ground, said Rebekah J. Poston, a former prosecutor and now a Miami criminal defense attorney.

"In talking to my associates, we felt there was no Massiah problem if Rolling contacted authorities on his own," said Poston, a partner in the firm of Fine Jacobson Schwartz Nash Block and England. "It is illegal if the officers initiated the contact."

The killings sent waves of fear through this North Florida college town. Thousands fled. Hundreds more bought guns.

The victims were all bright young students: Sonja Larson, 18, of Deerfield Beach; Christi Powell, 17, of Jacksonville; Christa Hoyt, 18, of Gainesville; Tracy Paules, 23, of Miami; and Manny Taboada, 23, of Miami.

The case against Rolling so far has been largely reliant on DNA evidence from the scenes. Investigators say they have a match between semen at the murder scenes and Rolling's blood type, although they have never publicly disclosed the strength of that evidence.

Still, investigators have been plagued by being unable to solve some mysteries in the case.

One is: Where's the murder weapon?

Tuesday, under a warm sun, investigators were dressed in jeans and T-shirts as they dug in the old animal pens. It looked like a construction site with huge mounds of fill. No guns or badges were visible.

To get there, you must follow a dirt road between two fences. The road narrows into a little-used path, which splits a meadow and an area thick with bushes.

The excavation is 50 feet down the path. Mounds of dirt are piled on the west side of the stable, which is surrounded by woods, swamp and a grassy area.

The old wooden building has about a dozen stables. Its aluminum roof was covered by leaves. Investigators operated two bulldozers. A third one sat idle. The search could go on for days. The crime scene area covers nearly an acre. (End of article)

****

In a related article dated February 14, 1993, the Miami Herald reported the following:

MIAMI (AP) - The man awaiting trial in the 1990 slayings of five Gainesville college students has confessed and is cooperating with authorities, the Miami Herald reported Saturday.

Danny Harold Rolling, 38, had pleaded innocent in the case and is serving a life sentence for a string of unrelated robberies. The paper, quoting four unidentified sources, said Rolling has given details of the stabbings to investigators, including why he chose the victims.

The five victims, all students at the University of Florida or nearby Santa Fe Community College, were found slain in campus-area apartments in late August 1990. Will Irby, spokesman for the slayings task force, said he could neither confirm nor deny the Herald report. A closed-door hearing in the Rolling case is scheduled for this week.

Rolling recently began talking to investigators directly, the Herald said, although much of the information has been passed through his inmate friend Bobby Lewis, who is serving a life sentence for murder.

Early last week, investigators searched an animal pen near the site of one killing. The Herald said they were looking for a knife, rubber gloves and body parts Rolling confessed to burying nearby.

Police found something, but refused to say what, the newspaper reported. (End of article)

Photos from the Miami Herald

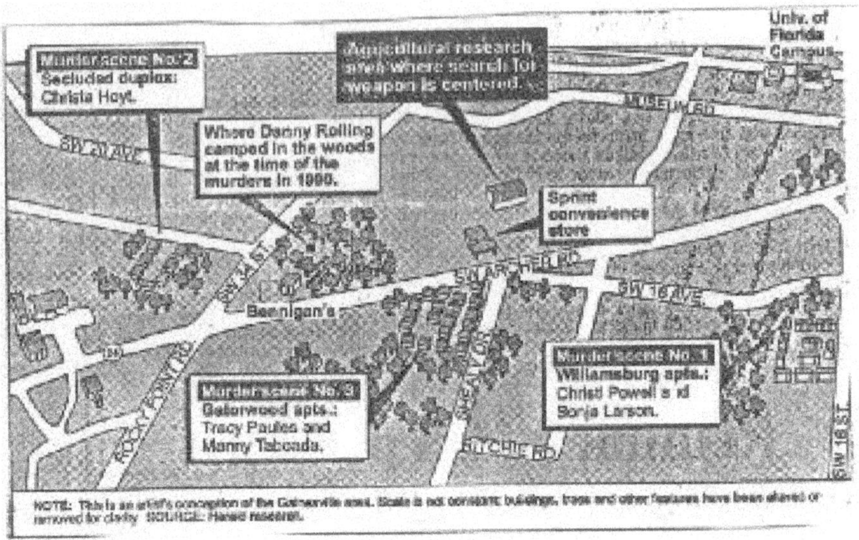

LOOKING FOR EVIDENCE: An investigator in Gainesville searches an abandoned stable site near the University of Florida on Thursday for clues to the August 1990, murders of five students.

Being Danny Rolling confessed to the co-ed murders of 1990 on the eve of his trial, no trial date was set. He was sentenced to death and executed October 25, 2006.

5

LOOK TO ME

The impact of this whole ordeal left me with more questions than answers. Obviously, there is more outside the norm than our everyday experiences. Paranormal is just that...outside the norm. I've had readings by psychics, clairvoyant classes and teachings, and dabbled with a Ouija board, which can have serious repercussions. However, none of these things were filling the void or satisfying my hunger for knowledge and understanding. I was endeavoring to understand my experiences intellectually, when the experience itself was supernatural.

Some months after my conversation with John Donnelly, of the Miami Herald, I was enjoying my morning coffee pondering my whole experience, all the while gazing at the wooden door where all the manifestations began to appear sometime prior. Gazing over the images I noticed something quite different that stood out to me. It was not there beforehand. Lo and behold... what to my wondering eyes should appear......the face of Jesus?! Jesus, as in Christ, complete with His crown of thorns?! To say I was incredulous, dumbstruck and awed is an understatement!

Just at that moment, I heard my wife's footsteps coming down the spiral stairs. I said to myself, let's see what she sees. We exchanged our good mornings at the breakfast counter, while outlining our day over coffee. After a few moments, I said, "I want you to look at the door in the upper left hand corner and tell me what you see."

"Oh no", she said. "Not again", she said. "Please say it isn't so", she said.

"What do you see?" I prompted. She didn't answer right away, but continued looking. Again, I urged, "What do you see?" still nothing. I'm thinking to myself can she not see this? I didn't want to influence her lest I "project" the image onto the door, as erroneously stated by Dr. Brown from the Institute of Parapsychology.

Then, with a hushed voice, she responded with, "I see the face of Jesus with His crown of thorns."

With that acknowledgement, we both simply stared at one another. "I don't want to talk about it", she said.

But, we did talk about it. We asked each other what was this about? What significance does it have? What does it mean? Where are we going? We weren't "religious" people. We were raised Catholic, but were non- practicing as we fell away from the Catholic Church teachings. We were no longer in lock step with some of their doctrines.

A few nights later, in the wee hours of one morning while I continued to be dragged into this family of God, I was awakened by the sensation of my body physically moving in an upward direction. The feeling was similar to the perception of falling that one experiences in a dream; the exception being I was propelled upward rather than downward.

As a result of God placing me in the right place with the right people, I was to learn this experience was a trance. Some do call a trance an open vision and vice versa. However, for my experience I will refer to it as a trance.

"During a trance, most, if not all, awareness of your natural surroundings is obscured and you are transfixed on the events in the trance as opposed to an open vision where you observe something transpiring. In a trance you participate in a scene through your actions. They can last any length of time, from a few seconds to several hours. Church history is filled with accounts of God speaking through trances.

Trances are found in the New Testament. Peter fell into a trance in which God profoundly spoke to him. Through obedience to the instructions he was given in the trance, Peter received a revelation that the gospel was for the Gentiles as well as the Jews (Acts 10:34) When he acted on this message, the door of faith was opened to the Gentiles. (You May All Prophesy by Steve Thompson)

In my trance, I was watching a man in a long white robe bearing a wooden staff. He advanced slowly toward me from the rolling clouds. He stopped at some distance from me and said, "I know you, Tom Kapinos and I know your wife Marianne." He paused, tilted His head, smiled and with the

Wisdom of the ages He related how my wife and I met some twenty five years ago at the Southgate Plaza.

Quite accurately he recounted that yes, indeed, we did meet at the Southgate Plaza. More precisely on February 19, 1970, my friend, Dave, then 21 years old, and I, age 19 years, had blown a stop sign at the Southgate Plaza while tooling around in Dave's prized rag top, yellow MGB. Being the middle of winter and slamming on the brakes of a summer vehicle caused the little sports car to slide effortlessly across the ice slicked parking lot. We narrowly missed t-boning a little Volkswagen bug travelling perpendicular to our vehicle. Unbeknownst to me, driving that robin's egg blue bug was to be my future wife.

The Lord's account of our past was to serve as evidence to me that what I was seeing, hearing, and experiencing was true and He was real. How profound were His words that He knew us! The truth of the revelations culminated over several months. My encounter at the brook where the image stretched out His arms with rays of light coming down to me as my knees buckled, the image of Christ wearing His crown of thorns manifesting on the door, the image of the Man with His staff saying that He knows us, were all Divine revelations of Jesus Christ Himself. He was wooing us, calling us, dragging us to Himself, which at this juncture, we had yet to understand. It would take years to grasp the enormity of the divine calling on our lives.

Here I would like to say that many a mainstream denomination issue an invitation at their altar call to choose Jesus; to ask Him into your life. Consequently, as the lines of the ready and willing stream forth, many exalt themselves believing that they choose Christ. But, my friend, the reality is He chose us in Him before the creation of the world. (Ephesians 1:4)

Where does one go to learn of these things? From our Catholic Church experience, no one talked about spiritual matters. Church was church on Sunday only! We decided to speak with the only person that could possibly shed light on our situation....Aunt Mary.

Sometime in the early 1990's I had a conversation with my mother's youngest sister, who being a charismatic Catholic, was worried that we were, maybe, not on the right side of the spirit realm. She suggested that we attend a charismatic meeting in her Catholic Church basement to better understand spiritual things. Having finally convinced Marianne to attend, she verbosely admonished me not to eat or drink anything that was offered! The leader of the group insisted on praying over those who had not yet received the gift of tongues.

The experience was and is still unexplainable. Being told to just make sounds 'til, what, the cows come home in hopes the gifting manifests itself, was a little weird. Stranger things have happened. Marianne was totally put off by the event. She thought it was absolutely ridiculous that a grown man would be telling someone to say "ta ta ta" over and over again.

The teaching was that if you don't speak in tongues, you have not received the Holy Spirit. However, that night as we were driving home from the meeting we were discussing what needed to be picked up at the grocery store. As my wife commenced reciting her grocery list she started speaking in some weird language that neither of us understood. "You're speaking in tongues", I said.

"I am not!" she vehemently denied. Oh yeah....she was.

"I guess we'll now be accepted into the group", I joked. However, neither of us returned to those charismatic meetings in Aunt Mary's church basement. We learned speaking in tongues is a spiritual language between God and self. It comes from your most inward parts, when your own words are weak and paltry, crying out to Abba Father! The experience is one we look back upon and reflect that it was but a stepping stone in our spiritual growth.

6

LEARNING TO HEAR

One sunny summer morning, as was our norm, my wife and I were heading to our window and floor covering business. As our schedules were diverse that day, we opted to take two vehicles into the small town in upstate NY where our business was located. With Marianne in the lead we pointed toward our destination. Up, around and down we traversed the hilly countryside leading to the main road that would take us to the southern expressway heading north into town. Upon making the requisite right-hand turn just passed the intersection, my wife promptly pulled off to the side of the narrow road, where county workmen were causing an even greater meager passage. Her car had stalled out as it had the occasion to do.

As I observed the intersection and the county workmen across the road taking their break, I checked for traffic on the left where the road curves and also includes a blind grade. All was clear as I proceeded into the turn and pulled behind my wife's car. Before I exited my van, I, once again, checked for oncoming traffic. There were no vehicles approaching from either direction, so, I turned on my four way flashers, opened my door and advanced toward her car. Being there was no room on the passenger side shoulder of the road I strode to the driver's side window where there was a minimal, but safe distance, between her car and the road proper.

As I was listening intently to what Marianne was saying, my attention was interrupted with the internal thought to "move to the front of the car". Without equivocation, I did just that. As I turned toward the windshield to face my wife, still in the driver's seat, a profound sense of foreboding enveloped me. Right on the tail of that portentous warning, I caught a fleeting gander of the backend of a pick-up truck that had just barreled passed us, right where I had been standing. The truck was wildly bouncing up and down, kicking up dust and rocks, as its driver struggled to gain control and get back onto the pavement from the shoulder of the road.

Hundreds of thoughts and emotions scurried across my unsettled mind as I attempted to assimilate what had just taken place. Marianne was visibly shaken as I, once again, approached her driver's side window. "Oh my God, what made you walk to the front of the car?" she quaked. "I was explaining about the car stalling and you just walked away in mid-sentence." She went on to explain that, dumbfounded, she watched me walk away from her. Immediately, her attention was drawn back to the driver's side window where she witnessed the distracted driver of a speeding pick-up truck veer toward her car as he waved to his buddies on the roadwork crew. "The pick-up truck came within inches of the side-view mirror exactly where you were standing! It happened so quickly there was no time to warn you! You were already to the front of the car before I could react. Thank God!"

Continuing the discussion, the cognizance of what had just occurred was jolting. I was shaken to my core as the adrenaline surge subsided. This could have had a very different outcome. Had I not heeded the premonitory, life as I knew it would have been severely curtailed. Being gravely injured, at best, or dead, at worst were not scenarios I wanted to think about!

Now, to have someone tell you that they hear the voice of God sounds ludicrous, crazy and delusional. I know! I know! But I am here, today, to bear witness to the fact that had I not heeded the Lord's voice within me, I most probably would not be here!

 At one time, in my arrogance, I put limitations on God who created the heavens and the earth and everything in it. Imagine that, me, dictating to the Lord how He is to communicate with His own.

So, what was the lesson here? What was I to learn? I'll tell you exactly. The closer we draw to the Lord, the better we understand how we hear Him.

7

LEAVING OUR COMFORT ZONE

Somewhere between 1993 and early 1994 we were invited, by a recent business acquaintance and friend, to attend a church service where she would be leading worship that day. Community Fellowship Church was an evangelical Protestant denomination church. Coming from a Catholic background we were not familiar with any service outside of the Catholic tradition. Even though we had not attended a Catholic mass in years, the idea of attending a Protestant church felt uncomfortably awkward.

Ultimately, I decided not to attend this particular service. My wife did attend out of deference to her friend. However, when Marianne returned home, we discussed the service and its merits.

She described the congregation as small, open and friendly as everyone fellowshipped over coffee. Singing and the playing of instruments preceded the sermon. Growing up Catholic and taught by Catholic nuns in a parochial school, we were not able to talk or laugh in church. It was so serious. Comparatively speaking, it was a refreshingly unregimented atmosphere. Marianne felt somewhat conflicted. Attending the Protestant persuasion was totally opposite of our Catholic experience, while at the same time pleasantly comforting.

After continuing our discussions, I decided to join my wife at Community Fellowship Church. Although it took me several weeks to come around, come around I did. We felt a strong desire to be in God's house to draw closer to Him. Our aspiration was also to further our understanding and education of all things encompassing God.

As we attended church services, bible studies, breakfasts and dinners, we grew more comfortable with our surroundings and the people there. Many Sundays were spent in fellowship 'til late afternoon, which is contrary to the thinking of many regarding the "get in get out" in forty five minutes mentality. We, too, believed, at one time, those forty five minutes were much too long for a church service and couldn't wait for it to end. Now, here we were, spending most of a day doing that very thing.

As a result of this quality time spent, we felt relaxed enough to share our supernatural experiences with Pastor Sal and his wife Donna. This, needless to say, raised a few eyebrows as it was not something this particular denomination cottoned to. Sal had to be very cautious as to what he introduced into his congregation. Any teaching or worship outside the traditional teachings of the denomination had the propensity to offend the more conservative minded members. The long-time congregants might not embrace anything outside their comfort zone, become upset, leave the church and report him to the superintendent. Sal had a family to take care of and could quite possibly lose his job and paycheck. Also, Pastor

Sal, at this time, was more inclined toward the traditional slant. One could say he had more of an intellectual gifting, rather than leaning toward spiritual matters outside his denominational doctrines, to readily introduce them into his congregation.

Being outside Sal and Donna's ability to mentor us, we were later introduced to ministry friends of theirs. Pastor Ted and his wife Karoline pastored a church in the southern tier, of which I do not recall the denomination. However, they possessed a different attitude toward spiritual giftings than their denomination allowed; they chose a disparate path. The faithful from the church they pastored complained about their teachings and practices. Consequently, they were summarily relieved of their duties.

As a result of the predicament they found themselves in, Pastor Ted and Karoline were invited to Pastor Sal and Donna's church as guest ministers. As was the custom, a special monetary offering was taken for them at the service. No one, at this time, was privy to their dilemma. Gradually, over the next few months, Pastor Ted was invited back as a visiting minister. During one of these visits, Ted offered that anyone who wished to be prayed over should sign up for a Wednesday time slot. So, we did just that.

As our Wednesday appointment rolled around, we drove to Community Fellowship Church, to find just a few people in attendance. We were the last couple to be called into the small room off the sanctuary where the ministering was being conducted. Uncertain as to what to expect, we were both excited and nervous. However, any lingering anxiety was relieved as we made small talk with Pastor Ted, his wife,

Karoline and Pastor Sal and Donna, who were also in attendance. "Ok," Pastor Ted intoned. "Are you ready?"

Pastor Ted began by asking for God's grace upon this ministry time. As Marianne and I held hands, we bowed our heads in supplication and awaited Ted to continue. He laid his hands on Marianne's head as his wife Karoline laid hands upon her heart. "Thank you, Lord", Ted said, as he began to relate just what the Lord was showing him.

From this point forward, the experience is better told by my wife.

As Ted and Karoline prayed over me, a comforting cradle of love, safety and security was made manifest like a giant cocoon. Clinging to my husband's hand was a lifeline as contrariwise, giant tears of abject sadness flowed from a submerged well deep within a swamp of despair. Softly, Ted shared just what the Lord was making plain for him to bring forth.   Seeing a heart riddled with stab wounds, Ted articulated, some large, some small, some dings, and a lot of scars, I unabashedly allowed the tears to flow. The memories being solicited, rooted in painful recollection and held tightly by the chains of time resisted the pull to daylight. However, in the Lord's loving embrace, using Ted and Karoline as His adjuncts and my husband as my human anchor, I allowed the ministering of the Lord to smash those chains that held me hostage for so long. Allow me to explain.

8

MARIANNE SMASHING THE CHAINS

In the autumn of 1950, I was born to a mother who had a strict Catholic upbringing, whose older brother would eventually ascend the priesthood to become a monsignor, a mother who was superstitious, a mother whose favorite holiday was Halloween and a mother who was shown little familial love. My mother believed that a wife should be married for at least two years before conceiving a child. I am not sure if that was the case with me or not. Pertaining to that fact, I have no details. She believed things like if you wore a pearl choker necklace while pregnant, you would choke your baby and if you were left-handed your child would be a thief. Ironically, I am left-handed as was my father. For the record, I am not a thief; neither was my dad.... as far as I know.

Growing up I heard the stories of my mother's bizarre behavior, sometimes by conversations with my family, other times by eavesdropping. From what I recall these things I am about to relate happened before my time, but give insight into the mind of a woman I would have otherwise loved to have been nurtured by and love to call mother.

My father shared that Betty would do odd things like lock the door behind her whenever entering or exiting a room. Whether she was moving into the living room, dining room, kitchen, bedroom or bathroom, she would secure the door firmly behind her.

The young kids in the neighborhood would love to walk behind Betty as she strolled down the avenue, with her department store paper bags loaded to the top with who knows what, dropping coins and candy as she went. This anecdote conjures up an image of what we would, today, call a bag lady. However, according to my father, Betty was anything but a bag lady.

My father, Buddy, was a bus driver employed by the NFT, making a modest, but comfortable income; enough that he and my mother owned their own home in South Buffalo. Betty was a homemaker as was the norm for wives and mothers of that era. If anything, I would daresay, she was eccentric.

However, with the birth of her child, me, things took a dramatic turn. As is the model of a mother giving birth, her newborn is brought to her hospital bed at feeding time. Most mothers, though exhausted, are elated to share in the joy of this moment of bonding. Unfortunately, for Betty, this was not the case. Her immediate reaction, as shared with me, via my dad and grandmother was, "Get that ugly thing away from me!" The attending nurse stunned, left the hospital room, forthwith, coddling the rejected infant.

Today, we know this to be called "baby blues". Baby blues is described as a mild form of depression, occurring within days of the birth of one's child. It usually lasts up to a week. Sadly, for Betty and me, her "baby blues" morphed into, I believe, postpartum depression. As related previously, Betty was always somewhat eccentric, so, perhaps, she was predisposed to this condition. Postpartum depression is a type of depression that affects some women shortly after childbirth. The origin is unclear. A contributing cause may be related to sudden hormonal changes in the brain during and after delivery.

Symptoms of postpartum depression may include loss of interest or pleasure in life, not wanting to engage in social situations, loss of appetite, rapid mood swings, episodes of crying or tearfulness, poor concentration, memory loss, difficulty making decisions, difficulty falling or staying asleep, feeling of irritability, anxiety, or panic, restlessness, fear of hurting or killing oneself or one's child! (Lifescript website)

Postpartum depression was not readily recognized as such during the middle of the last century. It was diagnosed as a mental illness remedied by shock treatments.

The newborn rejection narrative occurring at the hospital coupled with several others shared throughout this chapter, resulted in my mother being institutionalized in a mental hospital, whereby she received shock treatments regularly. My father was adamantly against these treatments, but was soundly admonished by hospital doctors.

Mental illness or perceived mental illness was not a topic that was discussed openly then, as it is today. It wasn't until the seventies amid renewed scientific interest in mental illnesses that discussions were freer. In general, postpartum depression gained new recognition. Even then most women continued to struggle with this debilitating affliction on their own.

Betty developed other incapacitating issues, courtesy of having received so many anti-psychotic drugs and shock treatments at the facility. Consequently, one new mother had no chance to experience motherhood in all its wonder, while one child was deprived of her mother's love.

My paternal grandmother became my sole protector, advocator and champion. My grandmother's daughter, who just happens to be my aunt, nicknamed Sis (given name also Helen), stepped into the role of rescuer.

Grandmother Helen was a woman of such unselfish love she took in an infant at age fifty years and raised me as her own. Her own children were grown and her husband had passed away some two years prior. As a matter of fact, my Aunt Sis had a daughter of her own, with another baby on the way.

What would then possess this woman to complicate her life with an infant belonging to her second eldest son? Love. Pure, unadulterated love!

Even though my Gram was lovingly unselfish, she was also brutally honest, perchance to a fault, and did not suffer fools gladly. Therefore, when another family member encouraged her to say my mother had died in childbirth, she would not and did not fabricate such a thing. She would not shy away, she stated, from any questions I would have concerning my mother, and above all she said she would not lie to me about my background.

Accordingly, when I returned home from fourth grade one late spring day, where I currently resided with my Gram, aunt and uncle and four cousins, with the question of, "How come I don't have a mother like everyone in school"? Gram did, indeed, tell me exactly why I did not have mother like everyone in school. Over the next hours, days, months and years, Gram and I would have many, many hard to hear heart to hearts correlating to her daughter-in-law and her brokenness.

One of those exchanges centered on an episode when I was a very young infant, perhaps a newborn. As told to me, my mother would creep into the bedroom where I lay asleep, lift me from my crib and unceremoniously drop me to the floor.

This was not the first or only dangerous episode to arise from my mother's hand. I thank God, my father, as I was told, was at the right place at the right time, and able to intervene.

Could these events be the reason for the two partially fused disks in my neck today? There is no other explanation my doctor could provide. I have not had neck surgery nor was I ever in an accident involving a neck injury.

The fallout of this antidote on my young impressionable mind and heart, while not life-threatening, left me feeling unloved and devastated. Like I said, my Gram was fiercely honest. Holding back the tears, my heart was breaking. Was my own mother actually seeking to kill me? Was she not cognizant of the consequence of her actions? Why would another human being do such a thing to an infant, let alone a mother to her own child? Whatever happened to a mother's instinctual maternal love? I was her first and only born, but whatever maleficence invaded her consciousness mired her mother's love in darkness and, I daresay, hatred for her own little baby.

My own misery did not stifle my quest to learn more about my mother. I pestered my aunt and uncle and grandmother for more enlightenment. Eventually, my father's sister shared that one day she visited my mother and her new niece. My Aunt Sis shared that as she came into the living room, she could see me on the dining room table where my mother had just finished changing my diaper. I was probably about six weeks old. However, what she witnessed turned her blood cold.

Becoming agitated because she could not find the nipple to my baby bottle, my mother was slapping me and yelling, asking me what I did with it.

In those days, baby bottles were made of glass that had to be sterilized before use as did the rubber nipples and caps.

Stilling her fears, my aunt, who was all of nineteen years old, suggested that maybe the bottle nipple was in the kitchen and Betty should go check there. Apparently, my mother thought it a good idea and went to check.

On cue, my aunt wrapped me up in the receiving blanket I was laying upon and stole into the night. It was cold and windy and with nothing more than a baby's thin receiving blanket, she scurried to my grandmother's house.

It is from this point in time I learned how I came to be raised, off and on, by my Gram.

So, where was my father all of this time, you may be wondering. He was spending all of his time at the mental hospital where my mother had ultimately been sequestered.

Let's give some background that led to this point.

Because of my mother's increasingly dangerous state of mind and actions, her doctor signed the order for her to be committed to Gowanda State Hospital. My father opposed this option but, it was painfully clear he had no alternative.

Enlisting the help of his brother-in-law Chuck, they concocted a story of taking a drive to the country. As they arrived on the hospital grounds, Betty knew she had been lied to. Needless to say, she freaked out to the point of being unmanageable. The orderlies had no choice except to place her in a strait jacket. The whole sordid sequence of events left both my father and uncle devastated.

As Betty fought the orderlies like a rabid wild animal two grown men openly wept as she was carted off like so much baggage.   Reaching out to hold his wife and beg her forgiveness he saw only anger, hurt, betrayal and utterly no forgiveness, whatsoever.

Buddy became despondent. He didn't work, eat or sleep. He stood vigil at the hospital. Eventually, he lost our home and almost lost his job, in his quest to see his love return home as his wife and my mother. However, that was not to be.

Buddy was quite vociferous in voicing his displeasure of the barbaric treatments employed to treat his wife. Summarily, he was thrown off the property. The hospital doctors banned him from the hospital, never to step foot on the grounds again. He was no longer a welcomed visitor.

The official reason given for outlawing Buddy on the premises...he upset Betty. And being my mother was delivered into the arms of a harsh institution, by her husband no less, this rationalization holds credibility.

In my eighteenth year, I took it upon myself to journey to Gowanda State Mental Hospital. Like every child, I craved a mother's love. I longed to see her, meet her, naively hoping against hope she was well. Now don't get me wrong, my Gram was the perfect surrogate, but as she reminded me time and time again she was not my mother, she was my grandmother.

Deaf to the dreadful stories I heard growing up and feeling abandoned by my father, I was bound and determined to go. I disclosed to no one my planned excursion save one. With a look of excited skepticism, my friend readily accepted my invitation for an adventure, on faith, not asking where our destination would take us.

As we arrived at the locked massive wrought iron, Gothic-looking barrier, there was little doubt as to our locale. Gowanda State Mental Hospital, in script straight out of a nightmare, was ominously inscribed above the access gate. The only things missing to complete the movie set was a dark night, a full-moon, a baying wolf, and crashing thunder and lightning.

At this juncture, contemplating retreat, I screwed up my courage the best I could and forged ahead. After all, it was a bright sun-drenched warm afternoon and the park-like setting that lay beyond the gates was, indeed, serene and welcoming, I reasoned.

A paunchy, middle-aged security guard greeted us politely, asking us to state our names and business. Apparently satisfied with our responses, and without ceremony, he unlocked the gates and directed us to the main office. The road was long and winding as the building sat way in back off the road. We parked in front of the Victorian structure which was opened in 1898 and made our way to the front door. As I raised my hand to knock, the door was opened by a nurse, with a friendly smile in a crisp white uniform and cap. She greeted me by name as we were shown to a normally orchestrated reception area.

Once there I was introduced to my escort George, a pleasant, albeit, no nonsense sturdily built medical personnel, whom I assumed to be an orderly. His instructions were clear. Do not walk around the hospital unescorted; do not leave an office or waiting room without his accompaniment.

Our next stop was to meet my mother's attending psychiatrist. His office was located in another building. To get there we had to traverse a gauntlet of several pathetic individuals. Entering a concrete stairwell, across the lawn from the main building, several men in various stages of affliction sat or lounged on the steps. The malodorous stench of urine filled one's nostrils as we mounted the stairs. Glancing back at my friend, Debbie, we shared a wide-eyed questioning look of fear and apprehension. Keeping us moving, George whisked us up the stairs in short order.

Arriving at the dimly-lit second floor hallway, we took in the 9"x 9" brown and subtlely speckled asphalt tiles beneath our feet, the institutional green paint on the walls, the tall dark wooden doors and the generally overall gloomy atmosphere of our surroundings.

As George firmly knocked upon the doctor's office door, we were beckoned to enter. Gazing upon the thin austere man with his stern countenance and shock of white hair, I saw little compassion. Anxiety and dread assailed me as introductions were made and George and Debbie were sternly commanded to wait outside by the no-nonsense doctor. Not to be intimidated, and disdainfully glaring at Dr. Fritz, George reassured me that he would be right outside the door whenever I was ready to leave.

With no small talk or pleasantries, Dr. Fritz bombarded me with questions in his harsh thick German accent. "Vhat do you vant? Vhy are you here? Vhat are you after? Now, you come now?"

Attempting to explain my heart's desire of seeing and possibly meeting my mother, he continued his interrogation as he hotly pitched a black and white, glossy, 8 x 10 photograph across his desk toward me. I began to sob and shake uncontrollably as he kept up his tirade. "Is this vhat you vant to see? This is your mother. Are you happy?"

No, I most assuredly was not happy. I could not fathom the reasoning behind this doctor's unexplainable anger directed at me. The photograph he had so viciously and dispassionately thrust at me was of my mother on the day she was admitted. Encased in a straitjacket, her long dark curly hair sticking straight out from her head and eyes wild with fear terrified me and broke my heart.

Evidently eavesdropping at the door, George burst into the room admonishing the doctor to stop. Dr. Fritz continued unabated until George shouted at him to "Stop, this instant! That's enough!"

With that George escorted me out of the office and into the hallway. Once there he assured me, "You'll be okay, you'll be okay", as we strode toward the stairway at the opposite end of the hall. George was either more than an orderly or he was a very brave one to reprimand Dr. Fritz in the manner in which he did.

With my mind and emotions in turmoil, after being verbally and emotionally assaulted by Dr. Fritz, I found myself in the dayroom with no memory of how I arrived there.

Being greeted by RN Rose, she laid out the plan of a possible meet and greet. If all went well and both my mother and I were receptive, we would meet. The ruse was for Betty to be measured for a new dress. My instructions included not to approach her or speak to her until her nurse, Florence, deemed her to be calm and receptive.

Nervous and shell-shocked, I waited and waited in the dayroom. Having time to compose myself, I began to second guess the sanity (pun intended) of my quest. George was called away on an emergency and forbid me to leave the dayroom until he returned.

Several patients were playing games, talking or simply milling around the brightly lit and charmingly decorated room. A woman, named Stella, dressed totally in black from head to toe, wandered up and down the hallway, outside the dayroom, grinning gleefully. From time to time she would peek into the doorway and wave to me with her happy toothless grin. I uncomfortably smiled and waved back until another woman in the room, patient or not, I have no clue, admonished me to not wave to Stella. Oh Lord, I hope that's not my mother, I lamented rather uncharitably.

Just then the moment arrived. Nurse Florence returned with a short, fortyish, somewhat round, curly headed woman. She was adorable. Longing to reach out and hug this little cherub, I clearly remembered my instructions, and simply returned her engaging smile.

"Come over here Betty", her nurse beckoned. "We'll get you measured." Obeying as she was told, my mother joined the nurse holding the tape measure. Right off the bat Florence opened with, "Do you know who this is, Betty?" Wait… what? I thought. She's not supposed to ask that. She's going off script. Still smiling my mother shook her head no in response. "This is your daughter Marianne" she offered. Hold on, Nurse Florence, you're not to be telling her that. At this revelation my mother again shook her head no, smile vanishing. She held her arms as though cradling an infant and said that her Marianne was a baby. "No, Betty," nurse Florence continued. "This is your baby girl all grown up!" With that declaration my mother began to worry the side of her dress with her fingers. My father had long ago explained the meaning behind my mother's nervous tick. Betty was becoming anxious and/or fearful. It usually signaled an outburst or an emotional episode on the horizon. Sweat trickled down my back as her nurse continued the onslaught. "Who is Buddy?" No answer. "Isn't Buddy your husband," she continued unabated

"No!" my mother insisted with fearful eyes darting one to the other and back again.

Before all hell broke loose, I bolted for the door. Hauling Debbie by her jacket sleeve, I wrenched her from her chair and we made a mad dash down the hall. How had all this gone so wrong? Spotting an exit sign I charged down the corridor, ignoring the male voice shouting my name.

In tandem, Debbie and I burst through the door marked emergency-only, heedless of multiple alarms sounding and sprinted for my faithful VW bug.

As we neared the car, George caught up to us. His was the male voice calling my name. "Wait," he implored. Shaking my head in the negative, I clamored into my car. Thank goodness I hadn't locked it. Once inside, I immediately pushed down the lock button.

"I understand that you want to leave", he said through the closed car window. "I'm so sorry for how everything turned out," he consoled. "Won't you come back inside?" Again, shaking my head in the negative, with slumping shoulders he replied, "If you ever want to try again, I'll be here to help you."

With that, I peeled out of the parking area, with no intention of ever returning. And yes, you can peel-out with a stick shift bug!

Returning home with a heavy heart, Debbie and I did not speak about where we had just ventured. Each of us lost in our thoughts, we did not speak at all on the long ride home. I believed I had alienated a friend, which turned out to be not the case.

I eventually shared my shattered experience with my Gram. She always had this sixth sense of knowing what you were up to without having to utter a word. Her loving response was typical of her way of handling things. Gram passed no judgment, or said I shouldn't have done that. She knew one day I would take it upon myself to take that long lonely road. "Well, you better call your father", was her only response.

With trepidation and shaking fingers, I made the call. My dad's reaction was not one I expected. He was terribly saddened to learn I would attempt an excursion of that magnitude on my own. He said he would have liked to accompany me, which startled me. In all these years I never gave much thought to my father's feelings toward the whole debacle.

We discussed the worthlessness of Dr. Fritz and my dad, actually called him a bastard for the way he treated me. He shared that Fritz was always bristly, no-nonsense and just plain mean. He was so very sorry I had to encounter him.

Finally, we got around to my visit with my mother, Elizabeth. Together, we softly cried as I related the whole experience. We spent some time conversing on the phone, much of the content I have forgotten over the years. My dad did end the conversation saying that if I ever wanted to return to visit my mother, he would gladly take that trip with me. I did not respond. It would be some twenty seven years until my next encounter with my mother.

At this meeting I was accompanied by my husband, as my father passed away in 1974. He never did get to see his wife and my mother again.

Tom and I learned that my uncle, my mother's brother, the monsignor, had passed away, prompting our visit to the funeral home. The year was 1995. With much prodding and coercing, my pit-bull husband, Tom, finally persuaded me to attend Father Dennis' wake.

Once there, we struck up a conversation with my mother's sister, Norine and her husband Joe who, along with the Knights of Columbus, were the only people in the funeral home at this time.

I learned from Norine, my mother was living with a caretaker in the city of Buffalo. We made an appointment with Teri, the caregiver and with my mother's social worker for a visit with Betty.

Upon arrival at Teri's home, Tom was not allowed into the living room where we all were to meet. He stayed in the enclosed front porch while I was instructed, once again, as so many years before, not to speak to her or approach her, or touch her in any manner. So, there I sat like a lump, on my hands, on the sofa, as my mother entered the room with Teri. Let's just say it was not a Kodak moment. There was no conversation, except for Betty's one word answers to the questions posed by the social worker.

Finally, apparently concluding Betty was calm enough Tom was allowed to enter the meeting. I still sat mute as briefed. Apparently, they had not advised my husband in the same manner, as to no speaking, no hugging, and no nothing.

My wonderful, lovable, beautiful mate strode into the room with a huge smile on his face and waltzed right on over to Betty. With the innocence of a child he gently kissed her cheek and exclaimed, "Betty, it's so nice to meet you! I've wanted to meet you for a long time!" Well, don't you know, my mother broke into a dazzling smile and giggled like a schoolgirl.

Abruptly, it was time to leave. Betty's TV programs were about to start and she was headed for the door; social visit over. Feeling flat, Tom and I donned our overcoats and said our good-byes to Teri and the social worker. They promised to keep in touch.

I never saw my mother again. She passed away in 2008 at the grand old age of 82 years.

After speaking with my father, I knew he felt that everything he did was for my safety and benefit. I still resented him on some levels as I felt he had abandoned me so many years ago.

It happened this way. Sometime around the age of six years, I had still been living with my Gram in an apartment on West Woodside, in South Buffalo. My father decided or perhaps, was forced to decide, that I was to live with him and his girlfriend and their two sons on Fillmore Ave. I did not want to do that. I cried and I pleaded with my Gram, all to no avail. Patiently and tearfully Gram explained that she had no other discourse. She uttered, that for reasons she would not share with me, I was not allowed to live with her anymore. "Go wash your face," she said, "your father will be here shortly." And that was that.

However, when my father came, I kicked and screamed and cried desperately urging my Gram to understand how much I didn't want to leave.

Ultimately, having no say in the matter, my suitcase and I were carried to the waiting car. A short two blocks from my Gram's apartment, my father stopped for gas. As he attended to his business, I silently opened the car's back door and took off running like the hounds of hell were on my tail. Actually, that's really how it felt.

I made it back to Gram's and pounding on her door, I pleaded for her to open up. Surprised to find me standing there she asked, "How did you get here? Where is your father?" It was unnecessary for me to answer because the man of the hour was already running up the stairs. The scene of earlier replayed and, once again, out the door and down the stairs to the still waiting car I went.

I have little recollection of meeting Gerry, my father's girlfriend. My half-brothers, Marck and Mike, who were three years old and, maybe, one year old respectively, were just that, half-brothers. My role, at almost seven years old, in this little family of five was as the nanny. It continued this way for, maybe, a year. My Gram would come to visit, occasionally, which was strained. Instinctively, I knew Gerry cared little for my Gram and the feeling was mutual.

During Gram's visits, I would beg in a tearful whisper for her to please, please take me back home with her. With eyes shining with unshed tears she would always answer, no, it wasn't possible.

One day, returning home from third grade, I walked into a living room almost empty of furniture, as were the kitchen and two of the bedrooms. My bedroom was intact except for my piggy bank lying smashed on the floor. Whenever my Gram would visit she would slip me a few dollars which I would stash away in the piggy bank she gave me. My father, who was working for the Niagara Frontier Transit Company, had what he called his belt. The spare belt contained coins from which he dispensed change to the bus riders. That was missing also. Gerry was not home and my dad was still working, but I knew he would be home soon.

As I wandered through the partially barren apartment, I happened to notice a letter propped up on the buffet cabinet. Being in third grade and learning cursive, I began to read the missive. It was a rant from Gerry to my father about this and that much of which I did not comprehend, except for the portion pertaining to me. Using very indelicate language, she assured my father if I was in the house when she returned to pick up the rest of her belongings, she would kill me!

Shakily, I attempted to position the letter in the same position I found it. Making my way to sit on the stairs in the hallway facing the front door, I hoped my dad would come home before she returned.

It seemed like an eternity before I heard the bottom door open. Looking up at me from the bottom of the staircase, my handsome father smiled a big ole grin. Using his nickname for me he greeted, "Hey Liz, wuttaya doin' sittin' out here? It's freezing!" I did not respond as he pecked me on the cheek and walked right into the nightmare.

Several moments later, he came back out into the hall and inquired if I had read the letter. Fearfully lying, I shook my head no, saying I could not read writing. With a sense of urgency, he instructed me to get my stuff and pack my suitcase.

Riding in the car for what seemed to be forever, we eventually pulled into the recently snow shoveled driveway of a home I did not recognize. My father did not turn off the car or say a word. We just sat there. Soon my dad tooted the horn and told me to go to the door. I did just that and I knocked and knocked, but no one answered. With that, from the safety of his car, my father motioned me to go to the back door. As I waded in waist deep snow, I finally reached the other door and knocked again. A kindly lady looked out the door window, smiled and attempted to open the damp swollen wooden door; all to no avail. She motioned for me to go back to the door from where I just came. Unsure of what she was asking of me, I just stood there. After a few moments, with the help of her husband, my uncle Chuck, the door swung partway open, virtually saving my life for the second time. This was, indeed, the same loving and brave aunt, albeit older, who had whisked me to safety some years before.

I turned, looking to wave good-bye to my father, but the spot where his parked car idled was now empty; he had absconded. Saddened and abandoned I tumbled into the hallway as I numbly stared into the faces of all four of my estranged cousins.

Shortly thereafter, my Gram joined me in Orchard Park. There we would remain with Gram's daughter and family until turning seventeen years old and working full-time, Gram and I moved into our own apartment.

As my ministry time concluded, a supernatural peace and joy flowed over me as I felt the all-consuming love of the Lord being made manifest. Experiencing a love greater than a mother's love that was so long denied me, the healing process began.

9

DUNAMIS POWER

After my wife's ministry time, Ted began to minister to me. He shared that the Lord showed him a mantle on my shoulders which represented a position of prophet. He explained this was a powerful prophetic calling the Lord had given me; one which bore, among other things, a great and heavy responsibility.

Having a Christian minister acknowledge the supernatural realm brought more clarity and more understanding to all I had experienced. Step by step we were learning by seeking the Lord in all things, He will order those steps.

Being comforted by this realization, I was led to the following Scripture, "Which of you fathers, if your son asks for a fish, will give him a snake instead? Or if he asks for an egg, will give him a scorpion? If you then, though you are evil, know how to give good gifts to your children, how much more will your Father in heaven give the Holy Spirit to those who ask Him?" (Luke 11:11-13 NIV)

Having ministered to us individually, Pastor Ted began to pray over my wife and me as a couple. Closing our eyes we received Ted's prayers and together we experienced an atmosphere of tranquility. There appeared to be no time or space, as Pastor Ted continued to pray over us.

Abruptly, our serenity was brought to a jolting conclusion as both my wife and I separately realized what could only be described as nuclear explosions. With eyes still closed, even though there was no sound, a bright flash of light lit up our field of vision taking the shape of a mushroom cloud. The color of my mushroom cloud was white, while Marianne observed an orange mushroom cloud, as we would later share our experience with one another.

Apparently, those in the room, who were observing us, witnessed the captivity of our being in the awesome presence of Almighty God. Our spiritually mind-altered state left our physical mind and body in an almost comatose posture of awe, causing someone to exclaim, "What's happening? What are you seeing?"

Slowly being pulled back from the spiritual realm and into the natural realm once more, we both described, to the best of our ability, all that had just taken place. We had no rational explanation of what just happened. But, perhaps, more importantly, what we had was a knowing, deep within, that what we had just experienced was a huge spiritual, life altering event. Still reeling from the effects of the encounter, we had no further insight to offer those inquiring minds.

However, Ted, responding to the commanding and powerful presence of the Lord, explained the (dunamis) power of the Lord had been released, illustrated via the nuclear explosion.

Strong's Concordance renders dunamis as follows.

Dunamis, 1411, a Greek word meaning **(miraculous) power, might, strength**

Short Definition: might, power, marvelous works
Definition: (a) physical power, force, might, ability, efficacy, energy, meaning (b) plur: powerful deeds, deeds showing (physical) power, marvelous works.

1411 *dýnamis* (from 1410 /*dýnamai,* "able, having *ability*") – properly, "*ability* to perform" (*L-N*); for the believer, *power* to achieve by applying the Lord's *inherent abilities.* "Power through God's ability" (1411 /*dýnamis*) is needed in every scene of life to really grow in sanctification and prepare for heaven (glorification).1411 (*dýnamis*) is a very important term, used 120 times in the NT.

Without God's **power** we cannot change on our own. It is His "dunamis" which empowers us to change.

Some may find the following scriptures to be many and lengthy. However, scripture by its own virtue is the **power** (dunamis) of God. Jesus is the Word, the logos, of God.

"For the word of God is alive and powerful. It is sharper than the sharpest two-edged sword, cutting between soul and spirit, between joint and marrow. It exposes our innermost thoughts and desires." Hebrews 4:12 (NLT)

God's dunamis keeps us through faith as illustrated in 1 Peter 1:5 "And through your faith, God is protecting you by his **power** (dunamis) until you receive this salvation, which is ready to be revealed on the last day for all to see."

God's dunamis gives us everything we need for living a godly life. 2 Peter 1:3 (New Living Translation)-"By his divine **power** (dunamis) God has given us everything we need for living a godly life. We have received all of this by coming to know him, the one who called us to himself by means of his marvelous glory and excellence."

Jesus is far above all others. Ephesians 1:18-21-(New Living Translation)-"I pray that the eyes of your heart may be enlightened in order that you may know the hope to which he has called you, the riches of his glorious inheritance in his holy people, and his incomparably great **power** (dunamis) for us who believe. That **power** (dunamis) is the same as the mighty strength he exerted when he raised Christ from the dead and seated him at his right hand in the heavenly realms, far above all rule and authority, power (Greek word *exusia*, #1849, Strong's Concordance meaning authority and influence) and dominion, and every name that is invoked, not only in the present age but also in the one to come. God has put all things under the authority of Christ and has made him head over all things for the benefit of the church. And the church is his body; it is made full and complete by Christ, who fills all things everywhere with himself."

Paul prayed specifically for the dunamis to be released in us. Ephesians 3:20(NIV)-"Now to him who is able to do immeasurably more than all we ask or imagine, according to his **power** (dunamis) that is at work within us."

The gospel is the dunamis of God for salvation. 1_Corinthians 1:18-19- "The message of the cross is foolish to those who are headed for destruction! But we who are being saved know it is the very **power** (dunamis) of God. As the Scriptures say,

> 'I will destroy the wisdom of the wise and discard the intelligence of the intelligent.'

Dunamis is in that place of trials and suffering. 2 Corinthians 4:7-10-"We now have this light shining in our hearts, but we ourselves are like fragile clay jars containing this great treasure. This makes it clear that our great **power** (dunamis) is from God, not from ourselves."

Jesus gave the dunamis to His followers. Acts 1:8-"But you will receive **power** (dunamis) when the Holy Spirit comes on you; and you will be my witnesses in Jerusalem, and in all Judea and Samaria, and to the ends of the earth."

God's dunamis begets life as in Luke 1:16-17-"And he will turn many Israelites to the Lord their God. He will be a man with the spirit and **power** (dunamis) of Elijah. He will prepare the people for the coming of the Lord. He will turn the hearts of the fathers to their children, and he will cause those who are rebellious to accept the wisdom of the godly."

Also, Luke 1:35-37-"The angel replied, "The Holy Spirit will come upon you, and the **power** (dunamis) of the Most High will overshadow you. So the baby to be born will be holy, and he will be called the Son of God. What's more, your relative

Elizabeth has become pregnant in her old age! People used to say she was barren, but she has conceived a son and is now in her sixth month. For nothing is impossible with God."

Jesus was anointed of the Holy Spirit and dunamis. Luke 5:17-"One day while Jesus was teaching, some Pharisees and teachers of religious law were sitting nearby. (It seemed that these men showed up from every village in all Galilee and Judea, as well as from Jerusalem.) And the Lord's healing power was strongly with Jesus."

Jesus could feel when the dunamis power left His body. Mark 5:30 (New Living Translation)-"Jesus realized at once that healing **power** (dunamis) had gone out from him, so he turned around in the crowd and asked, 'Who touched my robe?'"

God's dunamis heals the sick and raises the dead. Acts 9:32-42-"Meanwhile, Peter traveled from place to place, and he came down to visit the believers in the town of Lydda. There he met a man named Aeneas, who had been paralyzed and bedridden for eight years. Peter said to him, "Aeneas, Jesus Christ heals you! Get up, and roll up your sleeping mat!" And he was healed instantly ("dunamis" power was released). Then the whole population of Lydda and Sharon saw Aeneas walking around, and they turned to the Lord.

"There was a believer in Joppa named Tabitha (which in Greek is Dorcas). She was always doing kind things for others and helping the poor. About this time she became ill and died. Her body was washed for burial and laid in an upstairs room. But the believers had heard that Peter was nearby at

Lydda, so they sent two men to beg him, 'Please come as soon as possible!'

"So Peter returned with them; and as soon as he arrived, they took him to the upstairs room. The room was filled with widows who were weeping and showing him the coats and other clothes Dorcas had made for them. But Peter asked them all to leave the room; then he knelt and prayed. Turning to the body he said, "Get up, Tabitha" (dunamis power was released). And she opened her eyes! When she saw Peter, she sat up! He gave her his hand and helped her up. Then he called in the widows and all the believers, and he presented her to them alive.

"The news spread through the whole town, and many believed in the Lord. And Peter stayed a long time in Joppa, living with Simon, a tanner of hides."

****

Dunamis (**power**) is God's nature; it's who He is. God's (dunamis) **power** enables us to accomplish all His purpose. His mighty power protects us, bestows upon us the gifts of faith, healing, joy, trust and salvation. God's dunamis is everything we need for living a godly life.

True dunamis takes care of a heart that has become hardened, unbelief, riotous living, and an unclean mind. It is God's standard in us that reflect His honor and glory.

Today, because of God's mind-blowing demonstration of **power,** beginning on the day of our explosive vision, a higher clarity of conscience ensued. By that I mean, being even more aware of the darkness constantly bombarding our lives.

Learning to root out all that is evil residing in these unclean vessels. This experience focused us on becoming more like Him; to be holy as He is holy.

Everyone is a work in progress. One cannot simply flip a switch, nor is there a quick fix, to be like Him. We are being made into His image. We aren't there yet. If we were already made in His image, why would we need to improve? Why do we continue to sin? Why do we need forgiveness? It is a process that involves a lifetime of trials and tribulations, experiencing evil, dying to self and putting God first!

While the nuclear explosions symbolize God's **power** (dunamis), the white and orange colors are an extension of that power. God's dunamis provides the means to do His will in our life, while the colors illustrate the way it gets done.

For example, the color orange signifies fire. Hebrews 12:29, in the New International Version, says, for our "God is a *consuming* fire", while the New Living Translation renders this scripture as, "For our God is a *devouring* fire." Either way, these translations evoke a sense of destruction. Strong's concordance explains this Greek word (*katanaliskó*) #2654, to mean to use up, and it is only used in Hebrews 12:29.

Be mindful, we are not speaking of a literal, physical fire…no, not at all. This fire is a spiritual fire. God is spirit. (John 4:24) God is working on our spiritual life. He is burning up all which is worldly within us and purifying all which is worth keeping. Just as gold is refined by fire and made pure, so are we.

In times of old, the refining of gold involved a smith sitting next to a hot fire with liquefied gold in a pot being stirred and skimmed to remove the impurities, known as dross, which rose to the top of the liquefied metal. The resulting product is a muddy substance that is almost pure gold (99.999% or 24K).

White is the presence of all the light in the spectrum that we see. Symbolically, white is representative of God's attributes.

One of the attributes which the color white signifies is the righteousness of Christ. He is pure light and pure righteousness and when a sinner comes to Him in faith He washes them clean.

Isaiah 1:18 (NLT)-"Come now, let's settle this," says the LORD. "Though your sins are like scarlet, I will make them as white as snow. Though they are red like crimson, I will make them as white as wool."

When Jesus washes us clean from sin, He makes us "white as snow" by giving us His righteousness. We then begin our journey of growing in faith.

2 Corinthians 5:21(NLT)-"For God made Christ, who never sinned, to be the offering for our sin, so that we could be made right with God through Christ."

God is divine perfection, and our goal is to live in right standing before Him.

Isaiah 6:3 (NLT)-"They were calling out to each other, "Holy, holy, holy is the LORD of Heaven's Armies! The whole earth is filled with His glory!"

In a teaching somewhere along my journey, I learned that in the Jewish language, when something is mentioned twice there is great emphasis being put upon what is being said.

This is the reason that Jesus often said, "Truly, truly" or "verily, verily" because He was about to say something of paramount importance. So, it follows that when something is mentioned three times, it is super colossal important. The only attribute of God that is mentioned three times in the entire Bible is that He is Holy, Holy, Holy and the earth is full of His glory. "Qadowsh" is the Hebrew word for holy. It means "sacred" and "set apart".

God is also omnipresent (present everywhere at the same time), omnipotent (all powerful), and omniscient (all knowing). God also knows the past, the present, and the future and He lives in all three.

1 Peter 1:15 (NLT)-"But now you must be holy in everything you do, just as God who chose you is holy."

As mentioned earlier, not a one of us is perfect or holy, but we are perfectly forgiven and made the very righteousness of Christ as 2 Corinthians 5:21 teaches. However, in this scripture verse Peter is reminding us about our conduct. Our lives should reflect the holiness of God because we are His children. Although we will never be completely holy in this life, we should continually aim toward the goal of living lives that are set apart.

God's attributes include being sovereign, merciful, and immutable, meaning unchanging.

Of all God's immutable attributes, perhaps, Love is at the top of the list.

"God is love." (1 John 4:8) Read that again.

God. Is. Love.

God does not just have love. He is love! He is the Creator of all things and is the truest purest definition of Love.

His love is unconditional, which unlike human love is conditional. Human love is based on our feelings or emotions. True love is an action. God sacrificed His only Son, who gave His life so that we could be reconciled with the Father. We were created for that very reason...to have a loving relationship with Him and Jesus willingly sacrificed His life so that we could.

1Corinthians 13:4-7 encourages us from The Message translation.

"Love never gives up. Love cares more for others than for self. Love doesn't want what it doesn't have. Love doesn't strut, Doesn't have a swelled head, Doesn't force itself on others, Isn't always "me first," Doesn't fly off the handle, Doesn't keep score of the sins of others, Doesn't revel when others grovel, Takes pleasure in the flowering of truth, Puts up with anything, Trusts God always, Always looks for the best, Never looks back, But keeps going to the end."

While the vision of nuclear explosions was literal and real in the spirit realm, we were able to view its manifestation in this realm via our consciousness. We encountered a demonstration of God's awesome power and nature. The feeling was one of pure ecstasy at being in the presence of the Lord! It is a place you never want to leave.

The aftermath left our souls, that is, our mind, will and emotions, foggy and full and our joints weak and wobbly, for hours afterwards, with such a profound wonder of a mighty God. The feeling was so foreign to us, we questioned each other as to whether either one had eaten the blueberry muffins! Earlier in the day, before our meeting, we jokingly admonished each other not to eat anything as it may be drugged. However, today, we realize that we entered into a realm so wonderfully awesome, no drug could possibly replicate it!

Until now, we mixed all things spiritual. Everything was lumped together. Lily Dale, psychics, the Catholic Church, saints, demons and angels were all in the spirit realm. and we really made no distinction. Seriously transitioning from the secular world of new age theology to the body of Christ was all a part of our journey growing in knowledge and Truth.

10

TOM'S TESTING

As we continued flourishing in our spiritual gifts, the human element of skepticism presented itself within the church government. We were invited to a breakfast that unbeknownst to us, at the time, was contrived for the express purpose of testing my gifting.

In attendance were the pastor, his wife, and several of the church elders plus their wives. For Marianne and I this was quite an honor to be included amongst the church leaders. While exhilarated we were, at the same time, disquieted as to the purpose of our attendance.

After a lovely breakfast and pleasant chitchat, the pastor produced an envelope from his inside jacket pocket. He gave no clues or hints as to its contents. He held the non-descript white envelope aloft and asked me what I thought it contained.

Perplexed, I chuckled nervously and wondered to myself if he thought I was the Great Kreskin. Never before had such a thing been requested of me nor had I ever presented myself in that manner. At that moment, the realization dawned upon me that the pastor and elders were calling me out. "What"? I asked incredulously. "Nobody can know that." How would I know what is in the envelope, I inquired silently to myself. It could be anything, I thought; a ticket, a bill, a paper clip. How was I to know what was in the envelope? Seconds seemed like minutes as I sought the Lord's rescue.

As I reached for my bible and placed my thumb along its edge, not knowing where I was going, I opened to 2 Samuel. My eyes were drawn to the middle of the page where chapter 11 began. As I silently began to read the passage I realized it was the chronicle of King David's adulterous affair with Bathsheba. With trepidation, and a huge lump in my throat, I hesitated to share just what I thought the envelope contained. What if I'm wrong?

"This letter is regarding an inappropriate matter", I shared.

The pastor inquired, "What do you mean?" He wanted me to be more specific.

I hemmed and hawed for a moment or two then replied, "OK, it's regarding an adulterous affair."

As the elders looked one to the other and then at me the pastor exclaimed, "Holy moly!" and revealed that it was, indeed, a letter regarding an adulterous affair. It was written by an elder's wife, neither of whom was in attendance, confessing to the affair which had happened a couple years prior.

This was a revelation I did not want to share. Being a very intelligent man with an invitation to Oxford, the pastor was skeptical of my spiritual gifting, as were the elders, and understandably so.

However, I was being tested, and while disconcerting, I realized the Lord was validating me before the pastor and elders of the church. This enlightenment was tremendously humbling and also exhilarating. The Lord was backing me up! What better Champion to have your back? Not knowing how or when He would use me, I would be His willing servant.

11

TIM THE SKEPTICAL CHURCH ELDER

One of the elders at the pastor's breakfast meeting was not yet totally convinced of prophetic spiritual gifts. Tim was an analytical thinker; he was also a Ranger, and more of a science guy except when it came to his faith, of course. However, one Sunday his skepticism of the prophetic spiritual gifts was to be challenged.

As was his custom prior to Sunday service, Pastor Sal asked if there were any prayer requests. Tim requested prayer for his son, Eddy. It seems that Eddy was continuing to have respiratory issues in spite of the fact he had been to doctors, specialists and had even been hospitalized for a time. Nothing or no one was able to relieve his ongoing condition. The poor boy had been suffering for some time.

The following day, I inquired of the Lord regarding little Eddy's illness. What He revealed to me was a furnace. To me, the furnace spoke of being the source of Eddy's continued poor health.

I called Tim and shared that the Lord showed me his furnace may be faulty; or it could be your air ducts, I said.

He replied that he just had his air ducts cleaned, but he would re-check the furnace.

Tim called me the next day and explained that on the furnace he found a compartment that he never knew was there. He realized the compartment was attached to a humidifier, and the compartment contained mold. The mold was migrating into the ducts, exacerbating his son's condition.

Tim thanked me for being obedient to the Lord's leading. He was profoundly moved and grateful for the word of knowledge from the Lord. We prayed together and thanked God for His grace and mercy. Although Eddy was not completely healed, this word of knowledge pinpointed the cause of his exacerbation, and allowed his medication to beneficially treat his respiratory condition.

When one personally experiences the voice of God the prophetic becomes all the more real, as Tim testified one Sunday service some months later.

During one of Buffalo's notorious blizzards, Tim was travelling down the I-90 to Batavia, a 40 mile trek from Buffalo, for a work related assignment. The weather was snowy, with about two or three feet of snow already on the ground, but usual for a Buffalo winter. The conditions changed rapidly as the winds picked up, blowing the snow around which had already accumulated. Adding to the mix, the new accumulation was falling at a rate of 3 inches per hour, and Tim soon found himself driving in the middle of a lake effect snowstorm. The driving was treacherous, with gusts of wind limiting visibility to about twenty to twenty-five feet ahead of him. Tim was familiar with these conditions as he lived in the Southern Tier, right in the middle of ski country, where abundant snowfall is commonplace.

As he was cautiously travelling down the highway, he felt as though the Lord instructed him to pull to the side of the interstate. Very often it is far more perilous to pull over in a blizzard than it is to continue at a prudent pace. Be that as it may, Tim pulled over to the side of the thoroughfare.

Sitting in his vehicle with the flashers on, as cars passed, Tim prayerfully questioned why he was there. No answer from above. Puzzled and without answers, he waited a few more minutes, then turned his flashers off, and signaled to enter the lane. As he put his car in drive, his attention was diverted to his passenger side. A red color in the snow caught his attention. How odd, Tim thought, to see color in a blinding white snowstorm. Putting his car back in park and putting his flashers back on, he squinted through the windshield in an attempt to identify what he was looking at. The best he was able to ascertain was just sudden and brief flashes of red. Unable to distinguish anything Tim, the Ranger, exited the passenger side door to investigate, as his training taught him to do.

Trudging through thigh high snow and battling fierce winds stinging his uncovered face and eyes, Tim made his way toward the unidentified, out of place object. As he drew closer, he established the object was a car partially buried in the snow.

With adrenalin rushing, he raced toward the driver side of the vehicle, brushed the snow off the window and peered inside. He was just as surprised to see a woman sitting in the driver's seat, as she was relieved and overwhelmed to see him peering in at her.

Shoveling the snow from the blocked door by hand, and rescuing her from entombment, Tim escorted the woman back to his car where he called for a tow truck. The towing service advised him they would be unable to make it out there until the storm subsided. Tim informed them of the vehicle's color and approximate location, and then drove the woman to safety.

Along the ride, Tim's rescuee shared that as she lost control of her car, she slid off the road and down the slight embankment, plunging into three feet of snow. Unable to open her door, she realized she was stuck and had to wait for help (Keep in mind, this was the mid 1990's and well before everyone had a cell phone). However, being stuck there for several hours, she was afraid of becoming asphyxiated, as it was quite possible the tailpipe had become obstructed. She shut off the engine, turning it back on only periodically and briefly to keep warm, as the temperatures were in the low teens. Not knowing when or if she would be found, she feared for her life and was frantic as lake effect snowstorms can last for hours or even days.

With tears in her eyes the woman relayed to Tim how grateful and thankful she was that he came to her rescue.

As Tim ended his testimony, he could not adequately express how humbled he was by God's leading him to rescue a stranded motorist, possibly saving her life. Where skepticism previously reigned Tim now knew, without a doubt from his experience, that God does speak to us today.

12

POLITICS IN THE CHURCH

Following my testing and time on trial at the pastor's home, I realized as did he my gifting was, indeed, genuine. Even so, just as the highs are high, the lows are low.

Unbeknownst to me, Pastor Sal wanted to elevate me to the position of church elder. However, one of the congregants, who himself aspired to the position, made a lot of noise as to why I should not be elevated to the position of elder; the reason being I was still a baby Christian. In the government of the church, it is true; you must be "converted" for at least 2-3 years. As 1 Timothy 3:6 tells us, "He must not be a recent convert, or he may become conceited and fall under the same judgment as the devil." (NIV)

From our perspective, this was not entirely the case. We had a Catholic conversion way back in the late 1970's, which the Protestant church did not recognize as a valid conversion.

During this time, we felt the wooing of the Spirit and attended mass every day, purchased a Catholic bible, and felt a tremendous pull to those things we knew as taught to us by Catholic nuns, growing up in Catholic homes, and attending Catholic schools. We were baptized, made our first communion, were confirmed, and married in the Catholic Church.

We were searching for all things Spiritual, as we understood them. True, all of our earlier expressions of the Catholic faith were done by rote and ritualistic, rather than spiritual. Later we were compelled by the Spirit of God to seek Him, rather than the ritualistic practices of the Catholic Church. God is not in the rituals nor does He dwell in buildings. Rather, He dwells within us! "The God who made the world and everything in it is the Lord of heaven and earth and does not live in temples built by human hands." (Acts 17:24 NIV)

This pastor acknowledged we had accepted Jesus Christ into our lives as our Lord and Savior, and were converted. However, there was such uproar from this individual and his wife that the pastor had to consider his livelihood as pastor in the Community Fellowship Church. In addition, being a generous tither carried a lot of political church weight in the decision making.

Consequently, I was not promoted to elder, which I accepted without rancor, as I had not been seeking any position within the church. It was the pastor's decision to make and I abided in his wisdom and his decision.

However, that was just the beginning of our understanding of the politics in the church, and just how much of the world resides within its four walls.

13

CHARLIE

In the summer of 1992, my father, Charlie, was diagnosed with bladder cancer which had already metastasized from prostate cancer. It is a horrible and debilitating disease, which if it had been caught earlier, perchance, would have prolonged his life.

During this time, I was content to spend quality time with my father as his part-time caregiver, heedless of my all-consuming schedule. Illness held little sway over day to day business operations, caring for family, home and horses. These responsibilities could not be ignored. Our son and daughter had recently graduated from college and although formerly integrated into the family business, were now looking for full-time capacity. This was an additional challenge along with providing continued employment for our long-time employees.

The excruciating pain Charlie endured rendered me helpless. Although my compassion for him caused my heart to ache, it did nothing to alleviate his suffering. He was not under hospice care, at this time, and pain medication was doled out sparingly by his physician. Surgery was not an option due to his age and advanced condition.

With this knowledge, I was concerned for my father's salvation. Although he was raised Catholic, Charlie did not ascribe to much of the Catholic Church teachings, which includes attending the sacrifice of the mass, receiving Communion, transubstantiation, confession, etc. Therefore, Charlie had more Spiritual understanding than Catholic leanings. As a father with a young family he attended Sunday mass infrequently. Christmas Eve midnight Mass and Easter were about it. As he became older, he rarely visited church at all. And growing up Catholic one does not discuss religion at home. Your inner peace comes from rote and rituals.

The Protestant church has a very different idea of the meaning of salvation. Salvation is not through works, but through the sacrifice of Christ alone. "For by grace you have been saved through faith-and this not from yourselves, it is the gift of God-not by works, so that no one can boast." (Ephesians 2:8-9 NIV) On the surface, Protestants, for the most part, believe that accepting Jesus Christ into your heart and making Him Lord of your life constitutes salvation. Recite the sinner's prayer, they say, and you're in.

So to that end, I was not quite confident of where my father stood on salvation. Being uncertain of broaching the subject myself, I asked Pastor Sal from Community Fellowship Church to intervene.

Not knowing what to expect, Pastor Sal asked Charlie if he believed in Jesus Christ as his Lord and Savior. We held our collective breath as his prompt response of "Yeah, don't you?" caused everyone to chuckle and exhale a breath of blessed relief.

During the week, while I was agonizing over and empathizing with my father's condition, and not knowing what to do about it, I recalled reading an article about "laying on of hands for healing". From what I remembered this article had to do with a lay person, in a hospital setting, laying on hands for healing for several of the hospital patients. Even though this was a practice of my Aunt Mary's small charismatic Catholic group, albeit underground in the basement, it was not something that I was familiar with or even contemplated. It was certainly out of my league, I guess you could say.

What could it hurt to try? Upon entering my father's bedroom I asked him how he was doing on this particularly rainy and chilly evening. He replied that he was in a lot of pain and it hurt very much. I inquired as to where exactly the pain was and he pointed to the affected bladder area. With my hand hovering about six inches above the area and not really sure I was doing it correctly, I silently began to pray for a healing.

With some relief evident in his voice, he asked what I was doing. Now, I should point out right here that my father had macular degeneration in both eyes and was declared legally blind. He could not readily see what I was endeavoring to accomplish. I was somewhat embarrassed because, well, this was something kinda wacky to do in our family. It just wasn't done or even thought about for that matter. I tentatively asked him why he was asking. Charlie replied that he felt heat and it felt better as I continued to hold my hand in that position. It brought him a degree of much sought after comfort.

With that declaration I removed my hand. My father noticed the absence of heat and said as much. Although he was not pain free, it was visible by his countenance that he was still comfortable. I was astonished that he admitted to feeling relief from that simple act born out of compassion for his suffering. He was very tired and soon thereafter, we exchanged goodnights, and I told him I would be by the next day to visit with him.

On our drive home my wife inquired about the time spent with my father. I replied, "We visited and he was in a lot of pain". Excitedly, I added, "And, well, you won't believe this!" I then reminded her of the article regarding the laying on of hands for healing. She said she remembered. I then showed her how I placed my hand over my father's bladder area, demonstrating over and above her thigh.

 She responded, "I felt that!" I asked her what she felt. She said, "I felt the heat go straight through my bone!" We were both in wonderment of what had just happened, and to my astonishment, had happened for a second time. I went on to tell her how my father felt the same thing and how this elementary action brought him a certain degree of comfort and relief from his agonizing pain. We speculated as to how long the pain would subside and whether it was possible that he could have been healed. It was truly amazing!

However, our elation was short lived. Upon our next home visit Charlie's pain had returned. His condition was deteriorating and hospice was summoned. This was a virile man 89 years young with a sharp mind and a physique of someone much younger. My dad worked on the railroad until he was 76 years old, after working twelve years there as a switchman. He was very active in spite of the macular degeneration that claimed his sight. Now, this very intelligent and healthy specimen of a human being was betrayed by his own body. Septicemia, which is a blood infection, was voraciously conquering his immune system because the bodily function of elimination was deteriorating and causing his organs to shut down. When hospice could do no more Charlie was transported to the hospital where the prognosis, as one can image, was not positive.

One of my last conversations with my dad sticks with me. I can still hear his request in my mind. "Tommy, let me go", he beseeched me. I was taken aback. His expression of wanting to go was a shock to me. My first silent reaction was NO! But Charlie's entreaty drove home the reality this wasn't about me and my selfish feelings. It was about him lying in his hospital bed suffering beyond belief! God was extending His tremendous grace to my father to hang on through his pain until I was ready to let him go. Can you imagine that; until I was ready to let him go? Who was I? The unselfish unconditional love my father had for me was more than humbling. He was ready to go, but would not leave until he knew I was ready to let him go.

With a heavy heart, my wife and I journeyed down the corridor to pray at the hospital's chapel. It was paramount for me to reflect upon my father's appeal to "let him go". Separately and unbeknownst to each other, Marianne and I prayed the same prayer. We tearfully petitioned the Lord to take away his pain, to release him from the constant torment and agony. We asked that He send His best warrior angels to guard him and accompany him home. With anguished hearts we left the chapel without a word to each other.

The following day we were summoned to the hospital because my father's condition had changed. He was gone. On November 26, 1994, my father Charlie passed away. Our prayers for his release from pain and agony were remorsefully answered.

Although my father was not healed, I believe his faith in Jesus Christ and compassionate prayer, moved Jesus to grant this wonderful man a modicum of comfort. Throughout the bible, Jesus prayed for someone or healed someone when He was moved by compassion to do so. Why He chose not to heal my father, I'll never know. But I do know that His loving manifest presence was felt through His touch in the form of pain relieving heat flowing from my hand that brought my father comfort.

As time passed, I reflected upon the entire experience of my father's illness. An enlightenment of knowing and understanding rained down upon me that God is Spirit (John 4:24) and resides within us (the Comforter, which is the Holy Ghost, whom the Father sends in Jesus' name-John 14:26). He truly does not dwell in buildings made by human hands.

First and foremost, my father knew Jesus Christ as his Lord and Savior, was forgiven his sins, and spiritually, rather than physically, healed which is everlasting.

In this life we will experience illness, pain, heartache and death. It is part and parcel of the human condition. Jesus did not heal everyone, including Himself.

As a matter of many translations, Isaiah 53:3 tells us Jesus was "familiar with sickness" (Rotherham), "knowing illness" (Concordant Literal), "acquainted with sickness" (Young's Literal), "acquainted with infirmity" (Douay Rheims), Himself.

Yes, Jesus suffered sickness or disease Himself as further evidenced in Luke 4:23. After reading from a scroll quoting the prophet Isaiah "Jesus said to them, 'Surely you will quote this proverb to Me: 'Physician, heal yourself!'" (Isaiah 61:1) Jesus would not have made that declaration if it was not obvious to the Pharisees that He, indeed, needed to be healed of an infirmity.

Speaking to the apostles in John 14:12 Jesus proclaimed "Truly, truly, I tell you, whoever believes in Me will also do the works that I am doing. He will do even greater things than these, because I am going to the Father". The greater works meaning spiritual things, rather than physical things. "The Spirit gives life; the flesh profits nothing. The words I have spoken to you are spirit and they are life." (John 6:63) Wouldn't a greater thing be to raise a spiritually dead person to spiritual life everlasting, rather than to raise a physically dead person to physical life only to have them die again? Those with ears to hear let them hear what the Spirit is saying.

14

SURRENDER

First and foremost, the carnal mind has got to go. A carnal mind is a mind that focuses on worldly or fleshly pursuits. "Those who live according to the sinful nature have their minds set on what that nature desires; but those who live in accordance with the Spirit have their minds set on what the Spirit desires. The mind of sinful man is death, but the mind controlled by the Spirit is life and peace; the sinful mind is hostile to God. It does not submit to God's law, nor can it do so. Those controlled by the sinful nature cannot please God." (Romans 8:5-8 NIV)

The carnal mind is constantly at war with the Spiritual mind. Our war strategy was to read and study our bible, spend time with like-minded people, and spend more time in prayer and praise. Soaking our minds in the myriad of TV and radio ministries opened up a whole new world to us.

Sitting at home one fine afternoon, I tuned into the television ministry of a well-known Pentecostal minister. As the choir sang, the words to the songs scrolled along the bottom of the television screen. The people in the congregation were singing along, raising their arms in praise, and worshipping God with their whole hearts. Why I don't have the freedom in me to do that, I wondered. Do I not love God with all my heart, as well? Is my passion for Him not as deep as those worshipping on the television screen? Is it my carnal mind stopping me from worshipping in that way? The mere fact that I was asking those questions is, indeed, the Lord exposing my carnal mind, and bringing conviction to me that it's all about Him and not me.

Sitting in my own living room I had nothing to be embarrassed about, but I still felt awkward. However, being so moved by the words in the song, I slowly lifted my hands and began to sing along. A rush of emotion permeated me as tears streamed down my face. Putting Jesus first, with awkwardness and embarrassment gone, I soon realized I was surrendering myself to Him. His presence felt so close to me, I was consumed with His love. With the simple act of abandoning my self-consciousness, I was ushered into the presence of the Lord!

Taking my new found freedom into the church, however, was quite another matter. After the preaching the following Sunday, the worship team ascended the stage and led the congregation in song. No one in this church ever, to my knowledge, lifted their hands in praise. After all, this was not a Pentecostal church.

With arms shaking, sweat collecting on my forehead, and struggling mightily, I slowly began to raise my arms. I succeeded in lifting them to shoulder height, which constituted a monumental victory. Now, if I could muster up a tad more courage, I could raise my arms the rest of way. This feat seemed unachievable. The longer the worship team sang the heavier my arms became. The word "Surrender!" suffused my mind, as tears began to flow.

Finally, with hands literally shaking, inch by inch, I lifted them up higher. As I glanced to my right, my wife had lifted her hands in praise, as well. Amazingly and slowly, but surely, and to my surprise, one by one, many of the small congregation joined in. As each person lifted their hands in praise, the whole atmosphere in the room changed. A quaking in the spirit realm arose as the Lord touched each person in kind. A spiritual freedom reigned down upon God's own, and commenced to release all who struggled with unabashed worship just as I had struggled!

How is it we can exalt athletes, rock stars, television and movie stars, past presidents, war heroes, business people, millionaires, et al? Most of those mentioned deserve our respect, without a doubt. Their accomplishments are touted and lauded loudly, with bold fervor, in some cases; but we lack that same exuberance and wholeheartedness when it comes to exalting Jesus Christ, Creator of the Universe. Why?

For most of us, our feet are still firmly planted in worldly pursuits. For believers, things of the flesh are in constant warfare with things of the Spirit. And as any believer is aware "burning" of the flesh is not only painful, it stinketh! This is not a literal physical burning of the flesh; it is a spiritual burning up of those things that keep us from true fellowship with the Lord. "Therefore, since we are receiving a kingdom that cannot be shaken, let us be thankful, and so worship God acceptably with reverence and awe, for our 'God is a consuming fire.'" (Hebrews 12:28-29 NIV)

As we walk closer with God, conviction, which is the "burning" of the carnal flesh, becomes more intense, not less so. Layer upon layer of the onion of our self is peeled slowly and painfully away.

A common practice for many of my family, friends, acquaintances and me, was and is taking the Lord's name in vain. You know, say you drop a drinking glass and it shatters all over the floor. Suddenly, without thought, the expletive explodes from your mouth. Or say, a tight scoring Sunday afternoon football game where the quarterback is sacked. Jesus Christ, you exclaim. A seemingly innocuous knee-jerk reaction when one is frustrated, upset, or angry. It may be a knee-jerk reaction, but the habit is anything but innocuous! Taking the Lord's name in vain is disrespectful to His Holiness. The word vain means, among other things, useless or for no reason. God is Holy, Majestic, and Awesome. "O Lord, our Lord, how majestic is your name in all the earth! (Psalm 8:1 NIV) "He provided redemption for His people; He ordained His covenant forever-Holy and Awesome is His name. (Psalm 111:9 NIV) The first line of the prayer that most of us are familiar with, "The Lord's Prayer" says..."hallowed (or Holy) be thy (your) name." (Matthew 6:9 NIV)

I had become complacent and casual when referring to my Lord. Even simply saying things like OMG, Lord have mercy, or Good Lord, in everyday conversation, were just idioms, not said with reverence. Coming before His throne is only through His Grace. "Let us then approach the throne of grace with confidence, so that we may receive mercy and find grace to help us in our time of need." (Hebrews 4:16 NIV) We must never take that grace for granted! Only God's conviction, mercy and grace could bring me to this place of understanding.

15

TRUST ME

MARIANNE

Skepticism, one could say, is my middle name. To be fair, my thought process intuits that just because someone shares something or says something or is the "expert" on something, to me, doesn't make it so. Loftily, in all matters, I always theorized myself to be more in league with the Berean's who, in Acts 17:11, we are told, "Now the Bereans were of more noble character than the Thessalonians, for they received the message with great eagerness and examined the Scriptures every day to see if what Paul said was true."

Pessimistic and cynical, I am characterized by my friends; pragmatic, I retort. My dear mate even exclaimed, "I swear, if Jesus Himself stood before you and introduced Himself, you would ask Him for proof of identification!"

"Hmmph", was my response.

One evening, after returning home from a particularly harrowing day at the shop, I plopped myself down in my favorite chair, with my favorite buddy, Mich, and just wanted to veg out before fixing dinner. My husband was finishing up in the barn, and I was taking this time to chill.

Seemingly, not five seconds later, in the door sweeps by beloved exhorting me to come outside to see this. "What...this?" I queried.

"Just c'mon. It's incredible", he exclaimed.

"Oh, Lord, preserve me", I thought to myself as I trudged out behind him.

As we made our way outside, Tom jauntily, me reluctantly, to the driveway alongside the house, Tom spun me around to look up at the sky over our home. Staring and speechless, we beheld an incredible phenomenon. The otherwise black nighttime sky was blood-red directly over our home.

With analytical thoughts whirring, I felt a stirring of air to my left side; the knowing that someone is there. For certain, that someone was not my husband, Tom, for he was a few steps in front of me and to the right. Softly, a gentle touch settled upon my right shoulder as a flutter tickled my left ear. "Trust ME", He charged; emphasis on the word ME. I knew who this Someone was. He was my Lord and Savior, Jesus Christ. And this was not the first time He uttered those same words to me.

Many have remarked that our land and home in the Boston Hills of New York State was a portal to the spirit-realm and there was an inordinate amount of spiritual activity surrounding us. Be that as it may, I knew without a doubt, the crimson sky above our home was the sacrificial blood covering of our Lord and Savior, Jesus Christ, prophetically speaking.

Referring to the blood covering of Jesus is not a grisly scene from a slasher movie. The blood of Jesus among other gifts, gives life, pays for sins, redeems us, grants forgiveness, brings peace and reconciliation to God, allows us to enter with confidence and boldness into the most holy place, cleanses us from a guilty conscience, washes and sanctifies us. The life of the flesh is in the blood. (Leviticus 17:11 NAS)

As mentioned previously, this was not my first encounter of this magnitude.

Summertime and all was quiet in my drapery workroom. Everyone was elsewhere and I was quite alone working on a customer's order, my mind focused solely on the task at hand.

Without warning, the next moment I found myself trudging up a huge mountain. Being totally awake, I was wholeheartedly immersed, and participating in the cinematic scene that lay before me.

The cold and stormy black night ominously surrounded me. The sword hanging limply by my side was dull and rusted, and I was dragging my dented, dirty and gouged armor behind me. I had been slogging along for an eternity, and just had no fortitude to take another step. Collapsing right there and then, the realization hit me I had not made any progress up the forbidding mountain, at all. The impact of that recognition was dispiriting. Broken, battered and bloody, I wept bitterly. "Jesus", I cried, "please....help me!"

With that plea, I was instantly swept up the mountain, dirty armor and all. Not only was I swept up the mountain, but I was catapulted far beyond its summit. Here, wherever here was, I found myself in a room, that wasn't a room; there were no doors, windows or walls. All around a tempestuous storm raged; yet I felt safe in this room that wasn't a room. I was as a little girl; all dressed in white and full of wonder. My dirty, dented, and dinged armor was piled high beside me. And I was quite happy to leave it right there.

Far in the distance I saw a Man kneeling in front of a throne. "Papa?" I called tentatively. He held His arms open wide, and there was an incredible smile on His glorious face. "Papa!" I cried excitedly, as I ran toward the throne, "I knew it was You!" Again, I was there in an instant. He gathered me into His loving arms and onto His lap.

"What took you so long to come home?" He asked. Just as a little one would do I ducked my head to avoid answering Him. Instead, I showed Him my black eyes, bloody nose, fat lip, the big gashes on my back and legs, and the part of my belly where there was no skin at all, just my innards hanging out.

"Oh my," He soothed. With a gentle breath from His mouth all my wounds were instantly and painlessly healed.

I showered Him with kisses as His glorious laugh enveloped me, and He held me tightly to Himself.

Just as I began to slide down off His great lap He said, "Whoa, little one, not so fast." Uh-oh, I thought. "Because you have let things into your heart, he began, "things that aren't your burden to bear, the edges of your heart have begun to harden.

I have not given you a heart of stone, but a heart of flesh. A heart of flesh is what you must have to bind up the broken-hearted, to set the captives free, to preach the good news to the oppressed, and to loosen the shackles of those confined to the darkened caves!" With that admonition a strong Wind buffeted my chest.

In the next instant, I was kneeling before the throne all grown up. Jesus, as Commander of the Heavenly Host, was exhorting me firmly yet lovingly, "Come, it is time to return to battle. There are others who need reprieve."

As I looked to my right, the beautiful warrior angel that I have seen in other visions was holding my armor. It was magnificent to behold. My armor was shiny, golden and new. There were no dents or dings or gouges or broken straps. I immediately identified it as my armor because of the inscription on the breastplate. During my time in the heavenlies the breastplate inscription was obviously identified as mine, but upon returning to my workroom I was unable to remember what determined it to be so. However, while writing this narrative, some mature twenty years later, the inscription was revealed to me. "Nevertheless, God's solid foundation stands firm, sealed with this **inscription** (emphasis mine): 'The Lord knows those who are His....'" (2 Timothy 2:19 NIV)

Also, the breastplate was encrusted with jewels, mostly sapphires; row upon row of sapphires. There were also diamonds, rubies, emeralds and many more jewels that I did not recognize.

My breastplate was not akin to the sacred breastplate

worn by the Old Testament High Priest of the Israelites, which was embellished with twelve precious stones. The armor plate adorning my chest was similar to one belonging to a Roman soldier.

The breastplate was part of the Roman soldier's armor. It provided protection for the torso containing vital organs like the heart and lungs. Without a breastplate, a soldier would be vulnerable, as any attack could instantly become fatal. With a strong breastplate, the very same attacks become fruitless, as blows glance off the armor.

"Finally, be strong in the Lord and in his mighty power. Put on the full armor of God, so that you can take your stand against the devil's schemes. For our struggle is not against flesh and blood, but against the rulers, against the authorities, against the powers of this dark world and against the spiritual forces of evil in the heavenly realms. Therefore put on the full armor of God, so that when the day of evil comes, you may be able to stand your ground, and after you have done everything, to stand. Stand firm then, with the belt of truth buckled around your waist, with the **breastplate of righteousness in place**, and with your feet fitted with the readiness that comes from the gospel of peace. In addition to all this, take up the shield of faith, with which you can extinguish all the flaming arrows of the evil one. Take the helmet of salvation and the sword of the Spirit, which is the word of God. "(Ephesians 6:10-17 NIV)

The colored jewels found on my breast plate have biblical significance, as well. Gold represents faith in God and purity.

"In a large house there are articles not only of gold and silver, but also of wood and clay; some are for noble purposes and some for ignoble. If a man cleanses himself from the latter, he will be an instrument for noble purposes, made holy, useful to the Master and prepared to do any good work." (2 Timothy 2:20-21 NIV)

Blue symbolizes royalty, sovereignty, rulership, power and authority, worthy of honor. "...warriors clothed in blue...." (Ezekiel 23:6 NIV) "Mordecai left the king's presence wearing royal garments of blue and white, a large crown of gold, and a purple robe of fine linen (Esther 8:15 NIV).

However, while the color blue is explained above, sapphire represents the throne of God and the platform upon which His throne rests, as well as, His tablets which are also taken from His throne of sapphire.

This was revealed to my ceaseless wonderment of God's awesomeness, as I read whereby Moses went up Mt. Sinai and saw something like a pavement of sapphire under God's feet. (Exodus 24:9-10 NIV)

Similarly, in Ezekiel 1:26 and 10:1, Ezekiel saw the likeness of a throne of sapphire above the expanse.

After I donned my armor, Jesus helped me to my feet and we walked back the same way I had come. Oh, I did not want to go. Please, no, let me stay, I silently thought.

Jesus answered, "It's time; you must return."

With that the Holy Spirit, in the form of the Dove lighted upon my right shoulder. Immeasurable peace flooded my being even though I still did not want to leave Him.

Jesus took both my hands in His. As we were standing face to face, He kissed my cheek and said, "TRUST Me!" The emphasis was on the word "Trust".

With those words, I found myself back in my workroom. Physically, mentally and logically, I was at a loss to explain what had just happened.

The apostle Paul, formerly Saul, shares an intriguing explanation in 2Corinthians 12:2-4a. "I know a man in Christ who fourteen years ago was caught up to the third heaven. Whether it was in the body or out of the body I do not know-God knows. And I know that this man-whether in the body or apart from the body I do not know, but God knows-was caught up to paradise." (NIV)

Was I caught up to the third heaven? I do not know-God knows. Paul goes on to say, "I will boast about a man like that, but I will not boast about myself, except about my weaknesses. Even if I should choose to boast, I would not be a fool, because I would be speaking the truth. But I refrain, so no one will think more of me than is warranted by what I do or say. (2Corinthians 12:4b-6 NIV)

What I do know is this was my experience, and it was natural as breathing.

16

THE BRIDLE OF ALCOHOL

MARIANNE

Whenever the stressors or pressures of life were getting the better of me, I would reach for my drug of choice. That drug being one, two, three or four bottles of Mich. I was not an alcoholic, but I was a binge drinker. My cousin and I, alone, were known to polish off a case within the course of a weekend. The goal was to dull the throbbing pain, and sink into the blessed oblivion of feeling nothing over the conditions I could not control.

If my husband would deign to say anything, even a word about opening another bottle, with flippancy and insolence, I would pop another top. I did not carouse in bars or bar-hop, my self-medication occurred within the confines of my sanctuary, which was the home we were about to lose.

We literally built our log home together. While some things like the concrete foundation and roof were sub-contracted out, and assistance with the longer and heavier logs was gotten, my husband and I oversaw much of the physical construction. It was our dream home that we designed. My husband took time off from our business, our livelihood, to achieve our dream. It took a year and a half to complete. Now, not only were we about to lose our humble abode, we would also lose everything we had worked for in our twenty-seven years of marriage. Our home, business, and income property would become just a memory.

During the time of home construction my husband, as I mentioned, took time from our business to complete our endeavor. Our son and daughter were fabricating and installing our vertical blinds and window treatments. I was going on sales calls, making draperies and other window coverings with my two workroom ladies, taking care of the office and books, and manning the phones and floor. An employee, who had been with us for eight years, looked after the showroom and warehouse, and answered the phones while the rest of us were otherwise, engaged.

He was also helping himself to the cash from sales out of the warehouse stock of drapery hardware, carpet and vinyl. Not only that, but this unscrupulous excuse for a human being, had the unmitigated gall to advise my cousin, my cousin, mind you, to help herself to any of the cash from things she sold! Can you imagine the impertinence? Did he really think she would not tell me?

Needless to say, once enlightened to his dastardly deeds, I did a cursory audit of just the previous two years he was in our employ. He was with us for a total of eight years. We never imagined he was stealing from us even though there were rumors that he was fired from his last job for a missing night deposit totaling ten thousand dollars! But I digress. Upon the completion of my audit, I found that he had embezzled from us to the tune of approximately seventeen thousand dollars in two years! I shudder to imagine how much he helped himself to in eight years.

Paying state sales tax and income tax was increasingly difficult. I was quite flummoxed as to why our coffers were empty or nearly so. We certainly were doing the business.

Well, it all became crystal clear as I was made aware of the thief among us! I confronted him on his dastardly deeds; he accused me of being greedy, and I threw him out the door, figuratively, of course. Actually, I did advance on him aggressively, motioning him out the door, but he was way bigger than me in height and width, so I refrained.

After much discussion, we declined to pursue the matter and press charges because we felt sorry for this employee who was a single parent with two young girls at home. Furthermore, he had no assets, and little funds for reimbursement. Time in jail for him would simply take him away from his girls, which is something we did not want to do.

However, by this time, the IRS was looking for us, as was the NYS Department of Taxation and Finance; not to mention the fact that our home, income property and business property were being foreclosed upon. We refinanced everything to take care of the mounting debt and put our home up as collateral. Big mistake!

The interest rate on this second mortgage, through a finance company, was a whopping fifteen percent. The prevailing interest rate, at the conventional banks, was seven to eight percent. However, being a small business and losing our favorite banker to retirement, we had no choice but to go to secondary financing. The scrutiny of primary funding would not allow a second mortgage.

Instead of being conducive to our plight, our refinancing was more harmful than helpful. The economy was tanking, big box stores were opening up everywhere, and taking over a good majority of the market share. Meanwhile, our monthly monetary obligations totaled twelve thousand dollars, which included an unreasonable payment plan to the government. Anyone who has dealt with these types of payment plans can attest to the hardened hearts of bureaucrats.

After much conversation and reflection, my husband and I decided the only way out was to declare bankruptcy. It was a hard decision to reach. We had worked hard for everything we had. Nothing was given to us. No handouts. It was nose to the grindstone, day in and day out, working twelve to fourteen hours a day, including weekends to accomplish what we achieved. To declare bankruptcy is demoralizing, embarrassing, discouraging, and depressing. We opted for Chapter 11, which is the reorganization plan. We hoped that with a little breathing room we could get back on track and pay all of our creditors; not just what the bankruptcy courts allowed, but we wanted to pay the total of all that we owed. After a year and a half in, we knew we were beaten. Even though we reduced our monthly obligations to eight thousand dollars, we were no longer treading water, we were drowning. Relief would only come by converting our Chapter 11 bankruptcy plan to a Chapter 7 bankruptcy plan which is total liquidation.

During this time between Chapter 11 and Chapter 7, I was wallpapering our great room. The great room was a combination kitchen and family room on the ground floor of our log home, boasting a circular stairway leading up to the living room, bedrooms and bath area. The black wrought iron circular stairs then continued up to the loft expanse, which included another bedroom and half bath. We designed the rounded bow window front to rise from the ground floor of the kitchen area all the way up to the cathedral ceiling at a soaring twenty eight foot roof height. The twenty foot open ceiling in the living room allowed us a nineteen foot Christmas tree to decorate with family and friends. Many wonderful and warm memories remain from those times we all spent together.

I absolutely loved the cozy dining alcove of the great room. The wide ruffled balloon shades that adorned the alcove were created to match the wallpaper. It was necessary to remove the beautiful mammoth shade from the window, done in a Laura Ashley steel blue mini-floral to allow papering the tricky curved width.

With tons of fabric and miles of cord to wrestle with, I was muttering, complaining, and swearing like a sailor as I endeavored to extract the shade from its mooring. In frustration, I collapsed onto the kitchen chair, and reached for my trusty and ever faithful companion...Mich. For the uninitiated Mich is short for Michelob, as in Lite, as in beer.

As I grabbed Mich up, I abruptly stopped on route to a swallow. Unbidden, I entreated the Lord to take this from me; "this" being my crutch, my need for a swill at every frustration or inability to control the circumstance. Without another thought, I rose from the chair, and made my way to the kitchen sink. Once there, I poured my nearly full bottle of Mich down the drain, without hesitation or remorse.

A shawl of peace descended upon my shoulders as I "heard" the clanking of chains fall to the ground, and a thought as soft as a whisper reminded me...."The God of peace will (soon) crush Satan under your feet. The grace of our Lord Jesus (be) is with you." (Romans 16:20 NIV)

The Lord was in charge of me and my circumstances. Choices we had made personally, and in business brought us to our present crises, but the Lord would keep us. This time of trial by fire was to be embraced, not feared or shunned. "In this you greatly rejoice, though now for a little while you may have had to suffer grief in all kinds of trials. These have come so that your faith-of greater worth than gold, which perishes even though refined by fire-may be proved genuine and may result in praise, glory and honor when Jesus Christ is revealed." (1 Peter 1:6-7 NIV)

Here I would like to share that in the midst of our tribulation, my husband and I remained unbelievably and eerily calm. Regardless of the worldly calamity raining down upon us an inner peace transcended all understanding.

Our son and daughter, being privy to our beleaguering woes, were stymied by our tranquility. A comment made by our son will remain with me forever. He said simply, "I want what you have!" Unsure of what he meant Tommy continued, "You have so much stuff falling down around you and yet you are so calm. How do you do that?"

His declaration initially gave me pause, and then filled me with incredible gladness. What we had and what our son was witnessing was the power of the indwelling Holy Spirit. Jesus promised us that "In this world you will have tribulation"; but, He also promised to "be of good cheer, I have overcome the world!" (John 16.33) And, trusting in Him, so would we.

17

GOD WHERE ARE YOU?

TOM

Losing things that you worked so hard for takes a tremendous toll on your soul (the soul is your mind or consciousness, will and emotions). Being in the prime of my life, these things weren't supposed to happen; or rather not supposed to happen to me.

My wife and I fully believed we had prepared ourselves for our old age. We owned income property to see us through after retirement, as well as a prospering business to hand over to the next generation. That was our life plan.

Our log home, in the country, was our dream home. We built a stable, which housed three horses, and enjoyed groomed trails to ride along. These trails were courtesy of the Tennessee Gas Pipeline who was the owner and caretaker of the gas lines that ran through the area.

Packing a lunch, which included hot dogs to roast over a fire by our secret waterfall, was a customary Sunday afternoon horseback riding excursion. Moonlit trail rides under a starry sky were a special treat. This was our aspired retirement, our security.

Why was God taking this from me? By turning to God and following Him, why was He allowing this to happen? We went to church on Sunday and bible study on Wednesday. We studied His Word daily. We supported the church community by teaching Sunday school, and volunteering for all manner of projects and potlucks. We were upstanding members of the community, with fair and honest business practices. We were floundering while the wicked were prospering. Why would He send a man destined to be our employee who stole thousands of dollars from our business, and caused all manner of chaos, if He was watching over us? By this employee stealing money and customers led to all manner of negative domino effects. The IRS was not happy, the State Sales Tax people were not happy, our mortgage lenders were not happy, and we certainly were not happy.

We were in constant turmoil juggling funds. Was it the economy, which was tanking at this time? Was it the big box stores, with merchandise from China that were making huge in-roads into the custom fabricated drapery trade? Yes, these all were contributing factors. Factors that made it very difficult to recover our losses. The stress of it all was taking its toll.

One night, lying in bed, I was asking the Lord, "Where are You in all this? Why have You allowed this? Why have You let this happen?" Immediately, a consuming embrace of dread, fear, extreme anxiety, grief and depression, a feeling of being forsaken and rejected smothered me. Mental and emotional agony ripped through me, wave after wave taking me deeper and deeper into the nightmare of the inky abyss. It was utterly and unbearably terrifying! Sweating profusely, my mind continued to swirl with the constant onslaught of black tormenting emotions which I could not control! All hope was abandoned. I was experiencing the suicidal melancholy of someone on the verge of no return.

Gripping the edge of the bed in the midst of the turmoil, and on the brink of losing my mind, I was unable to rationalize and normalize the mental state that was choking the life out of me. Death, I "reasoned", was my only reprieve; my only hope.

Suddenly, as though with the flick of a switch, I was released from the whirlwind of darkness. Just as quickly as the nebulous emotions turned on, they were turned off. I am uncertain as to how long I was insanity's prisoner, but it could not have been but a few minutes, at most, because that was all I would have been able to sustain on my own.

Liberated from this waking nightmare, comprehension lacerated me. My Lord had been there right along. His grace prevented me from being trapped within the confines of the isolation and desolation invading my mind.

My troubles were not the Lord's doing, they were mine. Remorsefully, I understood the choices and decisions I made were the very things that ensnared me in my current predicaments. I was experiencing life on this earthly realm. In spite of myself, the Lord was showing me myself. "Do not love the world or anything in the world. If anyone loves the world, the love of the Father is not in him. For everything in the world-the cravings of sinful man, the lust of his eyes and the boasting of what he has and does comes not from the Father but from the world." (1John 2:15-16 NIV)

The Lord initiated this petrifying episode to illuminate the outcome of my life's trials without Him. He illustrated the fragility and ineffectual efforts of my humanness without Him. He brought me to this place of desperate dependence-dependence upon Him –dependence upon Someone greater than myself. He showed me that when I am weak, then I am strong. (2Corinthians 12:10 NIV) He showed me that I can do everything through Him who gives me strength. (Philippians 4:13 NIV) He showed me that the God of Peace will soon crush Satan under my feet. (Romans 16:20 NIV)

"These things I have spoken to you, that in Me you may have peace. In the world you will have tribulation; but be of good cheer, I have overcome the world." (John 16:33NKJV)

The following evening, sitting in our great room, relaxing in my favorite rocking chair, I was reflecting upon the previous night's nightmare. The horrendous emotions tormenting me were something I have never ever experienced in my life! Even though the experience was such a short duration, it was enough to make a forever lasting impression upon me. I cannot imagine anyone not wanting God in their life! Is this what is to be expected for those condemned to the lake of fire; nothing but a black tormenting void absent of God's love, grace, hope, mercy, and protection?

I was being drawn deeper and deeper into the consciousness of entering another realm. The best way I can describe what was happening next was I could sense a slow moving "fog" rolling towards me from the other side of the room. It was not a literal fog; I could not see it with my physical eyes. It was a spiritual experience, a seeing and a sensing with spiritual eyes, ears, smell, taste and touch.

The presence of God was moving toward me; and as the "fog" rolled over me, I felt a great peaceful intoxication and a profound reverence for God, just knowing He was there with me, in the room.

As horribly low as the negative emotions brought me the night before, the presence of God lifted me wonderfully high. When the Lord is near He spiritually changes and charges what we perceive to be the natural order of the atmosphere; and everyone to whom He chooses to reveal Himself embraces it. It's not easy to explain the mind of God because God is Spirit and His manifest presence is not understood by our natural minds.

18

DELIVERANCE MINISTRY

During our time at Community Fellowship Church, Tom and I were introduced to the deliverance ministry under the tutelage of Minister Ted and his wife Karoline, as shared in a previous chapter. What is to follow is not a discourse on or a "how to" regarding a deliverance ministry. It is simply our experience, and a mini explanation.

A deliverance ministry, in Christianity, focuses on cleansing a person of demons and evil spirits. The "goal" of a demon is to pull you away from God. An unclean spirit can manifest in a person's life as a result of being given the authority to oppress and demonize.

Being oppressed or demonized is not the same as going through a trial, which is the fire of God cleansing from us those things which are not of Him.

Biblically, Jesus says it this way applicable to a deliverance ministry, "The Spirit of the Lord is on me, because he has anointed me to preach good news to the poor. He has sent me to proclaim freedom for the prisoners and recovery of sight for the blind, to release the oppressed, to proclaim the year of the Lord's favor." (Luke 4:18-19 NIV)

Every Christian has been, is, or will be oppressed or demonized by unclean spirits. No one who has the Spirit of God in them can be **_possessed_** by Satan or his minions. Possession signifies ownership. A child of God belongs to God. Christians can be attacked in their mind, will, emotions and body. They can be depressed, fearful, wounded emotionally or spiritually, etc., but this is not possession; it is **_oppression_** or harassment or demonization. Some simply prefer the term demonization. It is a plague of the human experience.

Every human being needs deliverance from evil. "....it is an experience of evil Elohim has given to the sons of humanity to humble them by it." (Ecclesiastes 1:13 Concordant Literal Version) Some translations render the word evil as task or burden. Nevertheless, they all stem from the Hebrew word *ra*, which is translated evil in Hebrew.

Jesus said, "The thief comes only to steal and kill and destroy; I have come that they may have life, and have it to the full." (John 10:10 NIV) Jesus is that life which is the light of men. The light shines in the darkness, but the darkness has not understood it. (John 1:4 NIV semi-paraphrase)

The methods of deliverance ministries are varied. We were committed to furthering our education and growing in spiritual things, which included this part of ministry. Investing much time to our education, we were dedicated to traveling weekly to the Southern Tier of NY for our instruction. The classes were roughly 3-1/2 hours from our home, and often times lasted well into the night. Our long drive home was filled with excitement, and fascination as we discussed, and reviewed, and shared all that each of us learned in that particular night's class.

As neophytes and part of our learning experience, Tom and I were instructed to attend a deliverance session as observers only. That's what we were told. However, as the session commenced everyone, including us, were instructed to sit on chairs in a circle with a chair in the middle of the circle. I guess it dawned upon us that we were to be more than mere observers. We were expected to participate in this deliverance session. There were probably a dozen people in attendance. Our team leader, Ted, led us all in prayer and worship. Earlier, intercessors had been commissioned to keep us all covered in prayer for our protection. The deliverance team had all previously fasted before this time of ministry.

A participant, we'll call her Sue, attending for deliverance sat on the chair in the middle. The minister then proceeded to touch each of us, in turn, upon the top of our heads. This action was accompanied by prayer to open up our spiritual eyes and ears.

Ted prayed over Sue. He admonished any unclean spirit or spirits to not manifest, not talk or harm this person or any person in the room, in any manner. This authoritative order was given very specifically. It is always most important that the demons understand whereby your authority emanates. The authority is Jesus Christ. Specifically, "We come in the name of Jesus Christ of Nazareth, Son of the Living God, Maker of heaven and earth, who was put to death, and on the third day rose victorious over death and hell, and after He ascended, is even now sitting at the right hand of the Father and is making intercession for us."

After several minutes the pastor handed out sheets of paper and asked each of us to write down what picture or symbol or word of knowledge we saw or heard spiritually. Some time passed, and we were then asked to pass our papers to him. Reading through each of the submissions, Ted abruptly stopped at one particular piece of paper. He asked, "Who saw the photograph of a woman?"

Being that it was my spiritual seeing, I was jolted to sit up straight. "Mine," I (Marianne) answered, never expecting to be singled out. He asked me to share more details. I explained the sepia tinted photograph was of an older man or woman. It was difficult to assess by facial features, but being the style of dress was definitively feminine the photograph had to be of a women. Her dark hair was cut short and semi-curly with a side profile of her face.

The minister, using the principle written in Matthew 18:16 explained my prophetic picture confirmed what he also witnessed. Matthew 18:16 reads "...so that every matter may be established by the testimony of two or three witnesses."

The old woman in the sepia-tinted photograph, which I "saw", represented a family ancestor of Sue's, while another team member "saw" a scroll written in red which represented a document, another "saw" a multi-strand cord. Still another team member "saw" a serpent.

A generational curse had been placed on Sue's lineage suggested by the multi-strand cord. Relevant to the other pictures and symbols, it was discerned somewhere in Sue's distant family history the woman represented in the photograph had made a pact with the devil. As a result, a generational curse or curses was visited upon the descendants of the family.

The exact generational curse afflicting Sue's family was not disclosed that evening. However, a generational curse is essentially an affliction, addiction, alcoholism, mental illness, poverty, divorce, lack, perversion, or the like, that is passed down from one generation to the next.

The minister, who was also the team leader, began his ministerial methods of breaking the curse line off Sue. In a very calm, serene and loving manner he also called out the unclean spirits of control, manipulation and lying.

Sue wept as a team member witnessed the demons flee, and the cord diminish in length. Just as Jesus drove the demons into pigs which ran down the steep bank and drowned in the lake (Matthew 8:28-32NIV), the deliverance team leader instructed the unclean spirits to go out the door, to the east and keep going until the east meets the west (Note: the east never meets the west).

After ousting the unwanted residents, it is necessary to disinfect and fill the holes left behind. Cleansing and healing of the wounds is performed by spiritually applying the Blood of the Lamb, Who is Jesus Christ and then the healing oil of the Holy Spirit. The spiritual application is akin to physically applying peroxide to a wound, then applying ointment and a bandage.

19

MORNINGSTAR MINISTRIES

While attending deliverance classes, we happened upon a booklet from MorningStar Ministries which was advertising a prophetic conference coming up in the near future. This was the path the Lord was leading us down, and we were very excited about the prospect of attending. However, our inquiries regarding this conference were met with an unenthusiastic response. No one was forthcoming with much information, which was odd. So we set about to find out the details on our own.

What we learned was that MorningStar Ministries was founded by Rick and Julie Joyner in 1985.

In 1992, MorningStar began sponsoring conferences as a way to help equip and train the future leadership of the church.

Thousands of people, from all over the world and across the spectrum of the body of Christ, flocked to the conferences. People were hungry for the supernatural power and move of

God, and MorningStar was anointed to teach and equip each and every person.

Soon after our decision to drive to Charlotte, North Carolina for our first of many MorningStar conferences, we received a call from the pastor of the church we were attending, at the time. He stated we should not go to this conference as we were not ready for an experience of this magnitude. "What?" we thought. We were very much uninitiated to the fact we needed permission from the pastor to attend a conference. Permission? To attend a conference? Attending a prophetic conference was something we were eager for, and had been for some time; people of like minds walking in the prophetic and learning from seasoned men wearing a prophet's mantle. (This mantle is a spiritual authority, and not a literal cloak.) The Lord was leading us to attend this conference, and nothing or no one was going to prevent us from going.

Pastor Sal stated he and his wife were not attending nor were any of the church elders attending. "Well," my wife replied, "Respectfully, we're going with or without you." So...they came with us.

This conference was for the gathering of prophets and prophetic people. The office of the prophet, which is part of the five-fold ministry of church government, is described in Ephesians 4:11-12 which says, "Now these are the gifts Christ gave to the church: the apostles, the prophets, the evangelists, and the pastors and teachers. Their responsibility is to equip God's people to do his work and build up the church, the body of Christ." (NLT)

While not everyone holds the office of prophet or has a prophet's mantle, many have a prophetic calling on their life. To have a prophetic calling, as we have learned and experienced in our own life, means to have the ability to discern spirits, to have a word of knowledge or a word of wisdom. Also included in the prophetic is the gift of prophecy, which is hearing from God and speaking (divinely) to men and women what you hear in order to build, comfort or encourage someone. "But one who prophesies strengthens others, encourages them, and comforts them." (1Corinthians 14:3 NLT)

Discerning of spirits is to distinguish between different types of spirits including angels, demons, the Holy Spirit or the human spirit. Discerning of spirits also allows the person so gifted to recognize anointings (the divine power and authority of God), mantles or a person's motivations.

A word of knowledge is when you know a specific something about a person which you did not know or hear in the natural. It could be information about their home situation, their job, their birthday, or what happened to them in the past.

A word of wisdom can give someone advice in a particular situation. It may not always be as exciting as a word of knowledge, but is perhaps, more valuable in many respects than a word of knowledge.

20

A CHARLOTTE ADVENTURE

TOM

After a grueling thirteen hour drive from Buffalo, New York to Charlotte North Carolina, which included lunch and multiple rest stops, we finally arrived at our long awaited destination.

The newly acquired space was MorningStar's distribution center for their journal publications. Hosting the conference at this site allowed upwards of five hundred people to attend, while at the same time, keeping the setting somewhat intimate. Not knowing what to expect at the conference we entered the commercial building, along with our fellow conference goers and travelling companions.

In the foyer, stood a group of middle-aged men kibitzing and greeting other conference goers. Among this cluster of people someone pointed out one of the men was a well-known prophetic voice.

"Hunh", I thought, "He doesn't look like a pastor." He was dressed in jeans, a fisherman's vest, and wearing cowboy boots, sporting a full beard and a mustache. That was not what I thought a pastor should look like. Not even wearing a suit? That's not my image of a pastor at all, I thought. Little did I realize my notion of what a pastor should look like would soon be challenged.

Walking past the little gaggle of gathered men, we entered into the building proper which was more of a warehouse, with its twenty foot ceiling. It was as though entering into another dimension. The manifest presence of God was overwhelmingly strong! People were in prayer, speaking in tongues, singing, and some were prostrate on the floor. It was quite obvious they, too, felt the presence of God.

Tapping me on my shoulder, my friend, Joe, pointed to the interior walls. As I gazed around the room, I was startled to see all manner of banners affixed to the walls encircling the room. Written on the banners were the Hebrew names for God. There was El Shaddai-Lord God Almighty, El Elyon-The Most High God, Adonai-Lord Master, Yahweh-Lord Jehovah, Jehovah Nissi-The Lord My Banner, Jehovah Raah-The Lord My Shepherd, Jehovah Rapha-The Lord that Heals, Jehovah Shammah-The Lord is There, Jehovah Tsidkenu-The Lord Our Righteousness, Jehovah Mekoddishkem-The Lord who Sanctifies You, El Eloam-The Everlasting God, Elohim-God, Qanna-Jealous, Jehovah Jireh-The Lord Will Provide, Jehovah Shalom-The Lord is Peace, and Jehovah Sabaoth-The Lord of Hosts.

What struck me, and the reason Joe tapped my shoulder, was because on our ride to Charlotte I shared with my companions the Lord showed me banners with Hebrew words on them. I didn't fully comprehend all of the written words were the Hebrew names for God. I did recognize some of the more well-known names, like Elohim, El Shaddai and Yahweh because they were included in songs we sang. However, Joe began to name some of the lesser-known, at least to me, Hebrew names for God, and I acknowledged the fact those could very well be the names that were written on the banners because the Lord showed me many banners.

We were all in awe of the artistry and creativity as we gazed around the room. A labor of love created the beautiful beaded, intricate patterns of golds, purples, blues, yellows, greens, oranges, and reds. They were simply mesmerizing and breathtaking.

As the four of us prepared to make our way to our seats, I was perplexed as to why, without warning, I could not pick my feet up to walk in a regular manner. All I could muster was an awkward shuffle. As I reached my seat I wondered what the heck was going on.

Suddenly, not only was I feeling weak and humbled but, at the same time, exhilarated. The realization hit me that just like all of the seasoned prophetic people here I, a newbie, could be sensitive to God's manifest presence in this place.

As the night's agenda unfolded our little group of sheltered, bottle-fed Christians stared in wide-eyed wonder. Maybe Pastor Sal was right-we weren't ready for this! We could now understand his concern, although at the time we did not want to admit it. In spite of our momentary doubt, we knew this is where we were supposed to be.

In addition to the usual guitars, drums and singers, this worship team also incorporated congas, chimes, and an electric fiddle into their repertoire. Not only was it quite different from what we were used to, but a woman was up on stage dancing! It was really weird! At the time, we thought she may be a witch casting curses! There had been a rumor circulating there was a coven of witches meeting down the road from where we were. Where was her pastor?! How could he allow such a thing?!

When the music started, we could see the people, who were there from all over the country and some from different countries, were of one mind and heart; and that was to worship God. The hunger for God's presence and to praise the King of kings was so authentic it was unlike any church service we ever attended.

Our initiation into the true prophetic exposed us to musicians with the heart of David. God testified David was a man after God's own heart. (Acts 13:22) Any musician can play an instrument and any singer can sing a song. But, it is the circumcised hearts of men which move and please God. The musicians on this worship team were not perfect; they were still men and women, after all. However, their hearts were pointed toward God with an unabashed desire to please Him.

As worship continued, the anointing (the divine power and authority of God) would fall in waves touching many with His power. Some were reduced to weeping, some just fell to the floor, and others travailed, crying out to God. Such compassion and love for God consumed the multitude and took me along with them.

Standing there basking in the anointing, with hands raised in praise, I reveled in the level of worship I was ushered into.

Abruptly, I found myself standing on a dusty, dirt road. In fact, the hot and humid air around me was dirty and dusty. Gazing at the ground, attempting to shield my eyes from the blowing sand and grit, I couldn't immediately fathom where I was or what I was doing here. Jolted by the foreign conversation around me, I jerked my head up. A short distance away I saw Jesus carrying His cross. There were men flanking Him; one on each side.

I now knew where I was. I was one of many spectators standing on this godawful road in Jerusalem. As I looked upon Him, I could see and smell His pungent sweat, and His blood, covering His torn and battered body, running down His bruised and swollen face. I saw His hair and beard were matted and caked with blood, as the horrendous, thorny crown had been deeply thrust into His scalp and forehead.

Mockers were laughing at Him, some were spitting on Him, and others were angrily shouting at Him. This is where I found myself-in the midst of a mindless atrocity.

Devastating sorrow wrapped its tentacles of agony around me. I began to sob, and my whole body trembled unabated as He approached me.

Then, without warning, just as I had been abruptly translated to the very streets of Jerusalem, I found myself back at the conference hall, unable to quell the violent quaking which still beleaguered me. Toppling to my right and into my wife she quietly, and without elaboration, guided me into my seat.

To ponder the crucifixion of Christ one could only wonder what it was like to be there. The Lord in His mercy allowed me to witness just a snippet of the times in which Jesus lived, and to observe the abhorrent suffering, ridicule, and pain He endured. Just that small snippet was more than I could bear, for I could bear no more. It is seared into my mind forever. To this day, I am brought to my knees as I relive my experience witnessing the unconditional love and sacrifice He made for us.

21

A CHARLOTTE ADVENTURE

MARIANNE

Walking into this huge building, as previously described by my husband, I was taken aback by the size of the crowd. People were jammed together everywhere with very little space to move let alone walk forward. Little groups chitchatting here, there and everywhere, not to mention those lying on the floor.

As I evaluated the best plan to make our way to our seats, I marveled at all the beautiful banners, with all the Hebrew names of God, lining the walls around the large hall. What absolutely talented and creative artists, I thought. These banners were exactly as Tom described them to us on our ride down to Charlotte.

Long about this time, we ran into our pastor, his wife, his father-in-law, and one of the elders from our church. Pastor Sal introduced us to Donna's dad, and we all decided to find our seats. Single file we attempted to make our way forward. Where's Tom? There he is. Why is he just standing there?

I made my way back the few paces to inquire as to his trouble. Tom voiced to me he was having a bit of difficulty lifting his feet. All he could do was shuffle like a much older man. I took his arm as we both made our way to our seats, with Tom shambling along. Discretion being the better part of valor was not necessary as it was too crowded, and no one was prompted to notice the rather abnormal gait of my husband.

Finally, finding seats near the front of the conference hall, we settled in. Waiting for the evening to commence, I gawked around the room and watched as others took their seats, making new friends and greeting old friends and acquaintances along the way.

The time had come for the worship team to assemble on stage to tune their instruments. An uncharacteristic exhilaration stole over me as my anticipation grew. The atmosphere became electric as the worship team began to sing songs of praise lifting up the name of Jesus.

I have never experienced corporate worship at this level before-ever. No one in the crowd was told to sing; harmonies were raised as one voice. No one was told to raise their hands or stand; every single hand was raised as praises were sung to the Lord. Worship was not choreographed or rehearsed rather, each song was sung with such fervor, and from the heart; it was spontaneous and Holy Spirit led. No one was coerced to participate as the musicians continued, and I was lifted higher and higher, consumed by the presence of God.

Without warning, I found myself, along with a multitude of unfamiliarly garbed people, lining the side of a dusty road. The air was hot, windy, sandy and reeking. Valiantly, and to no avail, I attempted to spit the sandy grit from my mouth, as sweat trickled down my face and body. I was dressed in a heavy, long robe-like, beige garment, tied around my middle, with a bulky faded blue scarf covering my hair. No wonder I was so hot and sweaty!

The stench of unwashed bodies packed tightly together, along with the malodor of animal dung was nauseating. Men held the reins of spitting camels, as women adjusted their belongings on the backs of braying donkeys, all the while laughing, rambunctious children chased excited, barking dogs.

A charged anticipation filled the air, as someone shouted, "There He is; He's coming!" I struggled to push my way forward to see who it was the children ran into the street to greet. Weaving in and out, dodging feet and elbows, I glimpsed Him. It was Jesus! Laughing, He lifted one child at a time into the air, ruffling their hair as He gently lowered them to the ground. He was dressed in the traditional clothing of the day; a muted striped beige colored gown, with dusty sandals covering His dusty feet. His beautiful brown eyes were kind, and His smile radiant, and full of love for all the children. He took joy in each and every child who ran to hug Him.

 As my heart pounded madly, He made His way closer. Ruffle my hair, I implored silently. But I was too far back in the crowd. I made my way to the front of the throng just as He passed by. I missed Him. Why didn't He ruffle my hair? I thought, dejectedly.

Suddenly, I was unceremoniously jostled from my left. I opened my eyes to find my husband, Tom, falling into me. As I helped guide him back into his chair, I realized I had returned from a wondrous journey.

As the evening's session ended, we made our way back to the missionary hostelry where lodging was graciously provided for a minimum charge. Sharing a late-night snack with our friends, we were laughing and joking uproariously over the kitchen wallpaper which was covered with adorable little monkeys, swinging on brown and green vines. Tom began making monkey chatter and screeches sending us all into gales of belly laughter. "Shh, Shh", someone cautioned, "its 11:30", which only served to escalate our hilarity.

The joy of the Lord consumed the four of us that evening. All was wonderfully light and merry, and just one of those moments where everything is hilarious.

 Lights out was at 10pm, so we were like the unruly teenagers at summer camp. Calling it a night, we retired to our respective rooms.

Once ensconced in our room, Tom excitedly, yet timidly, shared his improbable unexpected journey. Wide-eyed, I stared as he emotionally recounted the heart wrenching scene in which he had participated. After recapitulating the particulars, he asked me, "What do you make of it?"

Closing my dropped jaw, I disclosed that I, too, had been to Jerusalem. Now it was Tom's turn to gaze in wide-eyed wonder. "You mean you saw the same things I did?" he questioned. I revealed that although I was in Jerusalem during the same time period, I experienced an altogether contrasting day in Jesus' life. Long into the wee hours of the morning we considered both aspects of our journeys.

Tom participated in Jesus' sorrow, while I witnessed Jesus' joy from afar.

One early morning about a year later, after our shared journey to Jerusalem, I had awakened to a beautiful daybreak, ruminating on my previous year's sojourn during the MorningStar conference. Still not understanding why Jesus had not ruffled my hair, I was heavy-hearted.

My husband, who was facing the window, and away from me, was also just beginning to awaken; without a word he abruptly turned over and ruffled my hair. I began to weep.

First off, Tom is not prone to this sort of thing. Secondly, I was feeling sorry for myself thinking about the whole Jerusalem episode. Why wasn't I favored with His radiant smile?

Flummoxed by my blubbering, Tom apologized saying, "I'm sorry, what did I do? I don't know why I did that!"

"No, no", I answered. "There's no need for you to apologize. I was reminiscing about last year's conference and Jerusalem where Jesus did not ruffle my hair. Then out of nowhere, you go right ahead and do that very thing."

At that moment, I realized Jesus did not walk right past me; it was I who stayed where I was while the other children ran to Him.

22

A CHARLOTTE ADVENTURE-SESSION TWO

MARIANNE

Conference day two dawned clean and fresh as last night's gusty rain storm had been burned off by Charlotte's blazing morning sun. Laughing over last night's monkey hilarity, we enjoyed a simple breakfast with our friends. Excitedly anticipating the day's events, we had not yet shared our Jerusalem journey with anyone, as the timing to do so was not quite right. Finishing our bagels, orange juice and coffee, purchased last evening at a local convenience store, it was time to head out. Piling into Joe and Ruthann's vehicle, we deliberated over the best route to take to the "warehouse", as we had affectionately dubbed the conference hall.

Arriving early to ensure snagging a good seat up front, we were not the only ones with that idea in mind. Waiting our turn in line to enter the building, we discussed the prophetic teachers scheduled for the day's conference. Most of the men listed we had not heard of, but were told by many other conference attendees just how gifted, and down to earth the prophets and teachers were.

As we would soon learn none of the prophets, at the conference, ascribed this title or any other title to their name. They were simply Bob, Rick, Bobby, Ray and Larry.

Similar to the previous evening, this session commenced with the worship team, albeit, led by a different worship leader. Anticipating being taken to that lofty spiritual place, we were not disappointed. Although, we did not journey to Jerusalem this time around, we nonetheless basked in the anointing.

Worship time having ended much too soon, Rick initiated the evening by introducing the first speaker who was Bob Jones. Good naturedly, he ribbed Bob about dressing up for the evening in his sweatshirt containing remnants of the egg that he had enjoyed for breakfast. On a more serious note, Rick then explained that Bob was headed for knee surgery, the following day, as he beckoned him to the platform.

As I turned in my seat to identify the fellow, I was somewhat startled to gaze upon an elderly, white-haired, somewhat stocky, hillbilly-like man hobbling forward. He was clad in overalls, and the egg-stained sweatshirt Rick had just joked about.

Overwhelmed with unexplainable tears, I began to weep as Bob made his way to the stage passing right my chair. Now, I did not know this man from Adam. I hadn't a clue as to his reputation, nor had I ever met him or heard him speak. Being quite embarrassed by my display of emotion, I tried to stifle the sounds of weeping as Bob painfully climbed the three short steps to the stage.

Surreptitiously, glancing around to be certain no one from our church was witness to my discomfiture, the Lord "whispered" in my ear 1Corinthians 3:16 (NLT) "Don't you realize that all of you together are the temple of God and that the Spirit of God lives in you?"

Self-consciousness forgotten, I opened my bible as I recalled a particular bible-teaching on foundation gifts. Finding Ephesians 2:19-20 I read, "Consequently, you are no longer foreigners and strangers, but fellow citizens with God's people and also members of his household, built on the foundation of the apostles and prophets, with Christ Jesus himself as the chief cornerstone"; continuing with verse 21, "In him the whole building is joined together and rises to become a holy temple in the Lord." And finally verse 22, "And in him you too are being built together to become a dwelling in which God lives by his Spirit." (NIV)

With that Scripture, I understood what my spirit had already discerned. My impassioned demeanor was a direct result of my spirit witnessing God's anointing covering this humble man.

Bob Jones hailed from Alabama. Sometimes the words he brought forth were funny and sometimes embarrassing for him. Bob Jones was anything but a slick, polished, gold wearing, Mercedes Benz driving, jet owning televangelist. However, he was a real down-to-earth person and a lover of God and His Truth. Though the prophetic words he gave may sometimes have seemed out of place on the surface, they held deep spiritual truths. Here's just one account he shared at this prophetic teaching conference. Reading it with a southern Appalachian accent will give you a better flavor of the man.

"Right in the middle of awesome praise, I yelled out **macaroni and cheese**. Yep, just like you're doing here. My wife attempted to get behind me. The pastor came out and said I guess Brother Jones is hungry.

"There were visitors, pastors and others and an old mother among them. She huffed, got up and walked out and all the visitors went with her.

"Boy, I done it didn't I? Everyone looked at me like there he goes again. He drove 'em off!

"The woman in church was an old Pentecostal mother of eleven children. Ten sons and daughters were pastors or married to pastors. Youngest son was a backslider. Spirit of the Lord told her she was gonna die. She said I wanna know if my youngest son is gonna be saved. I raised him right. I'm gonna come home screamin' and yellin' unless you give me a word that I know is just for me.

"She spoke to her daughters just before Christmas and said get back up to Kansas City and you justify that prophet. He's been sweatin' long enough.

"Daughters came back up and told this story. Mama's been told she's going home. She told the Lord, I want a prophecy out of nowhere. Not from anybody else. I want you to tell me if my son's gonna be saved. I hear you got one up there and you speak to him.

"I never done that unless I was caught up in praise. Praise really helps prophets. It literally cleanses the mind out. Her son lived in Kansas City. He drove a truck. You know what he delivered? MACARONI AND CHEESE!

"So, sometimes what embarrasses you the most is the purest. You don't have the right to judge your own prophecies. I was sure embarrassed and the devil was doin' his best to keep me from sayin' anything!

"Well, I got back in favor after the girls came."

Being a prophetic teaching conference, Bob's way of encouraging us babes in diapers was to simply share his own experiences and foibles. All the while he admonished us to remain humble with the same directive the Lord gave to him…"If you ever do get a reputation, I'm a gonna take it away from you anyways!"

23

RELIGIOUS SPIRIT

Next up, in the dizzying array of prophetic teachings during this conference, Rick, a prophetic teacher spoke on the religious spirit. He also forewarned that if you had one (meaning a religious spirit) you were going to be offended by what he was about to say.

Religious spirit? What? We looked at each other like, "What the heck is a religious spirit?" We were soon to find out, and how it applied to us.

In order to bring you to the place where we were convicted of having a religious spirit a little teaching is in order-a very basic little teaching.

The religious spirit aims to be a substitute for the Holy Spirit in our life. Everyone struggles with the religious spirit-some more, some less than others. In order to be unencumbered with the religious spirit we must thoroughly surrender to the Holy Spirit.

If one declares, for example, "I start every morning at 9 a.m. sharp reading my bible for an hour", or "I go to church seven days a week, for hours, not just on Sunday morning", or you may take pride in the fact that you belong to the First Baptist Church (or whatever other church denomination), meaning you believe your church is above the others or perchance, you worship on Saturday boasting it to be the true Sabbath, then you, too, may be entertaining a religious spirit.

Without a doubt reading your bible and attending church are very good activities. However, we are to "never stop praying." (1Thessalonians 5:17) This means to walk and talk with the Lord all during your day, in the good times and in the bad times. It becomes a part of who you are, not just what you do. A religious spirit will keep you mired in rituals, traditions, prone to bragging and pride, rather than drawing closer to God.

 The outward signs of a religious spirit are many and diverse; too many and too diverse to discuss here for our purposes. There are many books and articles written which discuss the topic.

Our conviction of a religious spirit was to be realized. First, our idea of how and what a pastor or religious leader should look like, dress like, and act like was anything but what we encountered. If you remember, earlier I spoke of a pastor wearing a fisherman's vest, cowboy boots, and jeans. Not my idea of a religious leader, at all. No suit and tie, or spit shined wingtips, or carrying a bible around for effect, or sporting a collar, cassock, heavy cross, or rosary. His manner was somewhat gruff, and he was straight forward in his delivery;

reminiscent of an Old Testament prophet, without the oft times misused "thus saith the Lord".

As Rick continued his tutelage on the religious spirit, it became more evident that he was just like one of us; which was totally refreshing. There was no pretense, what you saw is what you got! He spoke the truth, from his heart, regarding the condition of the present-day church. This church leader is not a cookie cutter, just out of seminary graduate, who carries with him a certain way of talking, acting and a particular demeanor. Televangelists, Baptist tent meeting speakers, fire and brimstone preachers with their rhythmic modulation were not his style.

We had stereotyped the office of pastor as that had been our only exposure to the religious hierarchy in both the Catholic and Protestant institutions. This was our initial uncovering of the realities which were hidden under denominational blankets that elevated the office of pastor above its proper place.

 This conference leader spoke not only of the office of pastor, but the whole of the five-fold ministry of church government, and how it is meant for the church of today. While pastors, teachers, and evangelist are readily accepted, and are called to speak at various church venues, the offices of apostle and prophet have been blatantly excluded. There are certain Baptist sects, just to name one, who believe the gifts are not for today; illustrating those who are in church government and even whole denominations are not immune to the religious spirit.

****

Prior to that day's conference teaching the worship team took the stage to usher in the presence of the Holy Spirit. During this time of worship, a woman named Christine, stood behind her guitar strumming mate, who was leading worship. Christine was dancing there behind him, waving her arms and "mumbling" to herself. Her dance steps were reminiscent of Native American dancers. She had this wild grey hair, and as mentioned earlier, we thought she was a witch casting curses on everyone.

Lord forgive us our ignorance! Rick forewarned those with a religious spirit would be offended, and offended we were!

Christine, as a prayer intercessor, was petitioning and praying a spiritual shield of protection around her husband as he led his team and us in worship. As a spiritual warrior, Christine was engaging in spiritual warfare in the heavenlies as instructed in Ephesians 6:10-18 (NLT): "A final word: Be strong in the Lord and in his mighty power. Put on all of God's armor so that you will be able to stand firm against all strategies of the devil. For we are not fighting against flesh-and-blood enemies, but against evil rulers and authorities of the unseen world, against mighty powers in this dark world, and against evil spirits in the heavenly places.

"Therefore, put on every piece of God's armor so you will be able to resist the enemy in the time of evil. Then after the battle you will still be standing firm. Stand your ground, putting on the belt of truth and the body armor of God's righteousness. For shoes, put on the peace that comes from the Good News so that you will be fully prepared. In addition to all of these, hold up the shield of faith to stop the fiery arrows of the devil. Put on salvation as your helmet, and take the sword of the Spirit, which is the word of God.

"Pray in the Spirit at all times and on every occasion. Stay alert and be persistent in your prayers for all believers everywhere."

Christine's expression of intercession was foreign to our way of supposed proper conduct in a church setting. Was her fervor more powerful than someone simply sitting and praying in their seat? Who is to say? This was simply her style of praise and prophetic intercession. Who were we to condemn that?

The apostle Paul encourages us to "Test yourselves to see if you are in the faith; examine yourselves! Or do you not recognize this about yourselves that Jesus Christ is in you— unless indeed you fail the test? " (II Corinthians 13:5 NAS)

When our first reaction is to criticize that which is odd to us, or if we have a preconceived idea of what something or someone should or should not be, those thoughts, among others, will give an opening to the religious spirit; or is an indication that you already have a religious spirit. If someone nettles you, the better thing to do would be to pray, or intercede, for them. And in that prayer time, you just may be surprised to find that you are the one in error, rather than the one who offends you.

Finally, if you find yourself as the culprit, ask the Lord for forgiveness with a contrite heart, and then "Forgetting what is behind and straining toward what is ahead, I press on toward the goal to win the prize for which God has called me heavenward in Christ Jesus."(Philippians 3:13-14 NIV)

151

24

INTERCESSION

Some seven months after attending the MorningStar conference we, along with our friends Joe and Ruthann, were enjoying our local county fair in August, 1996. As we strolled around the fairgrounds, we happened upon a psychic's tent.

The oversized sign positioned at the tent's entrance offered readings, crystals, incense, tea leaf readings, and all things one would associate with mediums and psychics.

It is ironic those grieving and longing for contact with a departed loved one will turn to the psychic community for comfort and closure, instead of turning to Jesus, the Comforter, for closure. Or is it ironic?

God is Spirit and we are being made in His image. It is only natural we are drawn to the spirit realm because He is Spirit. However, being we are created spiritually weak, we gravitate toward the doctrines of demons. A doctrine is a held belief, conviction, dogma or principle. Therefore, the doctrines of demons are anything that would falsely influence us to believe in, be persuaded by or follow into darkness.

False prophets are charlatans who implement deception or sleight of hand for personal gain. In other words, false prophets are likened to magicians such as Simon from Acts 8:9-10 "But there was a certain man called Simon, who previously practiced sorcery in the city and astonished the people of Samaria, claiming that he was someone great, to whom they all gave heed, from the least to the greatest, saying, 'This man is the great power of God.' And they heeded him because he had astonished them with his sorceries for a long time." Simon used sorcery to display enough spiritual power that the people referred to him as "the great power of God."

Acts 8:9-10 addresses Simon, who deceived the people of Samaria with magic and not the power of God, while Acts 16:16-18 addresses the spirit of divination, also known as the python spirit. Paul and Silas, while "going to the place of prayer, were met by a slave girl who had a spirit by which she predicted the future. She earned a great deal of money for her owners by fortune-telling. This girl followed Paul and the rest of us, shouting, 'These men are servants of the Most High God, who are telling you the way to be saved (Concordant Literal Translation renders this portion as "who are announcing to you **a** way of salvation"). 'She kept this up for many days. Finally Paul became so troubled that he turned around and said to the spirit, 'In the name of Jesus Christ I command you to come out of her!' At that moment the spirit left her." (NIV)

So, you see, demons will appear to speak some truth, when it suits them; albeit, there is only "the" way to salvation, not "a" way, the slave girl was encouraging those at Philippi to listen to Paul and Silas. The python spirit only seemed to be agreeing with Paul and Silas, perhaps, for fear of being cast out of the slave girl; Paul discerned the deception and cast out the spirit of divination. Truth only comes from the Holy Spirit, not from a demonic spirit.

Many in our family, we included, in our circle of friends, and our acquaintances, have visited psychics and mediums. One recollection was disclosed to me by a business acquaintance. Julie's nineteen year old son, Jason, had recently passed away due to a drug overdose. The family suspected Jason dabbled with marijuana. However, they were not prepared for the pronouncement of a drug overdose as his cause of death. The family was utterly devastated; none more so than Jason's twenty-two year old sister Stephanie.

Grieving and hurting without remedy, Stephanie and her friends attended a local psychic fair. During the reading, the psychic relayed that there were two males present, with the younger male stepping forward. The psychic asked Stephanie whether a young male relative had passed away recently. Stephanie acknowledged that her younger brother did die a few months ago. The psychic replied with, "He wants you to know it was the fentanyl that killed him." Stephanie told her mother that Jason said he was very sorry for what he did, and for hurting everybody.

Ironically, the family had just received Jason's autopsy whereby, heroin laced with fentanyl was found in his system, and the cause of his death.

Stephanie confided to her mother that she felt some comfort from the words given to her by the psychic.

What is ironic relative to this whole dismal, mind numbing insanity is that Stephanie was receiving "comfort" from the very demon that took the life of her brother. The demon of addiction, or any other demon, for that matter, so directed by Satan, the adversary, is a deceiver and a thief and ….."comes to steal, kill, and destroy….." (John 10:10 NIV).

Tragically, Stephanie and most of those who frequent psychics will refuse to believe or are simply naïve to the fact, they are entertaining and being ministered to by demons. Rather, they believe contact is being made with their deceased loved one who has become an angel upon their death.

A great many people, Christians included, believe that when we die we become angels.

Factually, as it is written in the Scriptures, we do not become angels when we die. God created angels and He created us a little lower than the angels. We do become equal to angels at the resurrection. Jesus said, "For neither can they still be dying, for they are equal to messengers (*angels-italics mine*), and are the sons of God, being sons of the resurrection (Luke 20:36 CLV).

In fact, we will judge angels. (1Corinthians 6:3)

To reiterate, angels are created beings. They are not humans; they never were they never will be. They are spiritual beings and they are servants of God.

So, if we do not become angels at the time of death, what does happen to us? To put it bluntly, dead people are just that, dead; and when we die, we are dead. There is no consciousness in death. "For the living know that they shall die, But the dead know nothing whatsoever;" (Ecclesiastes 9:5 CLV)

When God imparts His spirit to our human body, we become a living soul. Humans cannot live without spirit. The soul is made up of a body and spirit (spirit is also rendered as breath-"*ruwach*" *Strong's Concordance #7307*, which is necessary for life). God created Adam out of the dust of the earth and when He breathed in Adam's nostrils the breath (ruwach-spirit), the man became a living soul (Genesis 2:7). Rotherham Emphasized Bible translation reads: "So then Yahweh God formed man of the dust of the ground, and breathed in his nostrils the breath of life—and man became a living soul."

When we die, God takes back His spirit. "....when you take away their breath (*spirit-italics mine*), they die and return to the dust." (Psalm 104:29 NIV) Our physical body returns to the dust. Our soul, which is our mind, will and emotions, or personality, character and consciousness, if you prefer, will only revive when God reunites our spirit (breath-ruwach) with a new spiritual body at the resurrection, when Jesus returns, which is yet future. There is no soul in death. The soul goes to the unseen (*"Hades" Strong's Concordance #86*). *Hades* in Greek or *Sheol* in Hebrew is not a geographical location, but rather a condition or state of the departed soul.

There are no dead relatives floating, wandering or flying around the ether bringing comfort. We are not immortal. Only Jesus has immortality. "Keep this commandment without stain or reproach until the appearance of our Lord Jesus Christ, which God will bring about in His own time—He (*Jesus-italics mine*) who is blessed and the only Sovereign One,

the King of kings and Lord of lords. **He alone is immortal**...”
(Berean Study Bible)

But, all hope is not lost. We will not lay in the grave forever.
We do become immortal. When? Listen up, this is important!

“But let me reveal to you a wonderful secret. We will not all
die, (*meaning there will be many still alive when Jesus returns-
italics mine*) but we will all be transformed! It will happen in a
moment, in the blink of an eye, when the last trumpet is
blown. For when the trumpet sounds, those who have died
will be raised to live forever. And we who are living will also
be transformed. For our dying bodies must be transformed
into bodies that will never die; our mortal bodies must be
transformed into immortal bodies.” (1 Corinthians 15:51-53
NLT)

In any case, the key to unlocking this truth is to know Jesus
Christ. If one does not know the Prince of Peace, he or she will
not have peace no matter how many psychics are consulted.
By searching for that all elusive peace without the Lord will
mire one in the deception of the counterfeit authority of the
occult; none of which will lead to the one true God and can
only come through Jesus Christ.

Once upon a time, and as lukewarm Catholics, with very little
biblical knowledge, we found no issue with these arcane
practices, as our testimony previously revealed. Our position
on the subject shifted, when we learned what God has to say
about conjuring up the dead.

In the Old Testament, Leviticus 19:31 admonishes, “Do not
turn to mediums or seek out spiritists, for you will be defiled
by them. I am the Lord your God.” Say What?! Or,

Deuteronomy 18:10-13 "Let no one be found among you.....who is a medium or spiritist or who consults the dead. Anyone who does these things is detestable to the Lord...You must be blameless before the Lord your God." Continuing with verse 14 "....The Lord your God will raise up for you a prophet like me (*meaning Moses*) from among your own brothers. You must listen to him."

Now you may say, as we did, that we are no longer under the law, but under grace. That's a true statement. However, "Jesus Christ is the same yesterday, today, and forever." (Hebrews 13:8) He does not change. He still declares spiritists and mediums detestable. Mind you, it is God Who is calling mediums and spiritists detestable.

He will not strike you dead, if you insist upon visiting a medium, but why would you want to? Don't be deceived as we were. Mediums will speak to your flesh, but they won't bring you the forever peace and comfort that transcends all understanding which you will find by seeking the Lord.

You must ask yourself, if you are not building your faith and beliefs on the strong foundation of Jesus Christ and Him crucified, what are you basing your faith and beliefs upon? Hearsay? Your life experience? A movie? Books you may have read? A good friend said so? You grew up this way? Your parents believed this way? Do you say I'm just not a religious person? You're an atheist or an agnostic? Psychics? Or is yours a cafeteria style theology where you pick and choose what suits you? Or do you say, "Oh, that's good for you?" If that is the case, you are deceived by the doctrines of demons.

Today, we still abide in the Ten Commandments even though they were given under the Old Testament Law. Does that mean it is okay to break anyone of them because we are now under grace and not the law? No, it's not okay, even under grace because God's laws are written on our hearts. "What then? Shall we sin because we are not under the law but under grace? By no means!" (Romans 6:15 NIV)

"If you sin without knowing what you're doing, God takes that into account. But if you sin knowing full well what you're doing, that's a different story entirely. Merely hearing God's law is a waste of your time if you don't do what he commands. Doing, not hearing, is what makes the difference with God.

"When outsiders who have never heard of God's law follow it more or less by instinct, they confirm its truth by their obedience. They show that God's law is not something alien, imposed on us from without, but woven into the very fabric of our creation. There is something deep within them that echoes God's yes and no, right and wrong. Their response to God's yes and no will become public knowledge on the day God makes his final decision about every man and woman." (Romans 2:12-15 The Message)

Life by the Spirit is summed up by the Apostle Paul, "For the entire law is fulfilled in keeping this one command: "Love your neighbor as yourself." (Galatians 5:13 NIV)

During our learning curve we were taken aback to learn just what God had to say about psychics. As we sought the knowledge of the Lord, we began to understand to fear (*reverence*) Him is the beginning of wisdom. "The fear of the LORD is the beginning of knowledge, but fools despise wisdom and instruction." (Proverbs 1:7)

For those familiar with the biblical account of King Saul and the Witch of Endor, you may be asking, as we did, "why did God allow Samuel to be raised up from the grave by the Witch of Endor? King Saul knew the law and the commandments and he did, after all, expel the mediums and spiritists from the land."

Remember, Saul did appeal to God first when he saw the Philistines assembled at Shunem, but because of Saul's disobedience, God would not answer him. So, Saul sought out a pagan practicing witch in Endor. He appealed to her to raise the spirit of Samuel.

Now, there are many debates and arguments as to whether Samuel actually appeared to Saul and the Witch of Endor. As to the spirit of Samuel actually appearing is hard to swallow for those of us who believe that when we die we are dead, to await a bodily resurrection at Christ's return. We contend that it was not Samuel, but the witch's familiar spirit (a demon).

God alone is omniscient. He does, however, send His messengers, both good and evil. Only the Lord and the messengers He chooses to send would know that Saul's kingdom would be given to David. Only the Lord and the messengers He chooses to send would know that Saul and Israel would be given over to the Philistines, and only the Lord and the messengers He chooses to send would know that Saul and his sons would be with Samuel on the morrow.

In Saul's case, God, Himself, effected this encounter to show Saul his fate by the medium Saul himself chose. God revealed the fate of Saul through the Witch of Endor. Samuel was never there. Saul did not actually see Samuel for himself. He made the assumption that the "old man", whom the Witch of Endor had described to him, had to be Samuel. Alas, it was not.

During this whole time, Samuel was unconscious and dead. Our "spirit" is conscious of nothing when we die. "Yes, the living know they are going to die, but the dead know nothing. They have no further reward; they are completely forgotten. Their loves, their hates, their passions, all died with them. They will never again take part in anything that happens in this world." (Ecclesiastes 9:5-6 Good News Bible)

No witch or demon has the power to bring a dead person back to life. "His spirit departs, he returns to the earth; in that very day his thoughts perish." (Psalm 146:4 NASB)

God speaks to and through His prophets, but He will use "lying spirits" to commune with evil people such as King Ahab in 1 Kings 22.

King Ahab called forth 400 heathen prophets and asked them if he should go to war against Ramoth Gilead or should he not. As one voice all the pagan prophets agreed and prophesied that the King would be victorious.

However, Jehoshaphat, king of Judah, who was sitting upon his throne alongside the King of Israel as the pagan prophets prophesied, asked for a prophet of the Lord to ask of him this same question. The king of Israel then sent for the prophet Micaiah.

As Micaiah had been admonished earlier by the messenger of Ahab to agree with the other prophets, Micaiah did exactly that. However, the king of Israel knew Micaiah was not giving him the truth because he said Micaiah never prophesies what he, the king, wants to hear. Ahab charged Micaiah to tell him the truth. Then Micaiah answered, "I saw all Israel scattered on the hills like sheep without a shepherd, and the Lord said, 'These people have no master. Let each one go home in peace' (verse 17).

Micaiah continued, "Therefore hear the word of the Lord: I saw the Lord sitting on his throne with all the host of heaven standing around him on his right and on his left. And the Lord said, 'Who will entice Ahab into attacking Ramoth Gilead and going to his death there?'

"One suggested this, and another that. Finally, a spirit came forward, stood before the Lord and said, 'I will entice him.'

'By what means?' the Lord asked.

"'I will go out and be a lying spirit in the mouths of all his prophets,' he said.

"'You will succeed in enticing him,' said the Lord. 'Go and do it.'"

"So now the Lord has put a lying spirit in the mouths of all these prophets of yours. The Lord has decreed disaster for you." (1 Kings 22:19-23 NIV)

In Ahab's feeble attempt to outsmart the word of the Lord given to him by Micaiah, he went into battle disguised, while he instructed Jehoshaphat to wear his own royal robes.

The king of Aram instructed his commanders to not fight with anyone except the king of Israel. When they saw Jehoshaphat in his royal robes, they thought for sure he was Ahab and turned to attack him. They realized this was not the king of Israel and stopped pursuing Jehoshaphat.

However, someone drew his bow at random and hit the king of Israel between the sections of his armor and that evening he died.

The king of Israel was brought to Samaria where he was buried. His chariot was washed at a pool where prostitutes bathed and the dogs licked up his blood, as the word of the Lord had earlier been declared through His prophet Elijah in Chapter 21:19. (1 Kings 22:29-40 paraphrased)

Let this be a lesson for all. Just because the popular majority brings forth a word (which you want to hear) and one lonely voice brings forth a word (which you do not want to hear), does not mean to follow the crowd and take the word of the majority. You could very well be entertaining a lying spirit.

Now when Jesus accompanied Peter, James, and John up the mountain to pray He showed them His glorified form, His deity. Moses and Elijah, who represent the Law and the Prophets, also appeared on the mountain with Jesus, where they were discussing Jesus' impending death. However, Moses and Elijah were not mortal bodies because they were dead in the grave.

This is what Jesus said. "And as they came down from the mountain, Jesus charged them, saying, Tell the vision to no man, until the Son of man be risen again from the dead." (Matthew 17:9)

What Jesus' disciples saw was a vision. It happened in their minds. Even so, just as with our experiences, be that as it may, happening in the mind did not make it any less real. Peter, James, and John really did see Jesus as He will appear in His kingdom via their shared vision.

Just as the psychic community of Saul's day was banned from the land, we believed that our local psychic needed to move on, as well. As our circuit bypassed the tent, once more, we headed toward the parking lot to our vehicle. On the way, as was discussed, we would engage in our first group intercession casting out the spirit of divination and sorcery.

Feeling pumped up, spiritually charged and motivated from our recent prophetic conference, we asked Father for divine intervention. We girded our loins with Truth, put on the breastplate of righteousness, shod our feet with the gospel of peace; we took up the shield of faith to extinguish all the flaming arrows of the devil, we put on the helmet of salvation and took up the sword of the Spirit. Holding hands and forming a circle, with our spiritual armor firmly in place, we were ready to kick butt! Rattling our swords and grasping our shields, we spiritually took aim at the demon blatantly taking up residence at the fairgrounds.

As we exited the grounds, riding high and reveling in our newly found spiritual authority, we were certain of an immediate conclusion.

As days and months passed, we heard no news as a result of our intercession. Humbled and deflated, we consoled ourselves with the fact that sometimes the Lord says no or says nothing at all. Perhaps, we fancied ourselves with more authority than we actually possessed.

So, one cold wintry morning, in January, after several months of wallowing in the self-inflicted wounds of doubt, it was necessary to restart the fire in our soapstone wood burning stove. The fire had burned itself out during the night. Being our only source of heat, the temperature in our home plummeted uncomfortably rendering us mighty frigid. I mean, I'm talking 43 degrees in the kitchen! B-r-r-r.

Emptying the spent ashes from the stove's grate and replenishing the logs, I gathered old newspapers from the storeroom to facilitate restarting the fire. Sheet by sheet, I crumpled each piece. During this process, I abruptly stopped crumbling as the words "Fair Fortuneteller" grabbed my attention. *"Say What?!"* Uncrumpling the newspaper, I set about to read the article.

FAIR FORTUNETELLER FAILS TO PREDICT BRUSH WITH LAW

"The future holds a day in court for a fortuneteller at the Erie County Fair who allegedly offered to rid a customer of evil spirits in exchange for $125.

Laura Nicholas, 52, of North Babylon, who identified herself as a gypsy, was arrested Tuesday evening by Hamburg Town Police and Erie County sheriff's deputies and charged with petit larceny and fortunetelling, a misdemeanor.

She was arraigned before Hamburg Town Justice Walter Rooth, who released her on $200 bail pending a court appearance at 10 a.m. Friday.

Town Police Capt. Thomas Best directed the investigation, which began after a woman complained about a psychic reader who claimed to see evil spirits all around her during a reading last Friday and offered to remove them for $125.

Police sent the complainant and a female undercover officer back to the psychic reader's booth near the South Park Gate on Tuesday evening. Authorities closed down the booth, and a variety of fortunetelling items were confiscated, including a crystal ball.

"We've turned up three people who were conned out of over $100 apiece," said Town Police Detective Frank J Panasuk, "and I'm sure there are going to be more."

Needless to say, my first reaction was one of astonishment. My second reaction was bewilderment. Why am I reading this account in January? As I checked the date on the article, to my amazement, it was dated August 14, 1996! I thought to myself, "Wow", this newspaper has been sitting right under my nose, in my storeroom, for five months! Why had I not seen this article earlier, like back in August, when it happened?

Then I realized, like any good parent, Father was teaching us to grow up. Mulling over the lesson being taught here, I already understood a relationship with Jesus is first and foremost. Without Jesus, we cannot come to the Father because everything is out of the Father and through His Son. Ok, so what was the lesson here? Why would He make us wait five months?

Pondering the question, the word patience came to mind, as if it was my own thought. Patience….ok….patience. Answers do not always come right away of that I am aware. Even though the outcome at the fairgrounds had been published back in August, we were not privy to it for months afterward; we were being taught patience wrapped in humility.

The medium we encountered did not just pack up, as if in a trance, and walk out that night. Our petition had to progress through a natural timeline because we live in a natural realm of rule.

Puffed up with a new "power tool", and with spiritually youthful exuberance, we charged forth to oust the demon of sorcery and divination, plying its trade at the fairgrounds. The Lord taught us to respect the power of intercession as the omnipotent warrior's tool that it is. To do so requires faith. Faith is being sure of what we hope for and certain of what we cannot see. Discipline, humility, and the Lord's wisdom must, also, accompany those who are destined to wield God's power tool of intercession.

However, we will not always realize nor understand what we believe should be the outcome of our petition because God's purposes will not always be revealed to us. "My thoughts are nothing like your thoughts," says the LORD. "And my ways are far beyond anything you could imagine." (Isaiah 55:8 NLT)

*NOTE-With respect to Christine's intercession, in the previous chapter, and ultimately learning just how significant true from the heart intercession is to garnering God's ear ("If you believe, you will receive whatever you ask for in prayer." Matthew 21:22 NIV), schooled us as to just how naïve, judgmental, and haughty we were in judging her.

25

WHEN PASTORS AND PROPHETS RESPECT THE OFFICE

Early on in our youth, before the advent of this stage of our spiritual evolution, many priests and nuns were put in our path by virtue of our Catholic upbringing. For us these servants of God laid the foundation of who Jesus was is and will be. For that life sustaining manna we are forever grateful.

Along the way, the Lord opened up a footpath for us to sit under today's gifted prophetic teachers, immersing us in the deeper things of God. Step by chastening step, enduring relentless trials and tribulations, we followed His lead which squired us to a vast field rich with hidden treasure.

Maturing to this point, though essential, was a mere baby step for what was to follow. Learning that normally docile sheep do, indeed, bite was a hard and bitter pill to ingest.

For the body of Christ to grow up and be fruitful, the prophetic ministry is necessary. We are exhorted to "be eager to prophesy" in 1 Corinthians 14:39.

Prophecy comes by the spirit of God. And when God, via His prophet, meddles with our complacent selves all sedateness is upended. As our lukewarm-ness sits in our "paid" for pews every Sunday, proud of the tithes we give, and the time we devote to all of our church activities, the prophetic ministry pummels this self-contented loftiness.

Humbly walking in a prophetic gifting or office within the church proper requires a relationship with the pastor of the church in order to address the congregation as a whole, or to minister to an individual. One cannot simply walk into a church and start prophesying. The churchgoers within the body are the pastor's responsibility to shepherd and protect.

What is to follow is a composite of our institutional church experiences. Our hope and desire is to address this section with humility and delicacy, but also with the hard hitting truth regarding the plight of prophetic people in the church today.

As was mentioned in a previous chapter, we began to understand just how prevalent politics' role in the church really is and how much of the world consumes today's house of worship. For many of those, Jesus is still at the front door knocking.

Reasons for politics and the world in the church today abound and are varied. A lukewarm age of a Laodicean church, a self-centered body, greed, deceit, jealousy, and hypocrisy, just to name a few, provide adequate evidence.

The inability to allow the Spirit of God to move unencumbered proves to be an obstacle few in authority within the institutional church are able to overcome. The initial experience of the move of the Spirit is exciting for the church. However, as piercing and compelling prophetic words are given to the flock, the atmosphere changes.

When a prophetic word is given and backed up by God, which is to say anointed, His presence is felt. My own experience testifies to this truth.

Over a year or so of having developed the trusted relationship needed with the pastor of this particular church, he had given me the authority to speak forth the word of the Lord as He (the Lord) anointed me to do so.

One typical Sunday morning, while the worship team was on the dais, the Lord spoke to me with a stern word for the body. Not a harsh word, mind you, but a stern word as a loving Father would speak to His children. He led me to a series of Scriptures, which essentially said that "if we would do this, He would do that". Once those words came forth, a strong manifestation of the presence of God was ushered into the room. People began to weep, as others cried out. Some on the worship team no longer able to stand simply dropped to the floor. The anointing upon me was so strong; it was as though Jesus, Himself, had spoken.

This Sunday morning service was completely altered by a word from the Lord. Spontaneously, speaking from in front of the worship team, not from the pulpit, the pastor changed his message to reflect the Lord's heart. It was anything but a routine service.

At some later point in time, the Lord spoke a harsh word for me to bring forth. I did not want to speak this hard word of rebuke to my church family. Perspiration beaded my brow. Battling jittery nerves, I chose to be obedient to the Lord and speak forth what I believed the Lord was saying.

This time the pastor was at the pulpit preparing to deliver his weekly sermon. Deliberately standing up from my seat, I made my way toward the lectern as all eyes shifted toward me. Infringing upon the pastor at the pulpit was not something that was done at this church. In fact, up until now, it was unheard of. Confident by way of 1 Corinthians 14:30 ("And if a revelation comes to someone who is sitting down the first speaker should stop"), that biblically I was in order, and having that all necessary relationship with the pastor, I continued forward. Interrupting him in mid-sentence, I delivered the Lord's message.

Once the word of admonition was spoken, my brothers and sisters in Christ began to cry out in repentance. "Forgive us Lord", they petitioned. Some prostrated themselves in the aisles weeping tears of contrition, as others sat praying silently.

Again, the pastor's whole prepared message shifted to the Lord's agenda with this spoken word. He invited those who may have fallen away, fallen into sin, or for whatever their reason, to come forward to repent or to rededicate themselves to Christ. The response to his altar call was immediate and robust.

It is undeniably difficult to convey the aftermath of emotions following a word given when Father backs up your proclamation. After battling, then defeating, the demons of fear, doubt and dread by proceeding forward, then to witness the effect on the body of Christ to a word just given will, admittedly, make one heady.

Beware this for the secondary battle is about to begin. The subtle ensnarement of vanity plots relentlessly, leaving many trapped in false humility. For those content to ride the coattails of pride and arrogance would do well to remember that "God opposes the proud, but gives grace to the humble".

In spite of God's dire warnings, many will continue down the road to perdition, bolstered by the spirit of haughtiness, reaping worldly rewards. If we choose not to humble ourselves before the Lord, He will do it for us, through humiliation, corruption, suffering, and striving in our own weakness, admonishing that we are just puny man.

Our high minded effort of operating out of our own ability is not unlike the tale of a bear cub being hunted by a mountain lion. Frolicking contentedly among the hills, the baby bear is completely unaware of being stalked from behind by a mountain lion. As the cub turned and recognized his enemy his little legs were no match for the powerful stride of the mountain lion. Terrified and losing the footrace, the cub cried and shook in distress. He clamored across a tree which had fallen spanning the swift flowing river, only to discover the timber did not reach the other side. In the meantime, the lion was inches from his lunch. Suddenly, the rotted wood, unable to support his weight gave way, and the cub fell into the water.

The lion stalked him along the water's edge as the cub valiantly attempted an escape to safety.

With little energy left in reserve and nowhere else to run, the cub turned to face his enemy waiting upon the rocks, which jutted out from the river bed. The brave little bear accepted the challenge of the mighty lion before he would accept defeat. He gave his best baby bear roar, as the lion swiped him across his muzzle drawing blood. Howling, he stretched himself to his full little bear height, and suddenly the lion turned and ran in the opposite direction.

Exhausted and bloodied, the cub turned around and discovered all eight feet of his mother, standing on her hind legs. In a fighting stance, unbeknownst to the cub, it was she who provided the power to banish the enemy.

26

WE WERE WARNED

All was right with the Lord and His church, until it wasn't. The enemy prowls around like a roaring lion looking for someone to devour. He comes to kill and destroy. Satan would much rather a mundane gathering where everyone's mind is somewhere else. Whether the focus is on their grocery list, preparing dinner, doing laundry or looking forward to watching the football game, it matters not. As long as the heart and soul of a man is not on Christ, but is, instead, on the things of the world, all is right with Satan.

The gathering of the body of Christ should not be a place of religious duty and activity. It should be an environment experiencing God's love and presence. Sadly, unconverted hearts, chasing worldly pursuits has reduced the assembling of God's saints to little more than a social club. Unlike the model of devotion like that of the woman with the alabaster jar, few jealously seek the heart of Christ.

Starting slowly and ambiguous enough, there were rumblings of discontent reaching our ears from among the church body.

Seeds of jealousy and malcontent were being sewn by long standing members, as well as from long-time leadership. They were bucking the change to the banal service to which they were so accustomed. Disgruntled gossip made its way to the ears of the church pastor, which in turn enabled suspicion and doubt.

Because of the critical murmurings in his ear, the church pastor began to fear he would no longer be the authority, but rather, the person or persons imparting the prophetic word would usurp his position and split the church, leaving with half the congregation; which, in some cases, not this one, but in some cases, is proven true. Ironically, this particular pastor, at one time, commandeered members of a men's group being pastored by someone else in order to start up his own church. Abuse is rampant on both sides.

Prophets are feared, shunned and often ham-strung by frightened and insecure leadership. It is the pastor's assignment to safeguard His flock not to become paranoid, jealously guarding his own posterior thereby, thwarting the prophetic ministry.

Prophets have a fierce sense of being accountable to God. Pastors are also accountable to God, of course, but they are also very keen on being obligated to the people in their congregations, perpetuating the status quo. Hence, they along with the elders will push back on the prophetic with a bureaucratic stance.

Wrong-headedly, but quite commonplace, congregants put the pastor on a pedestal no matter the denomination or non-denomination. Unfortunately, so do some in leadership who owe their position to the pastor and become little more than yes-men. Posturing, in the guise of "protecting" the pastor, the murmurings and complaining of the petulant if spoken long enough and loudly enough, gets into the head of the one in charge.

One of the seven things the Lord hates is one who sows discord among the brethren. Unfortunately, the damage has been done.

In spite of the repentance and healing brought to this congregation, via the spoken word anointed by God, Satan's strategy to conquer and divide is realized through false accusations, jealousies, envy and strife. So sad.

God uses the accuser, Satan, to strengthen us and teach us to be overcomers. Our purpose is not to please man, but to please God.

To counter the false assumption of usurping leadership's position, a crusade was implemented by leadership, in an attempt to take charge of the anointing, as if that is possible.

As someone once said, "you can't have the real unless you allow the false." What is meant by the statement is that in order to have the real anointing you have to allow the counterfeit anointing. The reason for this is such as to be able to discern between the two. Of course, it goes without saying, that if a word of prophecy does not line up with Scripture, it is a false prophetic word and should be rejected.

In a ridiculous attempt to remind all congregants of the leadership's lofty position, and to convey their ability to hear from God, a self-serving and pathetic plot was conjured up amongst them. A leadership tag team, pastor included, cooked up a scenario that what appeared to be a spontaneous word for the church spoken in tongues, was then interpreted by the co-conspiring assistant pastor. When in truth, this team had met that very morning in the pastor's office and put the scheme together. The aim, of course, was a lame attempt to mimic God's legitimate prophetic gifting. An enormously sad, but true story.

For the express purpose of self-elevation, as we have witnessed, you may have a minister who already knows a person's situation by natural means and gives a "word of knowledge or wisdom" under the false pretense of the word being from the Lord. Who are they fooling? The sheep which are being kept in a narcoleptic state, that's who!

Even under false pretense, the manipulating of the prophetic word can certainly be edifying for the recipient, but the motive is all about self-promotion. Some will even go so far as to affix an earpiece to their ear and have a partner with a microphone on the other end to relay information. Trickery in ministry is nothing new. Where, oh where, is the discernment in the body of Christ?

Biblically, pastors are held to a higher standard and will be judged more harshly. However, they are only human, just mere mortals, like the rest of us.

27

WATCHMEN ARE NEEDED ON THE WALL

Our teachers forewarned us of the hostile reception prophets receive from the brethren. Exposing the hidden things, the sinful things and reputed to be harsh in their delivery, prophets can be uncomfortable individuals to be around.

There was a man within the congregation who would continually turn away from me or look down, as if totally engrossed in his shoes, as I approached him. Well, I reasoned, perhaps, he simply does not choose to engage in conversation or he does not care for me. Josh was married and had children, attended church every Sunday, participated in church life, and was well-like by everyone.

One morning as he was heading into the sanctuary with his family, I was heading out to the lobby. As we passed by each other, one would expect the normal courtesy of exchanging pleasantries. True to form, Josh averted his gaze. He would not make eye contact. Abruptly, the word of knowledge the Lord spoke to me was "shame" because Josh was addicted to pornography.

After the service, I approached the pastor and relayed all that had transpired. I informed him of the word the Lord spoke to me regarding Josh. The pastor proposed I speak to Josh. Noting that I had no relationship with him, I believed and suggested it was prudent that he, the pastor, shoulder the responsibility.

The following Sunday, the pastor brought me up to date on the word I received from the Lord regarding Josh. Because of that word, Josh did admit pornography was, indeed, an issue for him. He accepted the pastor's offer to begin counseling to conquer his addiction.

Although uncomfortable to be around, an anointed prophet can facilitate a powerful spirit of breakthrough. Prophets have a way of messing up our masked skullduggery.

While a shepherd protects the flock, the prophet (or watchman), warns of approaching danger. This is another reason for a good and trusting relationship between the pastor and prophet. If the warnings of the prophet are heeded, the pastor is then able to carry out his responsibility of guarding the sheep.

On one occasion, the Lord cautioned me to be on guard concerning a stranger visiting the church the following Sunday. The warning was this man arriving possessed deviant ways because he was a sexual predator. "Be watchful of new male visitors attending church service".

Informing William, one of the elders, of the appearance of the demon oppressed individual, he eyeballed me sideways.

However, after a moment or two, he nodded and agreed to be on the lookout for him.

As was relayed to me, a meeting was set up by the pastor, with the elders, ushers, and greeters to be on their guard for any unsavory visitors.

Sure enough, as I was to find out about a week and half later, this man had, indeed, visited the church and spoke with Samantha, one of the female greeters. As was related to me his lewd narrative included a problem he was having with his non-working male parts.

Having been previously advised of a potential unwanted stranger did little to contain Samantha's revulsion and incredulity. Removing her shocked and shaken self from the conversation, Samantha immediately sought out the pastor.

As a result, the assailant was confronted, asked to leave and instructed not to return.

It is imperative for church leadership to allow the watchmen to operate in their gifting, as God designed. Only then can the enemy be thwarted at the gate.

A somewhat gross but very descriptive word picture of the job of a prophet was given by someone along my travels, of whom I cannot remember the name or where or when I heard it. He or she said something to the effect that watchmen or prophets are the bowels of the body which get rid of the crap that can cause the body to fill up with garbage and become polluted unless eliminated.

Oh, how wonderful it would be if all church leadership allowed the prophet to function properly within the body. Instead, the seat counters are more concerned with offending the small minded, religious spirits who are big tithers, with little or no discernment.

 Unfortunately, the world in the church rules through feelings, political correctness, and solicitude. Most choose to hear only the smooth things…. "and to the prophets, do not prophesy to us right things. Speak to us smooth things. Prophesy deceits." (Isaiah 30:10)

Not only will a prophet, sitting upon the wall, thwart the enemy from entering the body, but will expose transgression lurking amongst the sheep. To the pastor's credit he was ready, willing and able to do just that very thing, albeit, with an abundance of scriptural pressure.

Unfortunately, his decision was not shared by all. No one wants to see members asked to leave for their misconduct, even after repeated attempts at restoration. Confronted by scripture, the pastor had no choice but to capitulate to truth.

One Sunday after service, as was our routine, everyone gathered in the lobby of the church for coffee and snacks. As my wife enjoyed the lively fellowship, her eyes were drawn to two women, standing together chatting.

One of the women we had both known from our previous church. Ellie was about the age of our children, married, with two children of her own. Her and her husband Aaron visited our home, even helping with laying plywood for a floor in our new barn.

The other woman, Ruth, was not as familiar to us. She was married with children and somewhat older than Ellie. Ruth was part of the worship team and, as was well-known, attending marriage counseling.

As my wife observed the two women kibitzing, spiritually the words "unholy alliance" flashed within a banner above their heads. My wife shared the word with me, and I in turn, shared this information with leadership. The consensus was to have an individual sit down conversation with each of them. This measure was more of a probe, with meager results.

However, soon thereafter, Ellie and Ruth were summoned to the first of four meetings with leadership. Most within the church were oblivious to the unhealthy exchange between the two, in the sanctuary, after service one Sunday. Occasionally, this time was reserved to minister to one another, as needed. Nevertheless, Ellie and Ruth took the whole comforting idea to another level. A consoling hand morphed into a petting caress. Let's just say it did not take much discernment to recognize the obvious.

Being privy to the situation, we were aware that at the meeting with leadership Ellie and Ruth admitted to spending a lot of time with each other as friends, nothing more. How innocent you may think. Just two women seeking companionship with each other, you may think. But Ellie and Ruth were quite cunning when conferring with leadership; the pastors and elders bought their baloney of innocence.

Be that as it may, an unholy alliance does not conjure up an upright amicability. Delicately bringing to reason, this word of knowledge was further pressed upon leadership. Ellie and Ruth's friendship was not a pristine pairing.

As a result, a second meeting was called. Amid tears and what appeared to be heart-felt contrition, Ellie and Ruth admitted to an intimate relationship and vowed to break it off. Also, at this meeting, my wife was named Ellie's mentor and Ellie was to be accountable to her. She was allowed to continue helping out in the children's ministry, alongside the pastor's wife. However, Ruth was asked to step down from the worship team. In addition, during the time of restoration, Ellie and Ruth were admonished to stay away from each other.

On the surface, all appeared to be going great. However, on more than one occasion, my wife caught Ellie out and out lying. My wife, Marianne, advised Ellie that if she fibbed one more time that would be it. There would be no more mentoring and no more support for a phony restoration and, not to mention the fact, that she was jeopardizing her position in the children's ministry. Ellie vowed to be truthful.....until she wasn't.

Ted, our minister acquaintance, was in town for one week in the fall teaching several seminars on prophetic deliverance. Ellie was to attend with my wife and myself. She left a message on our answering machine stating that she would be attending the seminar the evening before because her cousin was coming in from out of town on the evening we were to attend together.

Discerning this to be another fib, on their next meeting, Marianne questioned Ellie further as with whom she did attend the seminar. In spite of her promise to break it off, Ellie belligerently admitted that she went with Ruth. It wasn't because her cousin was coming to town; it was because she attended the seminar with Ruth. (As a side note....taking a blind eye, the pastor's wife defended Ellie to the hilt. Seemingly, she did not want to grasp the importance of Ellie staying away from Ruth during their restoration. Perhaps, she reasoned, after so many years in ministry, this too shall pass). There was plenty of evidence by witnesses, who saw them out and about around the town, to confirm Ellie and Ruth were still carrying on despite all the protestations to the contrary.

Accordingly, a third meeting was convened to let them know this would be their last chance to get right with God. Stop this unholy alliance. Once again, they duplicitously assured everyone they would comply and do what was right. The reality of the matter was a joke. Smugly, they were covertly laughing at leadership, believing their scheme opaquely slick.

It appeared leadership just wanted the whole thing to go away. They would accept any assurance on the part of Ellie and Ruth to repent.....for real. After all, these two women were not baby Christians; they grew up in the church and knew the consequences of sin. They knew they would be called to account if caught. But they were also confident of being able to pull the wool over everyone's eyes and continue in their ungodly ways.

Needless to say, after much persuasion, a fourth meeting was necessary. Incredulously, the pastor and assistant pastor were reluctant to deal with the matter. Restoration is never to be taken lightly on either side. No one wants to see a brother or sister expelled from the church family. Be that as it may, Paul, the apostle, instructs us succinctly from *The Message,* 1 Corinthians Chapter 5:

"I also received a report of scandalous sex within your church family, a kind that wouldn't be tolerated even outside the church: One of your men is sleeping with his stepmother. And you're so above it all that it doesn't even faze you! Shouldn't this break your hearts? Shouldn't it bring you to your knees in tears? Shouldn't this person and his conduct be confronted and dealt with?

"I'll tell you what I would do. Even though I'm not there in person, consider me right there with you, because I "can fully see what's going on. I'm telling you that this is wrong. You must not simply look the other way and hope it goes away on its own. Bring it out in the open and deal with it in the authority of Jesus our Master. Assemble the community—I'll be present in spirit with you and our Master Jesus will be present in power. Hold this man's conduct up to public scrutiny. Let him defend it if he can! But if he can't, then out with him! It will be totally devastating to him, of course, and embarrassing to you. But better devastation and embarrassment than damnation. You want him on his feet and forgiven before the Master on the Day of Judgment.

"Your flip and callous arrogance in these things bothers me. You pass it off as a small thing, but it's anything but that. Yeast, too, is a "small thing," but it works its way through a whole batch of bread dough pretty fast. So get rid of this "yeast." Our true identity is flat and plain, not puffed up with the wrong kind of ingredient. The Messiah, our Passover Lamb, has already been sacrificed for the Passover meal, and we are the Unraised Bread part of the Feast. So let's live out our part in the Feast, not as raised bread swollen with the yeast of evil, but as flat bread—simple, genuine, unpretentious.

"I wrote you in my earlier letter that you shouldn't make yourselves at home among the sexually promiscuous. I didn't mean that you should have nothing at all to do with outsiders of that sort. Or with crooks, whether blue- or white-collar. Or with spiritual phonies, for that matter. You'd have to leave the world entirely to do that! But I *am* saying that you shouldn't act as if everything is just fine when a friend who claims to be a Christian is "promiscuous or crooked, is flip with God or rude to friends, gets drunk or becomes greedy and predatory. You can't just go along with this, treating it as acceptable behavior. I'm not responsible for what the *outsiders* do, but don't we have some responsibility for those within our community of believers? God decides on the outsiders, but we need to decide when our brothers and sisters are out of line and, if necessary, clean house."

Unfortunately, after almost a full year, with little headway toward restoration, this final meeting was to determine the future fate of both Ellie and Ruth within the church body. Crowded into the small office were the pastor Paul and his wife Darlene, the assistant pastor, Russ and his wife Denise, Ellie and her husband Aaron, Ruth, my wife Marianne and myself.

After quite some time conversing with Ellie and Ruth, who continued to deny any culpability, I noticed they were wearing matching rings. I inquired as to why they were wearing matching rings if the relationship was broken off. A fleeting dumbfounded and stunned expression was exchanged between the two of them. After a stammering and stuttering moment they explained the rings were purchased months ago. "Ok, so why do you still wear them?" I inquired. With no credible answer forthcoming, they offered to give up the rings; which, at this point, didn't matter either way. It was rather a "duh" moment. By that I mean nothing, whatsoever, had changed between Ellie and Ruth.

There were two heavy-hearted camps in the meeting room that night. One camp, headed by Russ, the assistant pastor, wanted to give Ellie and Ruth an additional chance to repent, turn from sin, and continue restoration. The second camp, headed by my wife and myself, proffered by way of 1 Corinthians 5, enough was enough!

Back and forth scriptural truths were volleyed. The assistant pastor served up his scripture and was soundly answered with the prevailing truth. Unaccustomed to being challenged, Russ became annoyed and somewhat exasperated with me.

Once again, he spat out a scripture to seal and finalize his position. I was at a loss to understand why Russ was so contrarily dug in, despite all the obvious proof. Perhaps, it was because as I recalled a prophetic teacher saying prophets see things in black and white, while pastors tend to allow their mercy gift to override their wisdom. Pastors regard prophets as merciless and unmindful of future consequences, while prophets discern pastors as making concessions and people pleasing. Nonetheless, by allowing them yet another chance, Ellie and Ruth were taking everyone for fools and making a mockery of our faith and beliefs.

As I pondered all Russ had said, a silence descended upon the room. The Lord then led me to a scripture in Hebrews, Chapter 6, and verses 4-8. With all eyes upon me, I considered my response. Not only did I want to be respectful to the leadership in the room that day, I knew I must be obedient to the Lord's leading.

Responding to Russ, I noted all he expressed. I shared his compassion for the two women and understood that as a pastor he viewed things through a different lens than me. I humbly asked that he indulge me with the reading of one more passage of Scripture. He complied. I then shared Hebrews 6:4-8, as the Lord inspired me to read.

"For it is impossible to bring back to repentance those who were once enlightened—those who have experienced the good things of heaven and shared in the Holy Spirit, who have tasted the goodness of the word of God and the power of the age to come— and who then turn away from God. It is impossible to bring such people back to repentance; by rejecting the Son of God, they themselves are nailing him to the cross once again and holding him up to public shame.

"When the ground soaks up the falling rain and bears a good crop for the farmer, it has God's blessing. But if a field bears thorns and thistles, it is useless. The farmer will soon condemn that field and burn it" (Hebrews 6:4-8 New Living Translation).

When I read the words "by rejecting the Son of God, they themselves are nailing him to the cross once again and holding him up to public shame", my heart filled with sorrow.

I grieved for both Ellie and Ruth because they would not submit to the consequences of their actions.

In my heart I knew the best discipline for Ellie and Ruth was to be put outside the church for a season. They needed the heart revelation that by continuing their actions they were re-crucifying Christ. As we believed, at this time, if either of them were to die on that day they would be condemned to hell unless they truly repented.

Once again, silence prevailed. Sorrow replaced the contentious atmosphere. After a few moments, the pastor called the meeting to an end. During the session he said very little. However, Pastor Paul was listening intently and taking every word to heart. He advised everyone he would make his decision within the next couple of days. One by one, everyone mutely filed out from his office.

Several days later, true to his word, Pastor Paul rendered his ponderous verdict. It was not an easy decision to make nor was it an easy decision to bear. The consequences of his conclusion could reap disastrous results. The church could split, people could just up and leave and take their tithes with them, or a mutiny could be the result.

Be that as it may, taking courage in God's written Word while weighing the evidence put forth, only one verdict could be returned.

 Ellie and Ruth were asked to leave the congregation.

This was not a joyful feat. It was a light shining into the darkness, exposing the hidden things, and pulling the Christian mask off evil.

Sexual immorality is not limited to the congregants, however. Reaching epidemic proportions, many area churches, as well as those across the nation, have sexual predators presiding at the helm. When exposed, a self-preserving and self-centered type of repentance, called attrition, is offered up. It is not heartfelt nor is it a God centered sorrow for doing wrong. It is simply a means to avoid further discipline and keep their position.

By using weapons of submission and a "lord it over you" authority, by those in church leadership, any attempts to further expose this sin is met with accusations of being unforgiving, and reminded that we are to forgive seventy times seven (Matthew 18:21-22); and not to mention the Lord hates a gossip (Proverbs 6:19), among many other Scriptural attempts of suppression.

True repentance comes from a contrite heart toward a God-centered obedience. It is a true desire for change and true sorrow for offending God and others. True contrition is turning one hundred eighty degrees from sin and running toward God. "The sacrifice you desire is a broken spirit. You will not reject a broken and repentant heart, O God." (Psalm 51:17)

Is it any wonder church attendance is drastically dwindling? Is it any wonder the world identifies Christians with hypocrites?

The penalty for sexual immorality within the leadership of the church should be resignation until such time when and if the offender is brought to wholeness through true repentance.

Darkness permeates today's church; and when the leader of the body is overtaken by evil, you may as well put a welcome mat out front saying, "All Demonic Minions Welcome." Demonic forces don a cloak of charismatic respectability; all the while cunningly vying for the mind, will, and emotions of those entrusted to their charge, by means of deception and manipulation.

The church has become a place where Satan resides and has his throne. He is now the master. All the while Jesus is on the outside knocking... knocking... knocking at the door.

If the true watchmen were in their rightful place on the church wall watching, perhaps most, if not all, improprieties could be and would be intercepted.

The day is coming when the Lord will raise up more of His true prophets and His true pastors, not church managers, to take up their lawful function within His governmental body. Let us humble ourselves before Him and each other so that when evil rushes the gates, the loins of His church are girded up with the whole armor of God and ready for battle!

28

GROWING IN HIGHER REVELATION

Jesus said, ".....Well done, my good and faithful servant. You have been faithful in handling this small amount, so now I will give you many more responsibilities. Let's celebrate together!" (Matthew 25:23 NLT)

There is no better commendation to receive than one from the Master Himself. Secular awards, titles, honors, and positions are all significant, praiseworthy and deserve recognition to be sure. But when it's all been said and done, they are meaningless. These rewards will pass away. They will not stand the test of time. These are the accolades of men.

How much more valuable it is to hear Jesus say, "Well done!" Promoting one to a higher level of revelation is unfathomable.

Wanting to clear my mind and put some distance between myself and the outside world, I put on my favorite worship tunes. As I entered into His gates with thanksgiving, and into His courts with praise, I was thankful to Him for all He is and all He does in my life. I worshiped His Holy name. My soul was comforted and I was renewed.

Just before I shut off the music, the Lord spoke to me about Sandy, the greeter from our church. I was to tell her that she was to have a dream and I would have the corresponding interpretation of that dream.

Sharing this revelation with my wife, Marianne, she said, "Well, then, you should probably call her."

"Not so fast", I responded. "That's a lot of faith. What if I don't hear the rest? That's easy for you to say." That's about the gist of my retort.

Back and forth, my wife and I traded our reasoning, until such time she assured me that it was best to be obedient to the Lord for the task put before me. She challenged, "Well, you did hear from the Lord...right? Do you want me to call her for you?" Marianne realized I needed that extra push as it was hard for me to step out with this word I received. To tell someone they are to have a dream and you are going to interpret that dream takes on a whole new level of faith. In the end my wife went ahead, with my blessing, and called Sandy informing her I had a word for her.

Oh boy, I thought. I'm at the point of no return. The next thing I knew the ringing telephone receiver was staring me in the face.

After exchanging pleasantries, I asked Sandy if I could share a word with her that I believed the Lord spoke to me for her.

"Yeah, sure, of course", she replied.

"What I believe the Lord said was that you are going to have a dream and I will interpret that dream", I said.

"Oh Tom", she replied apologetically. "I never dream."

I said, "Well, the Lord said you are going to have a dream."

Sandy graciously, but dubiously thanked me once more, reminding me that she did not dream. We said our farewells and that was that.

Fervently asking the Lord for the interpretation of a dream that I knew nothing about or I wasn't sure would even materialize, because Sandy "didn't dream", He answered me. He led me to three scriptures, which I wrote down and placed in my bible.

At the next Sunday service, I anxiously awaited an acknowledgment from Sandy, regarding her dream. It never came. Well, I thought, I missed that one. Maybe she didn't have a dream yet. Maybe I'm still on board. Have some faith, I told myself. It was a rather stressful wait, because if a word you proclaim doesn't come to pass, you are labeled a false prophet and the brethren want to stone you!

A tormented three weeks passed as I was sure I would be called up in front of the congregation by the elders holding their baskets of stones. I began to reason with myself. By faith, I believed the Lord really did speak to me. I believed that He really wanted me to share this word with Sandy. Ok, I rationalized, how many pastors or teachers would still be around if they were stoned for their mistakes? Not many I'm sure. Shouldn't the same grace apply to His prophets?

After service, I was lingering in the sanctuary. Most everyone had left by this time. Sandy approached me and informed me that she had spoken with William, one of the elders, about her dream. She went on to say that William did not have a clue as to the interpretation of her dream. He didn't know what it meant. He told her to speak with me, being I'm the one who told her she would have a dream and I would interpret that dream.

She went on to say to me that on the very night I told her she would dream, she did in fact, have a dream. "I never dream", she said sheepishly. "I can't remember the last time I dreamed. It had to be years ago! Well, Tom, here's my dream."

Sandy found herself at a large mall filled with joyful children. Delightedly, she merrily walked among them noting they were all very young. Each one frolicking about boisterously blowing bubbles without a care in the world. There were no adults present. There was no apparent supervision-just the children on their own. Sandy said she felt no fear or concern for the children. There was only peace and contentment. "The end. That's the whole dream", she chagrined.

My impression was that Sandy was still skeptical and unconvinced her "silly" dream had any significant meaning.

After waiting for those many weeks, it was necessary for me to refresh my memory. I asked Sandy to give me a moment to review my notes.

Satisfied, I turned back toward her and gave the interpretation to her dream as the Lord revealed it to me three weeks prior.

In the eyes of the Father, the joyful children were innocence and purity even though they were conceived out of wedlock or of illicit affairs. Sadly, their young lives ended tragically early. (This is the first Scripture the Lord led me to; the account of David and Bathsheba, their illicit affair and the child conceived which died as a newborn-2 Samuel 12).

Upon this revelation, silent tears streamed down Sandy's cheeks. Her whole countenance changed from feeling silly to feeling Father's presence.

Continuing, I told Sandy the bubbles represented all the aborted babies being kept in God's care, who were "just a vapor that appears for a little while and then vanishes away" (James 4:14-the second Scripture I received).

Mutely, the stream of tears continued to flow unabashed, down Sandy's face.

Lastly, I interpreted that the children, who died young and all of the aborted babies, belong to God, the Father. He keeps them safe and in His hand. "Before I formed you in the womb I knew you, before you were born I set you apart;" (Jeremiah 1:5 NIV-the third Scripture I received).

Concluding the interpretation of her dream, I glanced down at the floor and noticed a good size puddle of tears had formed at Sandy's feet. I witnessed this woman receiving a huge heart healing from the Lord. As I brought tissues to her, she shared with me a profound heartache and sorrow she has been carrying for some time, which no one else except her husband, knew about.

Sandy shared that one of her children was pregnant and to Sandy's dismay, did not want to keep her first grandchild. No amount of talking would convince her offspring to go ahead with the pregnancy. Ultimately, the baby was aborted. Sandy's heart was shattered and she grieved deeply.

Carrying this burden for so long, she was devoid of hope and could find no relief from the pain and anguish consuming her;

and yet she confided in no one, outside of her husband, until today.

The interpretation given to me by the Father, of a dream sent to Sandy by the Father, released her from her self-imposed prison. Father lovingly made Sandy aware He's got this. He's got her. She had no control over the decision of another. He holds innocence and purity in the palm of His Hand. She understood that she would see this beautiful child of God, again; but in the meantime, the baby was lovingly held in Father's care.

Some years later, after leaving the congregation which we attended with Sandy, my wife, my granddaughter and I were enjoying a late afternoon lunch. Sandy unexpectedly walked in, greeted us, and came to sit down across from us at our table.

She remarked on the word I had given to her so many years ago and the profound impact it still had upon her even to this day. Sandy said, "I will never, ever forget the word you gave me from the Lord".

29

POCKET FULL OF CHANGE

God created the earth and everything in it. And contrary to what you may assume, God's first language is not English. So, if you have eyes to see and are looking, ears to hear and are listening, you will discover what He is revealing throughout His creation. "For since the creation of the world God's invisible qualities--his eternal power and divine nature--have been clearly seen, being understood from what has been made, so that people are without excuse. (Romans 1:20)

If you are paying attention, a word of comfort during a rough time, a forewarning preventing you from harm or a strengthening of courage or exhortation from the Lord can energize your faith. Faith is being sure of what we hope for and certain of what we cannot see. (Hebrews 11:1 paraphrase)

There are no coincidences because......"There is an appointed time for everything. And there is a time for every event under heaven." (Ecclesiastes 3:1 NASB)

If your stiff-necked proclivity is to keep God buttoned up all nice and neat, you will be enlightened as to what He is revealing to the foolish, by taking off your cloak of intellectual religious snobbery. "Instead, God chose things the world considers foolish in order to shame those who think they are wise. And he chose things that are powerless to shame those who are powerful." (1 Corinthians 1:27 NLT)

In November, 1999, while emptying my pants pockets as I readied myself to retire for the night, I withdrew six nickels. No other coins, just six nickels. What an oddity, I thought. Normally, when emptying my pockets at the end of the day, I have an assortment of coins being tossed into the five gallon metal milk can my wife and I use for saving our change. As I believe there are no coincidences, I asked the Lord to shine some light on this seemingly mundane, albeit curious, occurrence.

"My ways are far beyond anything you could imagine", began the Lord. "Simply put, I created the universe on what you define as mathematical laws and numbers and those mathematical laws and numbers govern all of creation. Pay attention! Use your spiritual eyes!"

Heeding His gentle rebuke I called out to Him, "Lord, help me!"

He answered me and said, *"I'll tell you marvelous and wondrous things that you could never figure out on your own."*

Being the coins I possessed were nickels, the Lord began His revelation with the number five. Five is the number for God's unconditional Love and ultimate grace upon man.

How do I know that five is the number of grace? Aside from many teachings over the years subscribing to this truth, the Scriptures show this to be true.

The definition of grace is unmerited favor; meaning one does not have to do a thing to receive favor, blessing, or "good fortune", if you prefer.

In the Book of John, Chapter 6, Jesus feeds five thousand people from five loaves of bread and two fishes. The people did not have to work to be fed. All they needed to do was be obedient when instructed to sit down in groups. They received an abundance or unmerited favor through no effort of their own.

In Exodus 22, if a man steals an ox, he is to restore it fivefold to receive grace.

Now, number six, the number of nickels in my pocket, is the number representing man, his fallen nature and his works.

God created man on the sixth day (Genesis 1:27).

Six days were given to man to work (Exodus 20:9, 31:15).

The following morning, as I made my way downstairs to the great room for breakfast, my wife met me at the bottom of the stairs. Cheerfully, Marianne said she had a surprise for me. Grinning, she thrust out her hand and said, "Look what I found for you. Here you go," as she presented me with a nickel she found on the kitchen floor of our home. That makes seven nickels!

From our studies, we learned the number seven signifies completion, as in "By the seventh day God completed His work which He had done, and He rested on the seventh day from all His work which He had done" (Genesis 2:2).

Elisha sent a messenger to command the leprous Naaman to bathe in the Jordan River seven times to effect a complete cleansing (2 Kings 5:10).

In the Book of Revelation seven seals, seven trumpets, and seven plagues complete God's wrath on mankind.

Also, the book of Revelation, which is the testimony of Jesus Christ, who is, was and will be, was given to the Seven Churches of Asia. Seven represents the complete and total church down through the generations, which include the church of today.

Ok, so far I have seven nickels. Five is the number representing grace, six is the number representing man, and lastly, nickel number seven is representing completion.

Completion? I guess that's it then. Only God would lay out a pattern such as this.

What is up with the nickels, I wondered? What is the lesson He is impressing upon us? We both believe, without a doubt that Jesus Christ died for our sins and was resurrected to sit at the right hand of the Father; that He was made a sin offering for all who believe in Him and they shall not perish, but have eternal life and He will come again. These plus additional truths are fundamentals basic to Christianity. This is Christianity 101.

However, in Scripture, when the Lord repeats a thing more than once, a tremendous amount of importance is attached to what He is saying. And the more times He reiterates a thing, the greater importance is placed upon it. What were we not getting?

It would appear that the Lord was not done with His nickel lesson because the very next day our four year old granddaughter, who was in pre-school at the time, placed a sealed envelope on my desk. She said, "Here Papa. I got this from Miss Jones today. She said it's better to give than receive. So.....here." Miss Jones was Callie's pre-school teacher.

"Oh, thank you, Callie", I replied as I lifted her up in a big bear hug.

Eager for me to open her gift and impatiently squirming about she demanded, "Open it, Papa!"

"Ok, ok, hold on a second." After setting this wriggling mass of sweetness back down and not knowing what to expect, I grabbed the letter opener and slit the top edge of the envelope. And what to my wondering eyes should appear? A NICKEL! I kid you not. Nickel number EIGHT fell out of the envelope and into my hand.

The number eight represents new beginnings, new life, and regeneration.

"On that very day Noah and his sons, Shem, Ham and Japheth, together with his wife and the wives of his three sons, entered the ark" (Genesis 7:13). God saved eight people on the ark in order to have a new beginning for mankind after the flood.

The eighth day, in a seven day week cycle, would be the beginning of a new week.

Carrying on, I was uncertain as to whether the trend would continue. But lo and behold, several days passed and I found nickel number nine lying on my driveway as I went to retrieve the mail. How extraordinary that is, I thought, as I picked up the coin!

The number nine represents finality and faith.

At the ninth hour on the cross, Jesus succumbed (Matthew 27:46) and in John 19:30 Jesus declared, "It is finished." Jesus was obedient to His Father for the task placed before Him. He remained faithful to the end even though He asked for the cup to be taken from Him.

The Lord spoke to me, in a dream, that night relative to the number nine, which I will describe further along.

During a Wednesday night church cell group meeting, the topic covered was entitled, "Coming to Wholeness and Integrity". After the meeting, as was our habit, my wife and I took our routine stroll. As we discussed the evening's teaching we both spotted nickel number ten lying on the asphalt as we crossed the street. Just as two little mischievous kids would do, we turned to each other, smiled and then laughing out loud, raced to the shiny round coin to see who would reach it first.

It's the little things that lift our spirit. We don't need a lot. A mere nickel, five cents, compelled us to harken back to playful children. For us, my wife said, this was a Holy Ghost adventure!

Scripturally, the number ten, as in the Ten Commandments, symbolizes completeness of divine order.

Once again, not knowing what to expect or not knowing whether the tendency for nickels to pop up in front of me would continue, I went about my business. I did not spend my days looking for nickels. They found me!

A perfect example of this is while sitting in one of the pews in the sanctuary during a church seminar. I happened to glance down and noticed my shoelace had come untied. As I bent over to retie it my eyes bugged out as I spotted another nickel! For those of you keeping track, that makes eleven nickels!

Biblically, eleven correlates to disorder, chaos and judgement. For me to find this particular nickel in the church sanctuary was thoroughly unsettling.

Men rebelled against God in Genesis, Chapter 11, when they built the tower of Babel. By breaking His law, God's judgment rained down upon the people and chaos prevailed.

All things considered, if the nickel trend continued, the next one in progression would be nickel number twelve. And number twelve represents God's government.

The apostles, chosen by Jesus in Matthew 10:2-4, numbered twelve. Not only were the twelve disciples Jesus' closest followers, they became the primary teachers of His message.

Jacob had twelve sons who would become the twelve tribes of Israel (Genesis 49:28).

There is a twelve hour period to rule the light; and twelve hour period to rule the darkness (Genesis 1:5).

So, no one could possibly believe it a coincidence that nickel number twelve was given to me by Pastor Paul after service one Sunday. Laughing as he approached me, he said, "Hey, Tom, I found this on the floor of my truck this morning and thought you might like to have it." As I extended my hand to receive what he was offering, my smile vanished as I accepted nickel number twelve.....God's government. God's government....Pastor Paul....get it? Now, keep in mind, Pastor Paul did not know how many nickels I had already collected nor could he know the significance of the nickel he had just presented to me.

Whether or not I was to receive any more nickels was inconsequential. The Lord bombarded me with twelve nickels and an abundance of important revelation for the church.

My sojourn began with six nickels. Hmmm....six nickels....6, the number of man x 5, the number of grace....equals 30. Straightaway I mused thirty was the age at which Jesus initiated His ministry. The Son of God, who became man, made evident God's unconditional love for mankind and His ultimate grace upon us.

Jesus' ministry also brought radical change and disruption to man's religious order. "...he (Jesus) went into the synagogue, as was his custom. And he stood up to read.....All spoke well of him....." (Luke 16, 22 NIV).

But when Jesus spoke the truth by condemning Israel and showing favor to the Gentiles...."All the people in the synagogue were furious when they heard this. They got up, drove him out of the town, and took him to the brow of the hill on which the town was built, in order to throw him down the cliff" (Luke 28-29 NIV).

****

With number seven representing completion, I believe the Lord is saying the status quo of the way man conducts His (God's) business is coming to an end. He will expose the depth of corruption residing in the church. He is knocking at the door, but everyone is comfortable with the existing condition and no one will deign to get up and open it.

For Jesus to judge His Church is nothing new. During the Lord's ministry, the church leadership, that is to say the Scribes, Pharisees, Sadducees and Chief Priests, was nefarious and deceitful. The Scribes and the Pharisees were among the most rabid regarding the Law of Moses. Along with the Chief Priests, the Scribes and Pharisees were the ruling class of that time.

In Matthew 16 Jesus declared to the apostles to....."Take heed and beware of the leaven of the Pharisees and Sadducees" (verse 6). Here Jesus was not concerned about actual yeast in bread. He was referring to the false doctrines of the Pharisees and of the Sadducees (verse 12).

Witness the unthinkable accusations leveled against the religious leaders of Israel by Jesus in the Book of Matthew. Throughout Chapter 23, Jesus calls the Scribes and Pharisees – HYPOCRITES, BLIND GUIDES, FOOLS and finally, SNAKES and BROOD OF VIPERS. As the saying goes, "A snake is a snake to a snake-eating snake."

Even so, Jesus instructed the crowds and His disciples to obey the teachers of the law and the Pharisees because they sit in Moses' seat. But Jesus also instructed everyone not to do as they do.

Why did Jesus level vile indictments against them? He explains:

"But be careful about following *them*. They talk a good line, but they don't live it. They don't take it into their hearts and live it out in their behavior. It's all spit-and-polish veneer.

"Instead of giving you God's Law *(The Ten Commandments-italics mine)* as food and drink by which you can banquet on God, they package it in bundles of rules *(the 613 Mosaic Laws-italics mine),* loading you down like pack animals. They seem to take pleasure in watching you stagger under these loads, and wouldn't think of lifting a finger to help. Their lives are perpetual fashion shows, embroidered prayer shawls one day and flowery prayers the next. They love to sit at the head table at church dinners, basking in the most prominent positions, preening in the radiance of public flattery, receiving honorary degrees, and getting called 'Doctor' and 'Reverend.'

"Don't let people do that to you, put you on a pedestal like that. You all have a single Teacher, and you are all classmates. Don't set people up as experts over your life, letting them tell you what to do. Save that authority for God; let him tell you what to do. No one else should carry the title of 'Father'; you have only one Father, and he's in heaven.

"And don't let people maneuver you into taking charge of them. There is only one Life-Leader for you and them - Christ. "Do you want to stand out? Then step down. Be a servant.

"If you puff yourself up, you'll get the wind knocked out of you. But if you're content to simply be yourself, your life will count for plenty.

"I've had it with you! You're hopeless, you religion scholars, you Pharisees! Frauds! Your lives are roadblocks to God's kingdom. You refuse to enter, and won't let anyone else in either.

"You're hopeless, you religion scholars and Pharisees! Frauds! You go halfway around the world to make a convert, but once you get him you make him into a replica of yourselves, double-damned (Matthew 23:3-15 The Message).

Facetiously, could Jesus possibly be speaking to the church today? Yes, of course He is speaking to the church today! Can you imagine accepting such a rebuke to your church by such a radical disrupter? My inclination is to believe the response would be the same today as it was then…. "Crucify Him!"

****

As mentioned previously, the book of Revelation is the testimony of Jesus Christ, which is the Spirit of prophecy; and it was given to the Seven Churches of Asia. Jesus Christ who is was and will be is the Spirit of prophecy given to every generation. Seven represents the complete and total church down through the generations, which include the church of today.

Now I was beginning to draw a glimmer of understanding of the deeper revelation Jesus was declaring about the condition of the church today and the enormity of the falling away.

First of all, the Seven Churches in Asia depicted in Revelation 2 and 3 are Ephesus, Smyrna, Pergamum, Thyatira, Sardis, Philadelphia and Laodicea.

I had always believed that the church of Laodicea represents today's church. However, the Lord was shining His light on the Truth that all seven churches were representative of all churches then and now down through the ages.

Laodicea was chastised for being lukewarm-neither hot nor cold! Jesus wished they would be one or the other. They were the wealthiest city in Phrygia during Roman times for which they were quite proud of their financial wealth, huge textile industry, and a famous eye salve. Be that as it may, the church in Laodicea did not provide either healing for the spiritually sick or refreshment for the spiritually weary.

Jesus admonished the self-deluded congregation to buy gold refined in the fire from Him, so they would be rich, and to cover their nakedness, He counseled them to purchase white clothes from Him to wear. Jesus also advised His salve to put on their eyes, so they could see (Revelation 3:18-19 NIV).

Jesus was not talking only to the Laodicean congregants. He was speaking to all the churches then and down through history. "He who has an ear, let him hear (*spiritually*) what the Spirit says to the churches (Revelation 3:22 NIV). Jesus would repeat this command six more times.

To the church of Smyrna and the church of Philadelphia, Jesus accused some within the congregation to be "...liars" and "of the synagogue of Satan" (Rev 2:9 and 3:9 NIV).

The church of Sardis was upbraided for being dead (*spiritually*), while Thyatira tolerated Jezebel who misleads Jesus' servants into sexual immorality and the eating of food sacrificed to idols (Revelation 3:1 and 2:20 NIV).

Jesus castigated the church of Pergamum for eating food sacrificed to idols, committing immorality, and holding to the teaching of Balaam and the Nicolaitans (Revelation 2:14-15 NIV).

Lastly, the church at Ephesus was berated for "forsaking their first love" (Revelation 2:4 NIV).

Of course, there were many more churches in and around the region besides the churches in Asia, such as in Judea and in Rome, as well. However, these churches in Asia personified all that Jesus had to say to all the congregations everywhere through all generations to today. The revelation Jesus gave to the Seven Churches in Asia is a complete revelation for all churches even now. These seven congregations had within them all of the sins, weaknesses, and shortcomings of all congregations everywhere during all time.

And this is what Jesus has to say to His church. "Yet I hold this against you: You have forsaken the love you had at first. Consider how far you have fallen! Repent and do the things you did at first. If you do not repent I will come to you and remove your lampstand from its place" (Revelation 2:4-5 NIV).

Be that as it may, all of the churches in Asia also had at least a few names that were not spiritually defiled (that is to say they possessed spiritual character), which also applies to all churches everywhere even now. "For many are called, but few are chosen" (Matthew 22:14 NIV).

However, "The LORD is gracious and compassionate, slow to anger and rich in love" (Psalm 145:8 NIV). It has been better than two thousand years, after all. But make no mistake, Jesus will purge all the evil from His Church and bring all into the Father's Kingdom!

Jesus did not just reprimand the Seven Churches in Asia and leave it at that. He proclaimed His promise of rewards to all the overcomers, the called and chosen, the conquerors (referring to all those who are victorious in the battle (for it is a battle) of our Christian walk).

In the Book of Revelation, Jesus declares just what rewards are awaiting the conquerors. "... I give to eat of the tree of *(the)* life which is in the paradise of God" (2:7), "... shall not be hurt of the second death" (2:17), "... I give the power over the nations" (2:26), "...shall be clothed in white raiment; and I will not blot out his name out of the book of *(the)* life..." (3:5), "...I will make a pillar in the temple of my God.... and I will write upon him My new name" (3:12), and "...will I grant to sit with me in my throne" (3:21).

All of the rewards promised by Jesus to each church were promised rewards to all the churches, even now, down through every generation. In addition, all the rewards are actually one reward. And that One Reward is Jesus Christ....so simple, so child-like, so awesome!

It's interesting to note, as we studied these Scriptures in the Book of Revelation, most translations left out the article *"the"*, contained in the Greek manuscripts. A Conservative Version Interlinear, the Emphatic Diaglott New Testament, and Young's Literal Translation are a few of the translations that retained the article "*the*," however.

Retaining that one small three letter article is important. Because our rewards are not about our names being written in some book of life or eating from some tree of life somewhere. We, as conquerors, are to be written in the book of THE Life, eating from the tree of THE Life. That is to say, we, as overcomers, are partakers of Jesus Christ who is "the way, the truth and the life" (John 14:6).

****

Nickel number eight, representing new beginnings, was given to me by my granddaughter, sealed in an envelope. I believe the Lord has sealed this new beginning for those who will enter into His rest with child-like faith. He is restoring the church to its purest form.

****

Earlier I alluded to a dream the Lord had given me in relation to nickel number nine. It was a dream of devastating magnitude. I found myself in a residential area. Being this a dream, I do not know the why or the how of the circumstances bringing me to a neighborhood I had never visited before, even though there was a certain familiarity resonating from the streets and homes.

Without warning the earth began to shake as never before decimating homes surrounding the local church and its property. Just as abruptly as it began, the shaking ceased. The only thing standing was the church with a huge cross atop its spire.

What I could see from my vantage point was the church minus its doors. As I made my way to the stone and brick structure, I stepped through the door-less entryway. I gasped as I saw the concrete floors had heaved exposing the demolished foundation beneath it. As I gingerly stepped through the rubble of the building, I felt an eerie, contrary sense of peace that all would be well, in spite of what I was to discover.

As I sought the Lord for clarification, I reflected on the verifiable truth that as Christians our firm foundation must be built on Christ (1 Corinthians 3:11). Sadly, in this dream, the foundation of this church had been destroyed.

The roof signifying His covering was completely untouched; which is not surprising as "He will cover you with his feathers. He will shelter you with his wings. His faithful promises are your armor and protection." (Psalm 91:4)

It was not unexpected, however, that the four corner pillars, representing the four gospels, were still standing because "When the earth and all its people quake, it is I who hold its pillars firm." (Psalm 75:3)

The walls, save the four corners, were scattered across the decimated foundation. The few battered and broken pews that remained intact held emaciated, sickly, catatonic saints. These trusting souls bore the air of terminal cancer patients who were forfeiting the battle for life, in spite of the chemo drugs dripping into anemic bloodstreams. Most had scraggly little or no hair at all remaining on their heads, with shriveled blue veins visible beneath translucent skin.

The building stones of the church walls represent God's people. In 1 Peter 2:5 we are told..... "you also, like living stones, are being built into a spiritual house to be a holy priesthood...." However, in this spiritual house the saints were not just sickly, they ALL WERE DYING!!

Jesus spoke to me through Matthew 15:13-14 that "Every plant that my heavenly Father has not planted will be pulled up by the roots. Leave them; they are blind guides. If a blind man leads a blind man both will fall into a pit."

 Jesus declared that He is the Good Shepherd and spoke to me regarding the hired hands of John 10:12. He emphasized the hired hands don't own the sheep and don't care for the sheep. They are little more than church managers, who are in it strictly for the money. He said, they, along with every man who has built His church on self-promotion, hype, greed, and those who continue to tickle the ears of His people have become stains before Him.

Without a pause, Jesus continued from Joel 3:6 "You sold the people of Judah and Jerusalem to the Greeks, that you might send them from their homeland." The Greeks, He said, speak of humanism; psychology, philosophy and all manner of intellectual pursuits, rather than pursuing the things of the Spirit. Jesus threw down the gauntlet and challenged His bride to leave the Valley of Jehoshaphat, the valley of decisions, and choose Him; or does she prefer to stay in the world?

Relentlessly, and without a break, the Lord led me to Matthew 23:38-39 "Look your house is left to you desolate. For I tell you, you will not see me again until you say, "Blessed is He who comes in the name of the Lord."

As I grappled with the full import of the Lord's revelation, He showed me the well within the church is not the well of John 4:14. His well is a well which is a spring of water welling up to eternal life. Rather, the church's man-made wells are tainted with waters poisoning His people with self; self-serving, selfish ambition, self-centeredness and self-reliance. All who drank from this well are "falling into temptation and a trap and into many foolish and harmful desires that plunge men into ruin and destruction." (1Timothy 6:9)

Jesus Christ said in Revelation 3:1-6 "…….I know your deeds; you have a reputation for being alive, but you are dead. Wake up! Strengthen what remains and is about to die, for I have not found your deeds complete in the sight of my God. Remember, therefore, what you have received and heard; obey it and repent. But if you do not wake up, I will come like a thief and you will not know at what time I will come to you. You have a few people in Sardis who have not soiled their clothes. They will walk with me, dressed in white, for they are worthy. He who overcomes will, like them, be dressed in white. I will never blot out his name from the book of (*the*-italics mine) life, but will acknowledge his name before my Father and his angels. He, who has an ear, let him hear what the Spirit says to the churches."

The time is coming when all church doors will be blown off their hinges to reveal the sick and dying within. Even though all are dying, the sad and misguided belief persists there is no need for The Great Physician.

Continuing on with the number ten signifying completeness of order, that nothing is wanting, it is an easy leap to see that the Ten Commandments contain all that is necessary for a prosperous Godly life; no more or no less. The 10 Commandments are the perfect instruction of righteousness.

However, upon further revelation, the Ten Commandments were also the special test that God gave to Israel.

****

The Lord allowed another dream where I was meandering through a life sustaining panorama of abundance. Clear, pure streams providing water, ample oak trees for building homes, fertile soil awaiting planting for the fall harvest, cows, sheep and chickens to provide sustenance for the long haul, and people aplenty toiling in the fields were observed for as far as the eye could see. The labor was exacting and only a few of the inhabitants appeared content and happy despite being provided with abundance. Contrariwise, the malcontents who were the majority were leaning on their shovels and gazing across the field, dreaming of a better life.

As I followed their gaze, what I saw strategically placed throughout the teeming landscape, were many golden objects. Each golden object was centered within its own giant spider web. As I continued to survey the scene being played out before me, I observed the unsatisfied make their way down a long, broad, worn path toward the golden object of their personal heart's desire. As each man and woman drew closer to the webs I became transfixed as their lives became full of every kind of wickedness, sin, greed, hate, envy, murder, quarreling, deception, malicious behavior and gossip. In doing so, each became ensnared with little or no hope of extrication. Tended by various sized black spiders, some large some small, depending upon the degree of one's ensnarement, the deceived eventually became imprisoned within the silken strands.

Suddenly and without warning, the golden objects began to melt and liquefy. In horror, I beheld the river of gold consume each man and woman desperately clinging to the object of their covetousness. As the molten gold continued its downward path, the entirety of the spider webs and all they contained was completely destroyed.

The Lord revealed to me the golden objects are the golden calves His people put before Him, as did the Israelites of Exodus 34. He is applying His fire to those golden calves. He is purifying each man's (and woman's) heart. He is "Casting down imaginations and every high thing that exalts itself against the knowledge of God…" (1 Corinthians 10:5)

Just as my dream illustrated, the Lord is testing and purifying each of us by smashing the idols of our human heart in order for us to be brought to completeness, which is the state or condition of having all the necessary or appropriate parts. That is to say wholeness, completeness of divine order. He is burning up all which is worldly within us and purifying all which is worth keeping. Just as gold is refined by fire and made pure, so are we.

This is the true gold. The blessing comes in the form of being tested, judged and purified, now, in this life.

****

During the church conference where I found nickel number eleven, representing judgment, our daughter Jennifer, who was also in attendance, had an open vision of a map. Illustrated upon the map was a powerful rushing river. As the river surged mightily mammoth boulders, which had tumbled from the towering cliffs above, along with the ancient trees felled by a monstrous storm, created a dam of sorts. Instead of the formidable water steamrolling over the obstacles, the river branched off into two slow moving placid streams; one to the left and one to the right.

As Jen shared her vision with me, she asked, "What does it mean, Dad?" I explained to her I believed the Lord was showing her that being in the mighty river of God would exact a hefty price from this body of believers. There would be a church split relative to the carnal reaction of the moving of the Holy Spirit, I further interpreted.

The powerful rushing river denotes the awesome anointing and move of God. The boulders, which are more often than not immovable, depict those steeped in their religion come hell or high water. And the ancient trees, which one would believe to have deep roots simply because they are so venerable and majestic, actually had very shallow roots and are the reason they were felled by the mighty storm.

The splitting of the river into two parts illustrates the unwillingness of the shrinking saints to confront the obstacles put in their path. They would rather go around the impediments and not cause any waves, thus diminishing the powerful forging ahead. Shunning the mighty move of God enabled them to go back to their lukewarm ways.

Disdaining God's anointing would result in the withdrawing of His presence from the church. Who would the pastor choose? He could bow down to the pressure of the people, who paid his salary and guaranteed his retirement. Or he could obey God by jumping into the river with careless regard for the undeniable consequences.

Many attending this church clung to routines and rituals, unwilling to afford spiritual muscles a good workout. Regurgitating the milk of the word extracts minimal cost or effort. Those who can quote every Scripture verse verbatim often do not possess knowledge of the Truth. So, the thought of jumping into the raging River is absolutely terrifying.

Moses observed a similar situation in Exodus 20:18-19 "All the people perceived the thunder and the lightning flashes and the sound of the trumpet and the mountain smoking; and when the people saw it, they trembled and stood at a distance. Then they said to Moses, "Speak to us yourself and we will listen; but let not God speak to us, or we will die."

However, reading further in verse 20 Moses comforts the people. "Moses said to the people, "Do not be afraid; for God has come in order to test you, and in order that the fear of Him may remain with you, so that you may not sin."

Were we still so naïve to believe all God's kids desired His presence in whatever way He chose? Yes, yes we were. Apparently not every denomination or non-denomination is eager for the sometimes messy, prevailing spiritual chaos initiated by the Holy Spirit. And our involvement has shown us even the ones who crave the supernatural stirring of the Holy

Spirit want it on their own terms-nice and neat and quietly tied in a pretty red bow. Attempting to squash God into a teeny tiny box never results in anything good. What it will do is leave you right where you are in your spiritual growth-stagnant and complacent. And when living things stagnate, they begin to die.

****

Nickel twelve, you will recall was given to me by Pastor Paul and is representative of government.

During a particular teaching the Lord showed me He is raising up a new mindset of leadership. A new leadership will emerge from one of unrighteousness to one of holiness, from a self-centered ministry of gain and reward to one of honor and justice. A leadership which has a heart to jump into the river and eagerly await, with expectation, the next move God has for us.

The Lord is about to purge the Nicolaitan (**Nickel** – aitan) spirit from His body as part and parcel of His desire for wholeness (nickel #10), His judgment (nickel#11), and His perfection of His government (nickel #12).

The Nicolaitans were a heretical sect within the early church. Mentioned in the book of Revelation, Jesus and the church in Ephesus hated their practices, while the church in Pergamum had those who held to the teaching of the Nicolaitans.

220

Not fully understanding the nature of a Nicolaitan spirit, we conducted our own research through various means and sources.

The designation Nicolaitan comes from two Greek words...."Nikos" and "Laos". Nikos is defined as victory, triumph, a conquest, and by implication, dominancy over the defeated. Nicao literally means to dominate, intimidate, and manipulate. (Strong's Concordance)

Laos, on the other hand means the people or laity. Hence, Nikos and Laos together mean to be victorious over the people (Strong's Concordance); or those who exercise power over the people.

Furthermore, in Matthew 23, Jesus said to "obey the teachers of the law, but do not do as they do. Everything they do is done for men to see. They love the place of honor and the most important seats. They love to be greeted in the marketplaces and have men call them "Rabbi".

Jesus called them hypocrites and Peter admonished to not lord it over the flock, but to lead by example.

****

At the start of this chapter, I shared that the appearance of the nickels began in November of 1999. The Lord also gave me a dream, at that time, illustrating an imminent literal earthquake. Just before my wife and I left for a New Year's Eve prophetic conference, stepping out in faith, I told Pastor Paul we were going to experience an imminent literal earthquake in Western New York. The earthquake would be a confirming approval of the words God revealed to me using the twelve nickels. Earthquakes are a rare occurrence in Western New York, despite being situated on a significant fault line.

On New Year's Eve, the Lord revealed the location of the earthquake to me. The earthquake would happen near our home, which is south of Buffalo. As I considered the revelation, I had concerns for my family at home. But, once again, there was a peaceful reassurance that all would be well.

I did not know just how close the earthquake would hit until we returned home. Pastor Paul, incredulously, informed me there was, indeed, an earthquake just north of Buffalo. This was confirmed for me as I read in our local newspaper there had been an earthquake of a 4.5 magnitude twenty miles from our home; in spite of the ground shaking there were no reported injuries or deaths.

****

Our experiences witnessed the power-hungry brokers acting more like politicians and CEOs in church leadership throughout our area churches with which we were familiar. Not all authority leans toward such moral morass as this. However, there are those who desire to control the sheep through intimidation by weaponizing Scripture, all the while aspiring to a secret life contrary to what they preach.

As the Lord made plain, our gifting was not a good fit with the mindset of our brothers and sisters in the faith. Don't misunderstand. Most were all very good people with hearts of gold and they claimed to love the Lord. However, a paralyzing stronghold of fear gripped many in such a way they much more resembled church-ians (of or belonging to the church), rather than Christ-ians (of or belonging to Christ).

With that said, my wife and I both felt the pull of the Holy Spirit. It was for such a time as this for us to come out of the institutional church and move on.

30

WHERE TO NOW?

Ok Lord, where will You have us now? Lord...? Hello.... Lord....? No immediate answer was forthcoming.

In the meantime, as Christians are wont to do upon meeting other Christian acquaintances, we were condescendingly and unceasingly bombarded with "Where do you go to church now?" or "Who are you accountable to now?" And not receiving the answers they desired countered with, "You know Scripture says we are not to forsake the assembling of ourselves together" (Hebrews 10:25 paraphrase). Yada. Yada. Yada.

From our days spent in "religious" circles, those asked questions, except for the Catholic denomination, were a familiar mantra to anyone who left the four walls of the institutionalized church; but were the inquiries scripturally based or "come join our church" based? It was time for

Marianne and I to get down to the nitty gritty of the inquisition that we too, at one time, had been guilty of asking those poor "lost", "renegade", "lone ranger", "hurt by the church" souls-no matter their reason for leaving the church.

With many hours, months and yes, years, this was just the dawn of what we learned studying God's Word. Our education is ongoing and we are, continually, uncovering marvelous Truths revealed in Scripture.

What our zealous, albeit unenlightened, still penned sheep, aka Christian brothers and sisters, are referring to when they espouse "not to forsake the assembly" is, of course, "going to church"; preferably their church. The weaponization of Scripture has contributed to the sheep's misguided understanding that "church" is on Sunday, the Sabbath, and is situated inside the institutionalized brick and mortar construction. It just ain't so on many levels!

This is what the Lord says, "Do you not know that **you are a temple of God** and that **the Spirit of God dwells in you**?" (emphasis mine) (1 Corinthians 3:16 NASB) How many times have we read this Scripture?

And He assures us, "He is the God who made the world and everything in it. Since he is Lord of heaven and earth, **he doesn't live in man-made temples** (emphasis mine) ...." (Acts 17:24 NLT) How many times have we read this Scripture? Read on, o sleeper!

Paul advises the Colossians in Chapter 2 verses 16-17, "So don't put up with anyone pressuring you in details of diet, worship services, or holy days. All those things are mere shadows cast before what was to come; the substance is Christ" (The Message). How many times have you read that Scripture?

There are many, many incomparable Truths to be learned, if only we have ears of God's Spirit to hear and His eyes to see. We learned a bold Truth of just how the physical Sabbath Saturday, became the physical Sabbath Sunday. Read on and you will exclaim, "Are you kidding me?!"

The Sabbath day of rest is the seventh day of the week, or Saturday, because just as God rested from His work on the seventh day, so are we to rest from ours. So, how come we all "worship" on Sunday? Listen up.....

The Holy Roman Catholic Church, by its very name, came out of Rome. Rome was not Christian. It was a pagan city, and many of Rome's pagan beliefs were adopted by the Church of Rome. The Romans worshiped the Egyptian Sun god Ra, made into law by Emperor Constantine in 321 AD. So, it follows the Egyptians would worship on Sun-day, in honor of the pagan Sun god, rather than Saturday, the Sabbath. Is this warranted in Scripture? Heck no! Sunday, the Lord's Day, is not Scriptural, it is Roman Catholic.

In Charles J Hefele's *"A History of the Church Councils"* he wrote, *"Christians must not Judaize by resting on the Sabbath, but must work on that day, rather honoring the Lord's Day, resting then as Christians. But if any shall be found to be Judaizing* (meaning to keep the Sabbath, Saturday, holy- explanation mine*), let him be anathema from Christ."*

Wait a second here, didn't God say, "Remember the Sabbath day to keep it holy" (Exodus 20:8)? Yes, yes He did. But the Roman Catholic Church said to worship on the Day of the Sun. Who you gonna believe?

So, we're thinking, ok, ok, but that's the Holy Roman Catholic Church. How did the Protestants and almost every other denomination and non-denomination get misled into disobeying God? Read on.

There was a Catholic priest by the name of T. Enright who was president, at one time, of Redemptorist Father's College in Kansas City. Published in the Industrial American, out of Harlan, Iowa was one of his lectures regarding a decision made at the Council of Laodicea (363-364 AD).

"My brethren, look about the various wrangling sects and denominations. Show me one that claims or possesses the power to make laws binding on the conscience. There is but one on the face of the earth-the Catholic Church-that has the power to make laws binding upon the conscience, binding before God, binding under the pain of hellfire. Take, for instance, the day we celebrate-Sunday. What right have the Protestant churches to observe that day? None whatever. You say it is to obey the commandment, 'Remember the Sabbath day to keep it holy.' But Sunday is not the Sabbath according to the Bible and the record of time. Everyone knows that Sunday is the first day of the week, while Saturday is the seventh day, and the Sabbath, the day consecrated as a day of rest. It is so recognized in all civilized nations.

"I have repeatedly offered $1000 to anyone who will furnish proof from the Bible that Sunday is the day we are bound to keep, and no one has called for the money. If any person in this town will show any Scripture for it, I will tomorrow evening publicly acknowledge it and thank him for it. It was the Holy Catholic Church that changed the day of rest from Saturday to Sunday, the first day of the week. And it not only compelled all to keep Sunday, but at the Council of Laodicea, A.D. 364, anathematized those who kept the Sabbath and urged all persons to labour on the seventh day (Saturday-italics mine) under penalty of anathema. Which church does the whole civilized world obey? Protestants call us every horrible name they can think of-anti-Christ, the scarlet-colored beast, Babylon, etc., and at the same time profess great reverence for the Bible, and yet by their solemn act of keeping Sunday, they acknowledge the power of the Catholic Church." (December 19, 1889)

Pagan Rome appropriated many practices and beliefs from pagan Greece, who appropriated them from pagan Egypt and on into the Church of Rome, through the King James Bible and into Christian homes everywhere.

Yikes, isn't breaking one of the Ten Commandments a one-way ticket to hell?

When my wife and I were young, learning the fourth of God's Ten Commandments in Catholic school, we were taught to "Remember the Sabbath-day to keep it holy". Our perception, for all intents and purposes, was it simply meant attending church on Sunday (which we have since learned is the day dedicated to the pagan Egyptian Sun god Ra). We were not to work on Sunday, just go to church, which my parents and my wife's grandmother made certain each one of us did (even though they themselves rarely attended church).

However, as we matured in our walk with the Lord, we understood "Remember the Sabbath day and keep it holy" has a far deeper meaning spiritually, than on what day we should be attending church.

Genesis 2:2 from the Concordant Literal version of Scripture renders it this way. "And finishing is the Elohim, on the sixth day, His works which He does. And ceasing is He on the seventh day from all His work which He does." Wow!

All of God's works are finished and He is ceasing from the works of the physical creation of the heavens and the earth. The Concordant Literal version makes it plain that the seventh day is a day of rest and of His ceasing. God is not creating anything new, He is resting. We are living in His seventh day.

The fourth commandment, "Remember the Sabbath-day to keep it holy", given in Exodus of the Old Testament, was a law. Israel was to rest every seventh day of a week. But the law, according to Hebrews 10:1 is only a shadow of the good things to come. "The old system under the law of Moses was only a shadow, a dim preview of the good things to come, not the good things themselves." (NLT)

Delving further, we read in Hebrews 4:10, "For all who have entered into God's rest have rested from their labors, just as God did after creating the world." (NLT)

We are to spiritually rest from our labors just as God did from His. It is more than the keeping of the letter of the Law as did the men and women of Israel during the time Moses received the Ten Commandments; first comes the physical, the law, then the spiritual. (1 Corinthians 15:46)

It's all about God's **spiritual** creation-making us into His own **spiritual** image (God is Spirit- John 4:24). Now, I appreciate we were all taught that we are already made or created in God's image (Genesis 1:27 many translations). Be that as it may, when you look in the mirror do you see a person without sin? Are you sinless? Or maybe you believe God sins just like us? I don't think so. The proper translation reads, "And creat-**ing** (emphasis mine) is the Elohim humanity in His image. In the image of the Elohim He creates it. Male and female He creates them" (Concordant Literal). Sorry, but our creating in His image is an ongoing process. Unfortunately, we ain't there yet (sigh). And by the way, did you catch this creating, out of necessity, happens before the "fall" of Adam and Eve? Do you really believe that an omniscient God did not know Adam and Eve would sin and eat from the tree of the knowledge of good and evil? If they were already created perfect, in God's image, the devil would not have been able to tempt them.

The Israelites broke the law because they could not know the spiritual meaning of the Sabbath, and the physical law apparently held no profit for them. So, they broke it.

Physical resting does a physical body good. It revitalizes us to think better, to look and feel great. But what does physical resting do for us spiritually? Nada. Nothing. Neither does carrying out the physical rituals of carnal Christians. The physical letter of the law may give one a feel good experience of accomplishment, but all the traditions and rituals of men will not profit one spiritually.

There is nothing wrong with participating in altar calls, water baptism, Holy Day observances, lighting candles, icons, clean and unclean foods, prayer cloths, religious pilgrimages, circumcision, burning incense, doing penance, saying confession, being anointed with oil, saying the rosary or foot washing, Sabbath keeping, buying religious trinkets or prayer wheels. What is paramount to understand is all these things are but a shadow of what is to come and which point to something greater.

By coming out of the shadow (*meaning the law*), we will find rest (Luke 1:79). When we stand in the light there can be no shadow. Preferring the shadow of rituals, will forever keep you in darkness from spiritual understanding.

Jesus is the Sabbath. It is in His finished work on the cross we rest. There are no works we can accomplish on our own that will grant salvation. Jesus is the Sabbath; not Saturday, not Sunday, but every day we are to rest in Him.

****

And furthermore, when the concerned saints inquire as to "whom we are accountable" still does not bolster their faulty indoctrinated supposition that the faithful need belong in and to the confines of an organized religion with all their rituals and traditions of men. As Paul explained to those in Corinth in

1 Corinthians 9:19, "I am …..free from all human control…." meaning he was under no man's authority, but was under Christ's headship.

Be like the Apostle Paul.

Who we are accountable to is Jesus Christ and to each other. When the Spirit of God lives within you and His laws are written on your heart, you will be convicted of your sin. "…each of us will give an account of ourselves before God." (Romans 14:12 NIV) The key phrase here is "when the Spirit of God lives within you and His laws are written on your heart". Where is there another who is even conceivably superior to hold one to account than Jesus Christ?

In the natural, who is better to make one accountable than one's own Spirit-filled parents, spouse, significant other or best friend? That someone is one with whom you have a relationship, and who probably knows you better than you know yourself.

Now, if you are a babe in Christ, still drinking the milk of the Word, it's imperative to seek the tutelage of and be accountable to a mature, Spirit-filled Christian. Look for one who has the heart and mind of Christ; not one focused on touting the party line and spreading the infection of religious dogma! Whatever Christians you choose to gather with should, by definition, be mature in Christ knowing by experience that "I am crucified WITH Christ."

This takes time-years, in fact. Men can be so very convincing when teaching their church doctrines. To discern Truth the

Holy Spirit must first open the eyes of your heart. Spending time in prayer and seeking His face will open up a deeper revelation of Him and relationship with Him.

The same advice holds true if your circle of family, friends and acquaintances are not Christian. It is important to associate yourself with like-minded, Spirit-filled Christians. In our own experience we have found it next to impossible to pull up those who are hell-bent on pursuing things of the world to their own detriment, rather than on things of the Holy Spirit.

Of course, we are to be involved with people, our family, our community, government and typical social participation because we are to shine our light in this dark world. To be not of the world requires us to be free of worldly influence. (John 17:15-17) It means that we do not act as the ungodly world acts. We are not slaves to our sinful natures, but act in accordance with righteousness. "Could it be any clearer? Our old way of life was nailed to the cross with Christ, a decisive end to that sin-miserable life—no longer at sin's every beck and call!" (Romans 6:6 The Message)

****

Our Christian brethren reprimanded us with "do not forsake the assembly" from Hebrews 10:25. There is no quibble this Scripture is speaking of believers congregating to worship and study God's Word. This does not necessarily mean congregating in a cinder block building or crystal palace as the only venue available. For example, there are many Scripture verses that speak of house churches where believers of like-minds met to break bread and continue the teaching of Jesus Christ, thereby building His church.

The word "assembling" means more than simply "coming together", "meeting", or "gathering". Just because your little hiney is seated next to someone on a hard folding chair, or a cushy padded seat, or carrying out the traditions and rituals of men in a church building, does not demand what Hebrews 10:25 dictates.

*The word for "assembling" in Greek is "episunagoge". It is made up of the Greek prefix **epi**, meaning super...imposition...that which is above, higher than, highest, upon and the word **sunagogue** meaning assembly or gathering. So, together, **epi** and **sunagogue** mean the above synagogue, the higher meeting, the highest assembly, the higher than all gatherings. (J Preston Eby-"Forsake Not the Assembling" paraphrased) See? No hineys in cushy seats just sitting side by side here.*

By all indications, "episunagoge" is a meeting or gathering or assembling in the Spirit, on a higher plane, in a higher realm, in the apogee of Truth. "...the Holy Spirit, whom the Father will send in My name, He will teach you all things..." (John 14:26 NASB)

Episunagoge is used only one other time in Scripture and that is in II Thessalonians 2:1. This time the meeting in the Spirit is when we are being gathered to Jesus Christ.

Jesus said to the Samaritan woman, "Yet a time is coming and has now come when the true worshipers will worship the Father in Spirit and in truth, for they are the kind of worshipers the Father seeks. God is spirit, and his worshipers must worship in Spirit and in truth." (John 4:23-24 NIV)

If you are comfortably "doing your duty" by attending a brick and mortar church, or singularly following the rituals and traditions of men, or simply looking for a feel good Hallelujah, or swaying and clapping to the music of a good worship band Paul's message to Timothy in 2 Timothy 3:7 ".... always learning but never able to come to a knowledge of the truth" just might be meant for you.

"You're deeply rooted in him. You're well-constructed upon him. You know your way around the faith. Now do what you've been taught. School's out; quit studying the subject and start living it! And let your living spill over into thanksgiving." (Colossians 2:7 The Message)

As has been made plain, "do not forsake the assembly" is a far higher spiritual fellowship than just sitting side by side in church on Sunday.

We have experienced precious few episunagogues. However, when the meat of the word is taught rather, than the milk, when hearts are pure, when hearts are obedient, when repentance is real, and when the anointing falls the Spirit of God communes with His creation.

31

THE CROSS

Where to now Lord? Hmmm, still no reply.

Well, just as the apostle Paul exhorted the Colossians, we were going to go out and do what we'd been taught.

What we'd been taught, by men, was to win souls for Christ.

What we'd been taught, by men, was to have those who would accept Jesus as their Lord and Savior repent of their sins, recite the sinner's prayer and be saved. (You're in!)

What we'd been taught, by men, was all those poor souls who do not accept Jesus Christ as their Lord and Savior, who die in their sins, will burn in a mind-numbing torment, in physical agony beyond comprehension. They will be tortured endlessly in the pit of hell enduring misery and insanity for all eternity (And it's justified because they choose to!).

In Dante Alighieri's graphic depiction of hell, entitled Dante's Inferno, which many believe is literal, illustrates his revelation of the inhuman repercussion of sin. (Inferno is the first part of Alighieri's walk through nine concentric circles of hell in his 14th-century epic poem Divine Comedy. I would characterize Dante as the Stephen King of his day.)

This means many millions of good people, such as grandmothers, grandfathers, mothers, fathers, aunts, uncles, and children of Jews, Muslims, Hindus, Jehovah Witnesses, etc. and, of course, all pagans who do not know Jesus Christ will burn in hell forever and ever.

On our "nickel" budget, the mission of winning souls put before us was a big task to accomplish. How do we realize our part of reaching out to the lost multitudes, dying in their sins? How do we achieve our goal of exposing individuals to the gospel of Jesus Christ effectively and dramatically?

After much contemplative prayer a plan was born.

We would construct a ten foot tall cross with a base to anchor the cross and a platform upon which to stand. The platform allowed us to replicate the crucifixion of Jesus Christ by standing on it and strapping our wrists to the crossbeam. We also included a sign above the cross proclaiming the "King of the Jews". My friend, Joe and others, and I took turns depicting the role of Jesus. A brown wig, a crown of thorns, fake blood to simulate His wounds and a loincloth (sometimes a robe in cold weather) accomplished the makeover.

Flanking the cross, one on each side, was a two and one half foot by five foot banner. One banner read "Repent and be Baptized". The other banner portrayed the iconic Uncle Sam figure pointing his finger at the observer proclaiming "Jesus Wants You".

To complete the tableau, we all alternated the role of a Roman soldier dressed in a knee length tunic, along with a helmet, breastplate, greaves (shin guards), sandals and a sword. My wife and her friend, Ruthann, re-enacted the women at the foot of the cross.

Starting at 6:30 A.M. we took our cross to various highways and byways where there would be an abundance of motor vehicle traffic. We took our "Living Billboard", as it was soon dubbed, to locations visible to the interstate. It may have been a field or a dead end street where we would have access to a field adjacent to the interstate even, ironically, a New York State Fishing Access Park ("....Follow Me, and I will make you fishers of men." (Matthew 4:19 NASB)

Ten thousand cars per hour, according to NYS toll statistics, would witness our re-creation on their way to work and school or travelling through the state. A picture is worth a thousand words.

Prompted by dialog initiated by the "Living Billboard", Jesus would become the topic of conversation at the office, around the water cooler, in the lunchroom, in newspaper coverage, local and national radio coverage, television coverage and across the nation. It appeared we were meeting our goal of reaching the multitudes.

There were those who went out of their way to share with us the profound impact our re-enactment of the crucifixion of

Jesus Christ had upon each one. Being we were located in somewhat hard to find locations off the thruway, it would take some detective work and map searching to find us. But, find us they did! Only God knows how many souls collided with the power of the sacrificial Lamb upon witnessing His "crucifixion"!

One local television reporter enroute to work found her way to us one frosty morning. Laurie shared with us that at the moment she turned her radio dial, (and it just so happened to land on a Christian music station) which she described simply as spiritual music, she came upon the cross. Being brought to tears because she was so moved knowing it was no coincidence, she explained she just had to tell us the impact it had upon her. All the while her cameraman recorded the scene.

While speaking with the reporter, I was still up on the cross when a town police patrol car pulled up next to the news van. The officer hastily exited his vehicle and bustled to the cross. His first concern was for my safety. He received many calls saying a man was being crucified at the Fishing Park (I can't even imagine what was going through his mind when he heard this).He admitted to us that he was scared to death and uncertain as to what he would encounter. Once at the scene, he realized what was actually happening and placing his hand on his heart and mimicking buckling knees, he expressed his complete relief. He, once again, inquired about my well-being. "You're sure you're ok?" he asked. I assured him I was. As he turned to leave, he hesitated, turned back to me and said, "It's a good thing what you're doing. People need this." Then he went on his way.

Another memorable episode occurred on Good Friday, at what is called the Seven Corners. It is one of the busiest intersections in New York State where, as you would guess, seven streets converge. Reconstruction of the area has, since that time, taken place. One street, on both sides of the intersection, has been dead-ended and redirected to better facilitate traffic flow. However, to the locals it is still known as the Seven Corners.

The base of the cross was set up on a triangular patch of grassless ground, muddy from the previous night's rainfall. We placed the cross, quite conspicuously, to be viewed from all directions. Our plan was to be there from 12 PM to 3PM. Pushing the envelope, we had to "hit and run" as we called it. That means we had to set up, then dismantle at a moment's notice if and when the police told us to leave. Although we were doing nothing illegal, a police officer did stop after a number of complaints. He asked what was going on. Ruthann explained this was our ministry's outreach on this Good Friday. Accepting her explanation he held us to our designated timeframe and went on his way.

Shortly thereafter, a woman and her young daughter seemed to appear from nowhere behind us. I say nowhere because there were no pedestrian crossings or sidewalks with which to reach us. With tears in her eyes this mom said she wanted to teach her daughter what Easter Sunday is all about. She explained to her daughter right there that Easter is not about chocolate bunnies and Easter egg hunts. A teaching moment was given by a loving mother as she made clear to her ten year daughter that Easter began with Good Friday, the day

Jesus was crucified for our sins. Easter Sunday is when He rose again she explained.

A tender and encouraging moment was savored by all as Marianne and Ruthann prayed together with mother and daughter.

A short time later, a well-dressed man, in an expensive looking suit and tie pulled over and right up on our little patch of land. Startled by the suddenness of his arrival, we inconspicuously watched as he approached us, looked around, went back to his car and opened the rear passenger door. Reaching inside, he pulled out two sheets of paper. Walking in the drying mud in his highly polished wingtips, he placed the papers on the ground, dropped to his knees before the cross and began to pray.

What a blessing to witness such unadulterated love for our Savior, Jesus Christ. This man cared nothing for his expensive suit and shoes or who was watching as he compassionately knelt before the cross and had his moment with God. When he finished his time at the cross, he thanked us for being there and told us this is what he needed today....to be reminded of the reality of the sacrifice Jesus made. He shared he was going about his day when he spotted us as he sat at the red light. A feeling of guilt came upon him as Good Friday was the furthest thing from his mind. Sorrow and repentance came into his heart and he knew he had to pull over.

A young couple pulled into the parking area of Spagnoli Park (now Fisherman's Park), where we were stationed one morning. The young man departed his vehicle and made his way over to us. He said, "I just had to come over and tell you this story." He told us that he and his wife were travelling down the thruway discussing their dire situation. He just lost his job and they were expecting their first baby. They wondered if things could get any worse. "Lord, help us", he implored. "Give us a sign that everything will be ok for us." Within moments they came upon the cross. The young man shared their shocked reaction. Speechlessly staring at each other, for there were no words to describe what just happened, they both began to cry. They were so moved that God would answer them because neither one had ever experienced anything like it.

Although taking the cross alongside the interstate was our normal go to location, we would occasion to take the cross along an alternate, albeit still busy, route into the city. The plan was, once again, to catch the morning commute.

At 7 A.M., we positioned ourselves at the foot of the Skyway. Traffic became heavy as the work hour approached. With one eye on traffic, we observed motorists whipping their heads around to take in the spectacle of the man on the cross. Increasingly more and more morning commuters picked up their cell phones while gawking. Rush hour began to slow...way...down.

Congestion on the Skyway was not an unusual occurrence as all traffic ends at the downtown city streets, approximately one mile from our position. However, traffic came to a virtual halt. We had us a full-fledged gridlock. Later we would be enlightened that not only was there a gridlock, but it extended south for four miles.

The next thing we heard was sirens. Yep....sirens...as in police. Dumbfounded, we witnessed not one squad car or two squad cars or three or four or five, but six, yes six squad cars with all sirens blaring a cacophonous sound.

My first thoughts were, "What the heck is going on? Are those sirens meant for us? Is there an accident? I hope we didn't cause an accident! Please Lord, tell me we didn't cause an accident."

The good news is no, we did not cause an accident. The bad news is the cops and all their earsplitting sirens were there for us. Oh my...Six squad cars....Really? Certainly we were breaking no law.

Unable to reach us from the blocked Skyway, the police officers and their squad cars made their way to us via a secondary road. I remained up on the cross as I warily eyed the two police officers approach across a small strip of grass.

"Hey", the grizzled older cop hollered. "You gotta get down! C'mon, you gotta get down NOW! We've had a few hundred calls about a man being crucified on a cross." With a beet red face he continued, "You scared the hell out of us! Besides, you're holding up all this damn traffic. C'mon, get down....get outta here!"

Meanwhile, the captain and the three accompanying police officers who remained by their patrol cars, nervously guffawed once they realized our "Living Billboard" was only a re-enactment and not the real thing!

Immediately, Joe and I complied with the officer's demand. I quickly made my way down from the cross, as Joe began packing our gear into the van. Lastly, as we loaded the cross into our vehicle I noticed the Channel 7 news reporter, whose van skidded to a stop right on the heels of the six squad cars, begin his report for the evening news.

No interviews were asked for or given that day. However, the news coverage, which we were not seeking, was all positive. The Lord did, indeed, use the news media to promote the gospel. Each news reporter shared the Good News with an unbiased affirmative delivery, again reaching the multitudes we would not otherwise have access to.

 Most of our exploits with the cross were uneventful; some caused us a little fear and concern, but the last experience I'm about to share with you was a day to remember.

Here's one that shivered me timbers. It was just Marianne and I taking the cross out one beautiful sunny summer morning. We decided to take the cross to Route 5, which is a Lake Erie shoreline route into the city with lots of traffic.

Driving to the site, Marianne spied a skunk drunkenly meandering among the debris filled field. She said, "I have a bad feeling about this. We could be in for some trouble today." Skunks are nocturnal creatures, so to see one staggering in broad daylight was not a good sign. Heedless of the warning we prayed a hedge of protection around us, as was our norm, and continued on.

The place we settled upon to set up the cross was in the projects, with plenty of visibility to Route 5. This was an area, in predominantly Catholic Lackawanna, called "across the bridge or back the bridge." This side of the bridge is multi-culturally populated. Here I attended school and my grandparents, then my parents, owned and operated a "mom and pop", grocery store. I spent most of my childhood "across the bridge", and I was very familiar and comfortable with the area.

The first hour of the morning was uneventful. All was calm; all was bright-until it wasn't.

Out of the blue, a small mob of Baptist women descended upon us. As they approached the field where we were situated, they were picking up bricks and stones along the way. Marianne stood her ground on her side of the ditch as the Baptist women shouted at her. "Our Jesus ain't on the cross," they said. "Go back to your side of the bridge," they taunted. With this epithet they believed we were Catholic.

 Patiently and valiantly, my wife attempted to explain our position. "We know Jesus is not on the cross. We're showing the sacrifice of Jesus on the cross to those who don't know what He did for them." They were having none of it! And they were nasty! One woman threatened to climb up the cross and stab me with a broken bottle, not to mention the plans they had for the bricks and rocks. Marianne confided later that she was sure there was gonna be a crucifixion that morning....mine!

Finally, one of the women shouted, "I'm gonna call my pastor. Whaddaya gonna do about dat?"

"Oh thank you Lord, please do," my wife replied.

The next thing we see is three pick-up trucks skidding to a stop alongside the road throwing up throat clogging clouds of dust and gravel. "Oh Lord," my wife thought. "We're all gonna die. They've called in their re-enforcements."

Being some distance from the commotion I was still able to hear the louder of the threats being hurled. Immediately, I began to descend from the cross. I had no ladder and struggled to extricate myself from the wrist straps. At long last I was able to make my way over to my wife, as she stood alone facing the six women and three men.

Of the three men who showed up only one man came forward. He was a deacon, whom we shall call Henry, from a local Zion church. He asked what was going on here as he took in the scene. The women began clamoring in unison, reiterating the same mantra with which they assailed my wife. "It ain't right what they're doing," said one. "Jesus ain't on the cross," said another. "Why don't they go back to their own side of the bridge," shouted one more.

The deacon allowed these irate women to carry on hurling accusations and shouting unintelligible insults. Shrieking at the deacon, they continued to point and threaten us with the rocks and bricks still in their hands for what seemed an eternity. They appeared to be in the grip of a demonic influence. Deacon Henry said not a word. This was not a good sign.

When my wife was certain Deacon Henry was going to take their side and this might turn bloody, something remarkable occurred. As Deacon Henry calmly and deliberately lifted up his hands in a "be quiet" gesture, the women miraculously became silent immediately.

"Do you see what you're doing?" he asked them in a soft baritone voice. They did not respond. He waited. "Can you hear yourselves?" Again, there was no response from the gathering. "What they're doing here is a wonderful thing," he said. "But, do you know what you're doing?" he asked again. No answer. After a time, waiting for them to respond, he admonished, "You are no better than those who hurled insults and rocks and crucified Jesus."

With that we witnessed an incredible transformation of the "mob". The women promptly dropped their rocks and bricks and began to weep. It was remarkable. There was immediate humility and repentance. Not a one of them challenged or debated or argued with the deacon. It was so sudden. We were flummoxed by the scene playing out before us, having just been verbally threatened with bodily harm for the last half hour.

As each side made their way toward each other across the ditch, the glory of God enveloped the area. Our just moments before former enemies apologized emotionally, asking forgiveness, hugging us and calling us brother and sister. An initial atmosphere of anger and hostility morphed into one of love and repentance in the space of a few minutes. Only the Lord could orchestrate such an abrupt turnaround.

We forgave them as they were truly contrite as evidenced by their heartfelt demonstrative display. What started out as a possible situational crisis was instead used by an unassuming deacon to reveal the heart and mind of Christ to those harboring animosity and prejudice. It was quite a poignant and humbling undertaking.

Our adventures on the cross spanned the gamut. From the tattooed tough guy in his jacked up '72 Chevy brought to tears when he came upon the cross to prayer to a prophetic word for a police officer touched by the hand of God, and everything in between. We were insulted, called every name in the book, screamed at to leave, threatened with arrest, and threatened with bodily harm; but most of all we were blessed as the Gospel of Jesus Christ went forth.

32

YOU'RE IN!

In the beginning of a previous chapter we shared the teaching we received and experienced, on how to be saved. Simply put, one recites a twelve second (give or take) prayer something like this...."Dear Lord Jesus, I confess I'm a sinner. I repent of my sins. I believe Jesus died on the cross and shed His blood for me. Come into my heart and save me. I pray in Jesus' name. Amen." "That's it. You're in! Welcome to the family! Remember this date. This is the day you were saved!" they exuberantly proclaim. "Your life will never be the same! You will be blessed from here on out!" the mantra continues.

That's it? That's all there is? Recite a canned prayer and you're in, you're blessed forever? Heck yeah....I'm in...whoohoo!

Since those days, many years ago, we dug into the niggling concerns we had regarding the process of being saved practiced by so much of Christianity. Something wasn't quite right, something wasn't computing. Many great evangelists, whose crusades have reached millions of lost souls, implement the sinner's prayer methodology. No doubt the Gospel of Jesus Christ is being preached at the rallies and revivals and those whose ears are open will hear it. But, is anyone actually "saved" at revivals or rallies? Converted? Some, maybe, but saved? Only God is omniscient. Only God is the Judge of who is or isn't "saved" being it is He Who calls us to Him.

"And we know that God causes everything to work together for the good of those who love God and are called according to his purpose for them. For God knew his people in advance and he chose them to become like his Son, so that his Son would be the firstborn among many brothers and sisters. And having chosen them, he called them to come to him. And having called them, he gave them right standing with himself. And having given them right standing, he gave them his glory." (Romans 8:28-30 NLT)

During our adventures out on the cross, not one person recited the sinner's prayer; nor did we hand out tracts with the sinner's prayer printed on the back. The Lord never put that condition on our heart. We encouraged, we edified, and we comforted each person according to their need and request as directed by the Holy Spirit. No methodology was followed. Honestly giving an answer to anyone who asked us about Jesus was all that was needed.

Getting "saved" is not as simple as regurgitating someone else's words. It is the most arduous task to be undertaken. Jesus says, "But the one who endures to the end will be saved." (Matthew 24:13 NLT) So, this Scripture alone makes it plain that getting saved is not until the end for the one who endures.

There are a myriad of Bible Scripture verses disclosing how to be "saved". Call upon the name of the Lord (Acts 2:21), believe on the Lord Jesus Christ (Acts 16:31), be baptized (Mark 16:16), enter in at the door of Christ (John 10:9), by grace and through faith (Ephesians 2:8), believing the foolishness of preaching (1 Corinthians 1:21), come to the knowledge of the truth (1 Timothy 2:4), be reconciled to God through Christ (2Corinthians 5:19), confess with your mouth and believe in your heart that God raised Him from the dead (Romans 10:9). And these Scriptures are just for starters.

Whew, I thought. That's alotta stuff to do to be "saved". Be that as it may, we are told that our saving is not by works so no man can boast, but by grace through faith. "Lord, help my understanding."

Not immediately, but soon thereafter, a Holy Ghost light bulb illuminated the Truth. I asked myself what is the common denominator of all the above verses? Do you know the answer? Tick tock, tick tock.... Take a wild guess..... It is so simple......it was staring me right in the face. Do you give up? Ok. Ok....

Jesus Christ is the common denominator! Each and every Scripture pertains to Jesus Christ! If you have Jesus Christ, you have done all of those Scriptures because we are complete in Him (Colossians 2:10)! The Father has One message and that One is Jesus Christ!

Contrariwise, if you don't have Jesus Christ, I'm sorry to say, you are not complete. First we are called, "For many are called" (Matthew 22:14), and from the called, "few are chosen." (Matthew 22:14)

I believe it was Charles Spurgeon, (a popular English Baptist preacher, author, pastor and evangelist), who once remarked something on the order of "it's not hard to believe that **few** are saved; rather, that **any** are saved."

You know, in my younger days I used to think, "But I'm a good person. I'm probably not going to hell; purgatory, maybe, but not hell. I go to church, I don't swear or do drugs and I take care of my family. But the Spirit is contrary to what the flesh desires, if one is walking by the Spirit.

"You, my brothers and sisters, were called to be free. But do not use your freedom to indulge the flesh; rather, serve one another humbly in love. For the entire law is fulfilled in keeping this one command: "Love your neighbor as yourself." If you bite and devour each other, watch out or you will be destroyed by each other.

"So I say, walk by the Spirit, and you will not gratify the desires of the flesh. For the flesh desires what is contrary to the Spirit and the Spirit what is contrary to the flesh. They are in conflict with each other, so that you are not to do whatever you want. But if you are led by the Spirit, you are not under the law.

"The acts of the flesh are obvious: **sexual immorality, impurity and debauchery** (promiscuity, prostitution, incest, *crazy partying and wild nights, sexual innuendo, pre-marital sex, vulgarity and lust [Jesus says, "But I tell you that anyone who looks at a woman lustfully has already committed adultery with her in his heart" Matthew 5:28 NIV],);* **idolatry** *(Anything put above God including graven images. A graven image may be made of wood, stone or metal representing an animal or statue of a person that is prayed to or worshipped. In addition, praying to Mary, St Joseph, Padre Pio, St Anthony, St Peter, St Patrick, or in our area Father Baker or any of the other saints is idolatry because praying to anyone other than to Jesus Christ* ("For there is one God and one mediator between God and mankind, the man Christ Jesus" 1 Timothy 2:5 NIV), *is invoking the dead, [yes the saints are all dead, in the grave, only Jesus is immortal [1 Timothy 6:16], and putting them before Him. Idolatry encompasses idols of the heart, as well. Love of money or possessions, pride, religion or love of self are just a few idols of the heart)* and **witchcraft** *(Invoking the spirit of a dead saint or any deceased person to petition a favor. Televangelists employ a different type of witchcraft by asking the gullible to "sow a seed" of money to God, via their ministry, so that the giver may be blessed ten-fold by God. Many of the people being taken advantage of by this type of witchcraft are destitute or in debt because of illness or living paycheck to paycheck or seniors on social security believing the lie they are giving to God. Newsflash...God doesn't need their money! The only ones being blessed by the sowers of seed are the "spiritual leaders" themselves by means of jets, mansions, vacation homes, jewelry, fancy clothes and extravagant living. That's not to say one should not support their local church. Of course, it's important that one does and your money is much better spent. They have bills to pay such as heating, electrical, maintenance, salaries,* *and the like. We're talking about using witchcraft for gain here);* **hatred** *(Intense dislike or ill will. Jesus says we are to love our enemies and do good to them, lend and expect nothing back Luke 6:35 Good News Bible),* **discord** *(antagonism and opposition; Sowing discord among the brethren is an abomination to God [Proverbs 6:19]) and,* **jealousy** *(guarding or keeping what one has for fear it will be taken by someone else),* **fits of rage** *(uncontrollable anger),* **selfish ambition** *(winning at all cost, putting oneself above others),* **dissensions** *(bickering, conflict of opinion),* **factions** *(heresies) and* **envy** *(wanting what someone else has);* **drunkenness** *(intoxication- anytime, even if only on weekends),* **orgies** *(debauchery), and the like. I warn you, as I did before, that those who live like this will not inherit the kingdom of God (Galatians 5:13-21 NIV italics mine).*

And lest we forget, all liars will not inherit the kingdom of God (Revelation 21:8 paraphrased). Have you ever told a white-lie in order to not hurt someone's feelings? Were you ever evasive or have you ever told a tall tale or exaggerated? Have you ever told the cashier at a grocery store that you had a dozen donuts, when you really had fifteen donuts? Have you ever claimed you were sixty five years old, when you are actually sixty years old in order to enjoy a "senior" price? Have you ever said your child was younger than he or she actually is in order to pay a lower amusement park ticket price? I submit we have all been guilty of at least one, in some form or other, at one point in our life. We repent and repent and repent in the flesh....or not. "The human heart is the most deceitful of all things, and desperately wicked. Who really knows how bad it is?" Jeremiah 17:9 NAS)

Is there one among us who can claim to escape any of the above sins? Even after following any number of programs whose destination promises holiness, righteousness or a more perfect spiritual life, we all still fall short of His glory. "When we display our righteous deeds, they are nothing but filthy rags" (Isaiah 64:6 NAS) and "For the wages of sin is death…" (Romans 6:23)

If one is human, which I count myself among, we are going to sin; some more often than others, some to a lesser or greater degree. If God says our hearts are deceitful and desperately wicked, if our righteousness is as filthy rags, if the wages of sin is death, why does Peter, quoting Joel, say, in Acts 2:21 "Whosoever shall call upon the name of the Lord shall be saved." It certainly is a true Scriptural declaration and clearly says that's all we need do. Even with my newly acquired understanding of Jesus Christ as the One, which encompasses all of the Scriptures pertaining to being saved, what does Acts 2:21 mean exactly, being there is a whole litany of things to do in order to be saved?

The answer is revealed by the Lord in Luke 6:46, "Why do you call me Lord, Lord, and do not the things I say!" Wow! What a stinging rebuke! It was like the sharp crack of a whip jolting me from my tickled ear stupor! Our hearts must be spiritually circumcised. No reciting of a prayer or performing rituals or following a prescribed methodology will accomplish what only the Holy Spirit baptism of fire will. The flesh is constantly warring with the Spirit. Having the whole counsel of God is paramount for the working out of our salvation with fear (*reverence*) and trembling (*awe*).

We are baptized with Holy Spirit and with fire. John the Baptist said, "For I, indeed, am baptizing you in water for repentance, yet He Who is coming after me is stronger than I, Whose sandals I am not competent to bear. He will be baptizing you in Holy Spirit and fire..." (Matthew 3:11 Concordant Literal) Our God is a consuming Fire. (Hebrews 12:29 NIV) He will purge. He will purify. And He will perfect each one He has chosen. It is a process.

During this process, one will produce fruit; that is to say the fruit of the Holy Spirit. "But the fruit of the Spirit is love, joy, peace, forbearance, kindness, goodness, faithfulness, gentleness and self-control. Against such things there is no law. Those who belong to Christ Jesus have crucified the flesh with its passions and desires. Since we live by the Spirit, let us keep in step with the Spirit. Let us not become conceited, provoking and envying each other." (Galatians 5:22-26 NIV)

On numerous occasions, different forms of the following question have been patronizingly posed during the course of our ministry. "How many people have you saved?" Hmmm...good question, I thought. Well, aside from the fact even Jesus did not save or convert one person during His ministry, the answer would be none. It was not until Pentecost when His disciples were filled with the Holy Spirit and converted. (Not to mention we, of ourselves, save no one.) Gazing at the questioner with a posture of askance we would often wonder if our brothers and sisters in Christ really do not understand that......

It is all of God and none of us. He calls us. (1Corinthians 1:26-27) He draws (Greek word *"helko"*, Strong's #1670, means *to drag*) us to Him. (John 6:44) And it is Jesus Christ Who chooses us from among those the Father has drawn (*dragged*). "In His time, all men will be drawn (*dragged*) to Jesus." (John 12:32) "And every knee will bow and every tongue will confess that Jesus Christ is Lord" (Philippians 2:10-11) "...but only by the Holy Spirit." (1 Corinthians 12:3)

Once upon a time, we were taught it was our duty to "save" people, to "lead" as many as we could to Christ. Doing so would put another notch on our Christian belt, bolstering our position within the church. But that's not the Truth of it. Again, not once, in our ministry, did we have anyone recite the "sinner's prayer" or "lead" anyone to Christ. Why? It is not our job. It is the job of the Holy Spirit. What we did do, however, is proclaim the Good News.

33

FELLOWSHIP OF THE CROSS

Our fledgling ministry began in late summer of 2001 on the Lackawanna side of a local park. As we had just recently picked up instruments, namely the keyboard for my wife and I a guitar, our time spent there was one of making a joyful noise. We were no musicians by any stretch of the imagination. We were blessed by the many people who stopped by to offer a word of encouragement and prayer, as we prophetically ministered to those who were so inclined. Oh, we had some heckling, as well, but that was to be expected. Nevertheless, for us it was an outward expression of our love, joy and heartfelt gratefulness for the sacrifice of our Lord Jesus Christ, for our life, for our breath, for our very being and for our thankfulness for dragging us to Him.

In the fall of 2001, with the cold Buffalo winter approaching, we had some decisions to make. One evening after our four mile "stay trim" walk, we bought ice cream cones and sat on the steps approaching the entrance to St. Martin's church "kicking the can" and lamenting our position. Just like teenagers, even though we were over fifty years of age, grousing about wanting their own apartment, we complained to our Father that we wanted our own place for ministry and worship. What are we gonna do now? We can't continue in the park, it's too cold, but we could afford it because it was free! Our one bedroom apartment was too small, we couldn't go there. For a while we met at another couple's home however, we had different visions for ministry. We even considered renting a small, old, vacant clapboard church building, which dated back to the early twentieth century. Located on the property of a Lutheran congregation, it was conveniently located in our hometown of West Seneca. However, being the roof on the old church leaked, the pastor offered as an option, to rent a classroom to us for our evening meetings in the school situated on the grounds.

Joe, Ruthann, Marianne and I had recently ministered to a couple at their home in North Buffalo who we learned were members of the Lutheran congregation. It was through the North Buffalo couple, who shared our prophetic ministry time with their church, where we learned the Lutheran church was quite excited to accommodate us. What to do, what to do?

In the interim the Lord put a vacant space in our path that also met our financial resources. So, we had three spaces to choose from. Being the repair on the roof of the old church would take too long and the classroom setup would involve the mantling and dismantling of our equipment three nights a week, the Lackawanna space proved to be our only option. So, Lackawanna it was.

Our new indoor ministry, as was our park ministry, rested in the shadows of Our Lady of Victory Basilica. Why, oh why Lord, would you send us here? Why was this location our only option? Even with our child-like faith and exuberance, we were no match for the religious principality cloaking the city of Lackawanna. Be that as it may, we were not deterred.

We opened our doors to all denominations and non-denominations. Worship time, teaching and prophetic words, plays and skits, involving kids, made it a memorable season.

Our ministry kids gave prophetic insight to those being ministered to via their individual distinctive drawings. After the ministry team laid hands on the young ones, they were sequestered in another room while the "adults" prophetically ministered to individuals in the main room. As they were called back into the main room our amazing prophetic youngsters presented their artwork which spoke right into the matter of the heart of the person receiving ministry. Our God is awesome!

Having no desire to emulate a traditional church Sunday service, we gathered together on Friday nights. Illuminating the room, torches complete with "fire" adorned the Fellowship walls. Separating the conga drum from the guitar and keyboard was a large patio-sized fire bowl complete with "fire", which also provided a modicum of light. Yes, indeedy, we were way outside the box! Hallelujah!

The bowl held the incense which is representative of the prayers of the saints. The "fire" in both torches and bowl symbolized God's divine presence ("There the angel of the

LORD appeared to him in flames of fire from within a bush. Moses saw that though the bush was on fire it did not burn up" Exodus 3:2 NIV). The fire is the presence of God which brings the anointing. In addition, "Our God is a consuming fire" (Hebrews 11:29), burning up the idols of our hearts.

 Our ministry was housed on the first floor of a multi-purpose building facing a parking lot and Our Lady of Victory Basilica across the street. The parking lot side also included a side entrance to a restaurant, a vacant space, a bank and an optometrist. The perpendicular street side of the building was made up of a Chinese take-out, a nail shop and the restaurant's front entrance. Completing the menagerie was a boxing gym in the basement and studio apartments covering the three floors above.

Many of the restaurant patrons, coming and going on our side of the building entrance, who would covertly peek into our modest twelve hundred square foot glass double door space, believed us to be some sort of satanic cult, judging by the overheard comments. Suffice it to say, they did not understand the significance of the torches, bowl and fire.

Just remember Satan cannot create anything. He is a counterfeiter and a usurper and a destroyer. Satan stole the symbolism of fire for his glory. We took it back!

One particular warm summer Friday night meeting we had our doors thrown wide open, not only for better air circulation, but to create more of an inviting atmosphere to those who may have been too timid to open the doors and join us.

Many passed our Fellowship doors looking forward to a Buffalo favorite Friday night fish-fry at the restaurant just down the hall. An adorable blue-eyed blonde little boy of about eight years old stood gazing into the room as our worship team ministered, and our kids danced with flags and praise and worship tabrets*. He shyly accepted a tambourine offered to him and eagerly joined in with the other kids. That is until his grandmother appeared at the doorway. Taking in the torches and bowl with faux flames, she yanked her grandson off his feet as he passed by. With an angry thrusting motion she tossed the tambourine in the general direction of Ruthann, who attempted to engage the woman. Grandma then lit outta there like her hair was on fire, with her sobbing grandson in tow, muttering to herself all the while. I guess they don't praise and worship quite this same way in her church!

*A modern praise and worship tabret is unlike a tambourine in that it has no metal disks to jingle. Simply put it is two circular hoops, one fitting inside the other, rather akin to an embroidery hoop, with fabric stretched across and covering three quarters of the diameter, leaving a hand held opening. A symbolic form of an Old Testament tabret used as an expression of worship, spiritual warfare and battle, the modern tabrets are then embellished with streamers, tassels, braiding, and the like.

The tabret was commonly used by women during worship, dance and celebrations as described in 1 Samuel 18:6-"And it comes to pass, in their coming in, in David's returning from smiting the Philistine, that the women come out from all the cities of Israel to sing--also the dancers--to meet Saul the king, with **tabrets** (emphasis mine), with joy, and with three-stringed instruments;" (Concordant Literal)

Today, we wave the modern figurative version of the tabret before the Lord in worship and praise to His name.

Jeremiah 31:4-"Again will I build thee, and thou shalt be built, O virgin of Israel: again shalt thou be adorned with thy **tabrets** (emphasis mine), and shalt go forth in the dances of them that make merry" (American Standard Version).

Jeremiah reminds us that Israel will be rebuilt and the tabret, the ancient instrument of praise and worship, will be restored.

****

Returning from The Heart of David Worship and Warfare Conference at MorningStar, we continued our joyful noise in the Davidic tradition of worship, warfare, songs of deliverance and intercession with a prophetic proclamation. King David appointed thousands of singers and musicians who ministered day and night to the Lord. For 33 years, 24 hours a day, 7 days a week, 365 days a year they ministered. Not only did the singers and musicians minister to the Lord, enemies and demonic intrusions from idolatrous tribes were held at bay.

That's not to say we employed thousands of singers and musicians nor was it our aim to entertain. We longed to be in the Lord's presence, continually, and to usher in His presence to be among us, just as David did. We were not interested in being just spectators. And to that end we involved any who had a joyful noise, a prophetic song or word within their heart to express it without repercussion. Taking popular songs, the worldly lyrics were changed to ones of praise! It was a totally freeing, uplifting and joyful encounter with the Lord as He manifested Himself among us.

Music was a large part of our Fellowship. Worship time was accompanied by the traditional guitar and keyboard, but also included a conga drum and an ashiko. The kids participated with their favorite potato shaped shaker, a little triangle, a rain stick and a tambourine, among other instruments. In addition, every now and again real musicians would join us.

Our choice of worship music included very few hymns, which was frowned upon by some. And the fact that we included drums was even more frowned upon. A Baptist pastor friend of ours was a naysayer of the "rock and roll" beat. Apparently, the term "rock and roll" originated in the ghettos as a slang term for promiscuity; as in jumping in the backseat of a car to "rock and roll". You get the idea. Anyway, that is the argument against a "rock and roll" beat.

Others have said that the "off beats" can cause the heart to go out of rhythm and goes against the natural cadence of a one and three beat. Some "studies" claim plants and milk cows do not prosper with a certain type of beat. Devil worship and even murder are fueled by drum music, some say.

Are these studies valid? Maybe, maybe not. It's still being debated. Lyrics, screaming and incoherent voices can very well inspire those so inclined to commit all types of atrocities that, perhaps, are already in their heart; but music or instruments in and of themselves? I'm not convinced. I find no Scriptural basis to support the claim.

Psalm 150 lists all major instrument groups, even percussion instruments, which include drums.
"Praise the LORD!
Praise God in his Temple!
Praise his strength in heaven!
Praise him for the mighty things he has done.
Praise his supreme greatness.
Praise him with trumpets.
Praise him with harps and lyres.
Praise him with drums (*some translations have timbrel*-italics mine*) and dancing.
Praise him with harps and flutes.
Praise him with cymbals.
Praise him with loud cymbals.
Praise the LORD, all living creatures!
Praise the LORD!"

 A *timbrel resembling a modern tambourine, when covered with a skin, is a small drum. So, I would say if it was good enough for King David (a man after God's own heart 1 Samuel 13:14 and Acts 13:22), it is good enough for me.

What I do know is this. God created everything in the heavenly realm and on earth (Colossians 1:16). God is also the Creator of good and evil (Isaiah 45:7). Satan can create nothing and certainly is not God's equal! He is the god of this world (2 Corinthians 4:4). Satan is a deceiver (Revelation 12:9). Satan is a counterfeiter.

What I do know is God's music is perverted only when the wickedness of men give their hearts over to Satan. "The one who does what is sinful is of the devil, because the devil has been sinning from the beginning. The reason the Son of God appeared was to destroy the devil's work." (1 John 3:8 NIV)

Not all Baptists have an aversion to drums or certain beats we were to learn. When Ruthann, a member of our ministry team, suggested ministering with our music at her sister's Baptist church, we were not at all certain how we would be received; if, indeed, we were even invited.

Ultimately, permission was granted by the church's pastor. Ruthann's brother-in-law, who was the worship leader there, gave us a reserved "if I have to" thumbs up.

The appointed Sunday arrived and with excited anticipation we set up our instruments and mics on the raised platform. With God's anointing and a strong gifting of ministering through song, Ruthann captivated the hearts of all in the congregation with her solo of "Oh, Lord You're Beautiful" by Keith Green.

As our aim was to minister to the Lord in the midst of His people, we were off to a positive start. Neither the pastor nor his worship leader asked us to leave. However, with the next song we chose the outcome was not as certain. It is entitled "Our God Is Holy" by Don Potter. The flavor of "Our God Is Holy" is warfare, rather than prayerful exultation, as is "Oh Lord You're Beautiful".

After speaking an appropriate Scripture for the time, I grabbed my guitar and with Joe on the conga drum, and Marianne on the keyboard, I launched into "Our God Is Holy". This was a time of unease in the US as September 11, 2001, was just some several months prior. People were fearful and anxious.

With my focus solely on the Lord, the congregation fell away, the rest of the team fell away and all thoughts about being accepted by the Baptist pastor and worship leader fell away. I felt the anointing of God so strong upon me and understood the message He wanted me to bring forth. "Our God is Holy", as a warfare song, declared to all in attendance and to the demons of fear and anxiety, that our God is in charge and our God is a Holy, Mighty, Righteous Judge!

Our daughter, Jennifer, and granddaughter, Callie, were in attendance. Jenn later shared, to her amazement, those in attendance began to stand up, clap or raise their hands in praise, swaying in time to the music and calling out to Jesus. This was not a usual occurrence in this Baptist place of worship. God was most assuredly in the house!

Just as in 2 Chronicles 5:11-14, "The priests then withdrew from the Holy Place. All the priests who were there had consecrated themselves, regardless of the divisions. All the Levites who were musicians-Asaph, Heman, Jeduthun and their sons and relatives-stood on the east side of the altar, dressed in fine linen playing cymbals, harps and lyres, accompanied by 120 priests sounding trumpets. The singers and trumpeters joined in unison, as with one voice, to give praise and thanks to the Lord. Accompanied by trumpets, cymbals and other instruments, they raised their voices in praise to the Lord and sang: 'He is good; his love endures forever'."

"**THEN** (emphasis mine) the temple of the Lord was filled with a cloud and the priests could not perform their service because of the cloud, for the glory of the Lord filled the temple of God."

So, you see it wasn't until **ALL** were in unity, with divisions aside, that the Lord filled the temple.

If we go out to meet God clothed in white (purity), washed in the blood of the Lamb; if we go out, all making the same sound, regardless of our divisions; if we go out to glorify God, God will honor all the noise!

It's not emotionalism or just plain excitement, although it is emotional and exciting to be in the presence of the Lord. God comes down to acknowledge the praise. The power of God came down. The temple was filled with the power and glory of the Lord. Our body is that temple ("Don't you know that you yourselves are God's temple and that God's Spirit dwells in your midst?" 1 Corinthians 3:16 NIV) God wants to fill us with His glory!

This is exactly what happened at the Baptist church. No one criticizing, no one finding fault, no one concerned about a one three beat or a "rock and roll" beat or the fact we were not Baptists. All came together with the praises of the Lord on their lips and in their hearts.

When the glory of God fills the temple, it is impossible to remain nonchalant. Some of us have a tendency to act as though we are charter members of the "deeper life club". We take on an attitude of boredom believing this makes us appear "spiritual" or "godly". That's simply not true! When we enter into the presence of the Most High God, the Creator of the Universe and the Creator of everything in it, Jehovah, Elohim, Yahweh, Yashua Hamasiach, I guarantee you will not remain nonchalant!

Falling down as though dead is how the Apostle John reacted when he saw the Lord. (Revelation 1:17). He certainly was not nonchalant. There was a response. There is no other most excellent place to be than in the presence of the Lord!

At the conclusion of our worship time, the pastor took to the podium. Without preamble and to our wonderment, this modest and unassuming Baptist pastor repented before God and his congregation and us for his squelching of the Holy Spirit for years. With great humility he asked God first, then his congregation and us for forgiveness because of his disobedience.

Unprepared, dumbstruck and diminished witnessing this man's humble confession, I praised the Lord for this pastor's courage and obedience and contrite heart.

It's interesting to note, this is the first and only time we were called to minister, in this fashion, at another congregation. Why? Honestly, I don't know; our own fleshly lack of confidence and insecurities, perhaps. Right, wrong or indifferent, we never were ones to schmooze, network or promote ourselves even in our business. We did advertise in the major and minor publications, but did not participate in networking events. We always trusted in God to provide for us and He did. It was only through Ruthann, our ministry partner, as the reason we found ourselves at the Baptist church. It was all God.

So, you see one does not have to be a great or well-known musician, or a worship leader from a large congregation, or a musical prodigy for God to use you. With God's anointing, one becomes a musical virtuoso!

There are performers and there are worshipers. When one separates the two, there are few who care only to please God, rather than men. These are the worshipers. Performers focus on pleasing men. God will use whomever whenever He chooses... at any given time, anywhere, and anyplace....for His purposes!

Now, keep this in mind. There is no doubt that praising God through song and knowing His presence is awesome. However, true worship is far greater. True worship is living a Godly life. That is to say, doing what's right in the eyes of God every day. One can sing and praise on Sunday (or Saturday or whatever day you celebrate the Sabbath) 'til the cows come home, but if we hang out with Satan and his minions the rest of the week, it all comes to naught. Whether it's "just" cursing or carousing or any other behavior unpleasing to God, the praises from our mouth mean nothing. James 3:9-10 admonishes, "With the tongue we praise our Lord and Father, and with it we curse human beings, who have been (*correct translation- "are being"-italics mine*) made in God's likeness. Out of the same mouth come praise and cursing. My brothers and sisters, this should not be." (NIV)

True worship is obedience to the Lord. And with obedience, the Lord will inhabit our praise. We praise Him by lifting our hands, our voices, our shouts and our joy for all He is and does and is so far above anything we can conceive!

34

MARCHING TO A DIFFERENT BEAT

In the early 2000's, we joined the MorningStar Fellowship of Ministries, with the goal of fellowship, and the hope of ordination. During our time spent at the retreats, we met many, many wonderful godly people. Worship leaders, teachers and artists, pastors of churches, other ministries and outreaches and all walks of life coming together all with a hunger for God, with one accord, and with the mind of Christ. It felt like home. This was a respite, a time to reboot and energize before returning to the trenches.

At one meeting, admonishing all not to preach, Rick opened up the mic to anyone who had a prophetic word from the Lord. One by one whosoever was inclined came forward. About six people, one after another, gave words of trench warfare and Special Forces, each one building upon the previous shared word.

However, the word the Lord had lay on my heart the night before, had nothing to do with trench warfare or Special

Forces. Oh great, I thought. I questioned as to whether I was really hearing from the Lord. But He would not allow me off the hook. The opportunity presented itself. The moment was now!

Being I had never spoken before this group or any other group of this caliber for that matter, the "you're less than" demons were out in full force reminding me of my inferiority and inadequacy.

Now I had the chutzpah to get up there and give a prophetic word totally contrary to what everyone else was saying? What was I thinking? Well, I reasoned, it's just a word of short duration. I can do that much....right? Notwithstanding, I knew I had to be obedient to what the Lord had put on my heart.

As I stood to make my way to the microphone, was it just me or had the room become deathly still? (My wife later assured me that yes, the room had become deathly still.) I felt all eyes upon me as the Lord directed my steps, one foot in front of the other. The podium seemed farther and farther away.

Adding to my discomfiture, those at the main table craned their necks and turned around in their seats to see who or what was going on. It was just little old me, out of my comfort zone, walking the longest walk of my life to speak a prophetic word for the times in the company of all these mighty prophetic voices.

Reaching my destination, I drank in the sea of faces belonging to my brothers and sisters in Christ. My wife was silently weeping. As she would later tearfully share, the Spirit of the

Lord filled that place from the time I left the table. My going forward came as a complete surprise to her. She was not aware I was about to give a prophetic word.

The Lord settled my mind and gave me the confirmation and courage that it was, indeed, His word about to go forth.

I had barely begun to speak when shouts of amen went up from those gathered together in this place. The manifest presence of the Holy Spirit intensified as I spoke of a bountiful harvest coming. Whoops and hollers rung out 'til I was unable to hear myself speak. This was a "thus sayeth the Lord" moment and, let me tell you, I never say "thus sayeth the Lord"! The word of the Lord went forth and was confirmed by His presence. Little did we realize the profound significance this word would carry in the years to come.

Later that evening, one of the guest speakers was Bob Jones. He had not attended the afternoon session and to my utter surprise and astonishment he, too, spoke prophetically on the coming harvest. To say I was dumbstruck being on the same page as Bob Jones is an understatement!

This is where we belonged-right in the midst of all these peculiar people. "But you are a chosen generation, a royal priesthood, an holy nation, a peculiar people; that you should show forth the praises of him who has called you out of darkness into his marvelous light;" (1 Peter 2:9 American King James)

Lesson to be learned is this. If the Lord gives you a word which runs contrary or counter to what the rest of the crowd is prophesying, open your mouth and let the words roll off your tongue, knowing all the while the Holy Spirit will take care of the rest!

And don't be afraid to speak even if it's a simple word which you may believe too childish to share. My wife, Marianne will narrate her experience of just that very thing.

35

JESUS LOVES YOU MRS. JONES

During this same retreat, I saw Mrs. Viola Jones sitting at a big round table all by her lonesome. I noticed at other conferences Mrs. Jones did not interact with a lot of people, sitting sideways in her seat to make it impossible to talk with her or approach her. Her posture was very closed off from those around her.

I asked the Lord for an encouraging word to share with her at this retreat. What He replied was, *"Tell her that I love her."* Seriously? Tell her You love her? That's so childish. She already knows that! That's like coming from a three year old or maybe I'm making up a "safe" word to share. Everyone knows that Jesus loves them! *"Tell her, I love her very, very much"*, He insisted.

Self-consciously, I made my way over to the elderly forbidding looking woman. Eh, maybe this is not such a good idea, I thought. Ah, jeez... ok... step out... be obedient... what matter does it make if I look the fool? I be a foo' for Jesus, who foo' you be? I thought.

"M-M-Mrs. Jones?" I stammered. No answer. Ok… well… Quaking in my shoes, I cleared my throat and tried again. "M-Mrs. Jones, I believe I have a word from the Lord for you. May I share it?" Not only was there no answering reply, Mrs. Jones would not even look at me. Maybe I should leave. Yeah…I'm gonna leave. Just as I was about to do just that, she replied with a resigned sigh, "Yes, you may", but Mrs. Jones persisted in not facing me.

I thought to myself ok… wow… progress. Thank you, Lord. "The Lord wants you to know," I began then stopped. While gazing at her profile the Lord revealed not an off-putting, unapproachable woman but a heartbroken spirit. Tears stung my eyes as my heart overflowed with love and compassion for my Christian sister. My voice quavered as I continued, "that He loves you very, very much."

With that Mrs. Viola Jones turned to me, looked me straight in the eye, grabbed my hand and began to weep as she called out Jesus' name, thanking Him, over and over. She then hugged me and praised the Lord for my obedience, and exclaimed that was the most meaningful word she had ever received!

After a few moments, while still grasping my hand, Mrs. Jones composed herself and with the dignity and manners befitting this genteel southern lady, inquired where I was from, how many children, where were we staying, and other small talk. We both agreed on the beauty of West Virginia where we had spent the night on our journey to the retreat, and remarked on the incredible gathering of prophetic Christians in this one place.

For me, it was an eye opening experience. It doesn't matter how simplistic one believes a prophetic word to be. It is the anointed prophetic revelation from God at the appointed time, which blesses the recipient in spite of you.

****

Unlike the majority of conferences, whereby, there is teaching, along with ministry time, there is little opportunity to come up close and personal to some of the greatest prophetic voices and teachers of our time. However, we were invited to do just that during this retreat. Our personal ministry time with Bob Jones was compelling and humbling. Although he was known as a present day prophet with a great love for the Lord Jesus and His Truth, he never ascribed to the title of prophet. He was just Bob Jones.

Bob's greatest message was, "Did you learn to love? That's the only question the Lord will ask you when you die," he would say.

Bob Jones was one of our favorite speakers at conferences. He was genuine. He spoke from the heart of the Lord. He was one of us. My wife and I were deeply saddened when we heard Bob Jones passed away on February 14, 2014, awaiting his resurrection.

36

THE MOLE

During our time spent in ministry at the Fellowship of the Cross, the Lord opened our eyes to the deceitful wolves in sheep's clothing and, in one instance, the severity of His judgment.

It was not unusual for Christian brothers and sisters from local area churches to attend our Friday night ministry sessions. Some came to genuinely fellowship with us and be ministered to. Others made an appearance to check us out and report back to headquarters.

A particular couple, from a large local well-known Pentecostal congregation, dropped in on a few occasions. A rather considerable religious spirit was discerned covering the entire countenance of the husband. He didn't interact much during their premier visit, but had quite a lot to say on a subsequent visit.

Continually attempting and failing to coerce us to leave our ministry, he strongly suggested we come and join his church. Also, he didn't care for the fact that he could not identify the "leader" or that anyone was allowed to give a word from the Lord.

To which I replied, that although I was in charge and led the meetings, I did not lord it over the group. Unlike a large congregation where "church" revolves around one person, namely the pastor, here we on the other hand, are akin to the first century church as Paul in 1 Corinthians 14:26 instructs...."Well, my brothers and sisters, let's summarize. When you meet together, one will sing, another will teach, another will tell some special revelation God has given, one will speak in tongues, and another will interpret what is said. But everything that is done must strengthen all of you."

 In addition, everyone was respectful of one another and knew the protocol, with the exception of our visitor.

Declaring he had a word from the Lord for our ministry and it wasn't good, our visitor stated he wasn't going to divulge it. The whole episode was bizarre. The "mole" was so hell-bent on protecting his church's numbers he could not comprehend his own folly. Those seeking ministry outside the four walls of his church was an embarrassment and, for some reason, a threat to him. We were quite aware of the scuttlebutt. Although never attempting to recruit or draw others away from their home churches, we were a hazard to him and church leadership as we learned via "heard it through the grapevine" conversations. And even though our little Friday night meetings consisting of a half dozen on up to twenty five people tops, on a good night, were no match for Goliath, certain church leaders could not abide or tolerate our existence. What a shame! To abhor the idea of one of their sheep coming to another ministry for blessing by God's prophetic word is unconscionable. Disparagingly compared to a small "home" cell group (his disdain not ours), the aim was to put the kibosh on our little ministry.

It's funny to note shortly after his last visit, our once upon a time visitor's church started a Friday night ministry time modeled somewhat after our own. We must have been doing something right for the reactions we received.

37

ANANIAS

A Friday night ministry incident which will remain forever burned upon my heart involves the wife of a pastor or deacon, I don't recall which, from an inner city church. Lily came with two of her friends who were regulars at our Fellowship. Weeping openly and profusely, Lily recounted that her pastor/deacon husband was a drunk and beat her regularly, while putting on the guise of a pious leader to their church family and the outside world.

While Marianne and the intercessors prayed over Lily, the Lord spoke a word of knowledge to me regarding her dilemma. The Lord revealed to me that He was going to take Lily's husband out- as in out of the picture! What I told Lily was she need not be afraid any longer. Wide-eyed she gawped at me as I relayed this would be the last weekend she would need to deal with him. Lily asked me no questions and it was left at that.

Our intercessory group met the following Tuesday evening, which had been our usual designated night of the week to meet, and it was then one of the ladies informed me that Lily's husband had died of a heart attack the day before. No more needs to be said.

Anyone familiar with the biblical account of Ananias and Sapphira in Acts, chapter 5, knows that Peter had a word of knowledge regarding Ananias and Sapphira lying to the Holy Spirit (God). Ananias said of his possessions that he and his wife sold, he contributed all of it to the apostles; but he had not. Now, keep in mind, Ananias and Sapphira were not required to give anything at all. They offered to do so, which was commendable. The problem arose when first Ananias and then Sapphira declared they gave 100% of what they sold so that others would look favorably upon them and hold them in high regard; but Peter knew different. Peter knew they had kept a portion for themselves; which, again, was not the issue. By lying, they attempted to deceive not only Peter, but God. Seriously, did they really believe they could deceive God? Ananias and Sapphira, in their hypocrisy, sinned against God.

God's judgment was swift. When confronted by Peter, Ananias was struck dead on the spot. Sometime later, Sapphira, not knowing what had happened to her husband, was asked the same question posed to Ananias. She, too, attempted to deceive God and was struck down just as her husband had been.

Akin to Ananias and Sapphira giving the illusion of being something they were not, so did Lily's husband. Professing to the church and the outside world to be a godly man when in fact he was abusing his wife and an alcoholic, God's grace expired and His judgment fell upon him, just as it had with first Ananias, and then Sapphira.

There are those who may believe that God does not act upon His judgment while one is still occupying his earthly vessel. But I, and all who were present at the meeting, are here to tell you and can testify that, yes, He does!

38

LACKAWANNA SIX

Coming from a city which hosted the Lackawanna Six sleeper cell, this next experience made real the enemies of the cross and how certain radical members of the Muslim faith will come against anyone outside of their faith. Labeled an infidel, the radical Muslim declares that all infidels deserve death!

As a window covering dealer, my task was to install vertical blinds in the home of a Yemeni woman, living across the bridge. Being the weather was brisk and without a second thought, I grabbed the only coat hanging on the coat rack. It happened to be my letterman styled street ministry jacket with John 14:6 emblazoned on the back. "I am the way and the truth and the life. No one comes to the Father except through me" (signed) Jesus. The scripture lettering was done in bright yellow with the signature of Jesus in bold red making the statement as bright as a neon sign!

My knock on the door was answered by the lady of the house just as two young men, who I assumed were her sons, pulled into the driveway and followed me into the modest home.

I unpacked my tools and set up for my installation as the young men followed their mother into the kitchen at the back of the house. Ascending the steps of my ladder with vertical track in hand, I heard all manner of commotion emanating from the kitchen area. Shouting and hollering in Yemini Arabic, along with the slamming of drawers and doors, and the sound of something metallic hitting the ceramic floor reverberated off the walls as mother and sons engaged in a heated exchange. This continued on for roughly ten minutes. Fear prickled my neck as I realized the young Yemeni men most probably read the back of my jacket as they were behind me when we entered the home.

A short time after the ruckus in the kitchen had settled down the home telephone located in the kitchen rang. I could hear the missus assure the caller that I was fine, I was OK, and was almost done. The person on the other end of the phone call was my wife. Marianne had had a check in her spirit that something was not quite right over on the job site. Her ruse in phoning the installation site was that my next appointment called the shop wondering where I was.

Wasn't it odd that the missus assured Marianne that I was fine and Ok when the inquiry posed was whether I had left the job site yet? As the Mrs. handed me the portable telephone, I realized the Lord and the mother had been protecting me from her sons.

Some years later it was uncovered that our fears were not unfounded as Arafat Nagi, one of the sons, was a radical extremist and an ardent supporter of the Lackawanna Six sleeper cell. He was arrested for attempting to join Isis and for the attempted shooting and attempted beheading of his own daughter.

For all who are not familiar with the Lackawanna Six, allow me to share a brief account.

In the spring of 2001 a group of six Yemeni-American childhood friends traveled to Afghanistan to visit the "al-Farooq" terrorist training camp, returning to the US later that year.

An anonymous letter was received by someone residing in Lackawanna, in June 2001, who knew the Yemeni community. Essentially, the letter warned of the young Yemenites and the two recruiters meeting Osama bin Laden and staying at his camp for training. The letter went on to name the twelve young men involved.

In September 2002, one of the men was arrested in Yemen and the other five were arrested in Lackawanna and eventually pleaded guilty to *"providing material support or resources to a foreign terrorist organization."*

The trial of the Lackawanna Six sleeper cell uncovered a potential plan of a terrorist cell to detonate briefcase-sized dirty bombs in Western New York. Some contend the assertion was not true but was, instead, fake news as we call the liberal news media today. The same liberal news media that seeks to protect those whose sole aim is to do harm to Americans.

Even so, six young Yemeni-Americans were arrested, thwarted from joining Isis, becoming terrorists and returning home to wreak havoc. (Niagara Gazette, Wikipedia, Spectrum Local News, etc.)

At the start of this chapter we asked why the Lord would send puny us into the shadow of a Catholic Basilica for ministry.

Lackawanna is a culture unto itself. With a bar on every corner, the pool hall a preferred hangout, buying your "stash" from the friendly neighborhood dealer and the "Lackawanna slide" through stop signs the norm.

The city I grew up in is where gambling is a source of church revenue, lawn fete beer tents a debaucher's haven, where the name of Jesus Christ is called upon in every other sentence and it's not to praise His Holy Name; pitching quarters against a store-front wall and spitting in the street a favorite pastime in my day, and just being Catholic is a free pass to heaven-not to mention the large Muslim community. What dent were we to make in the culture? We weren't even able to keep the church folks from commandeering our parking area. Signage threatening to tow their vehicles and polite pleas to desist was scoffed at with belligerent arrogance.

Lawlessness was a virtue for the majority of inhabitants including the politicians and police department! It seemed there was always some scandal or other. Lackawanna was a rare place where one had two full-time jobs and only had to work eight hours!

For teenagers, Lackawanna was the city of "Rocks", a moniker describing one's group affiliation. Our dress code was black...black tee shirts, black jeans, black boots and jackets; our "gang" even wore black berets. Dangling a "Marlboro" from the side of your mouth and owning a stick shift, on the floor, souped up '57 Chevy was cool. You were the man! Being a punk was celebrity. All those growing up in the sixties or those who saw the movie "Grease" know what I'm talking about!

Now, don't get me wrong here. This was my hometown hangout. Most of my family lived and played and died in Lackawanna. Living on the Lackawanna/West Seneca border I am a product of the same culture. So, I knew first-hand what a tough nut the Lackawanna bros were to crack.

It would appear obvious His purpose for our presence there. So, in spite of our perceived inadequacies we interceded continually for the area.

For six short years, we fought the good fight. However, with dwindling attendance and an air of indifference from our ministry partners, we were not able to sustain the financial burden of the ministry. To that end, with sadness, we closed our ministry doors.

Feeling defeated and deflated, I regressed within myself. My carnal mind, rather than the mind of Christ, tossed me to and fro. We had been programmed, by men not God, to understand success is measured by big numbers (of people), and with people comes big money. Without those two components, men not God will say, a ministry is deemed a failure.

Resigning myself as the armpit of the body, I was devastated. I mean, that's the truth of it. In spite of all the Lord had showed me and brought me out of, and all the times He used me to minister to His people, dejection and rejection doggedly kept pace. Setting the ministry aside and putting down my guitar, I embraced the roll of the shunned stepson. True enough, I was engaging the demon of self-pity. Be that as it may, good, bad or indifferent that is the muck and mire where I found myself wallowing.

For the next ten years, my wife and I would wait on the Lord for direction. During this time, we repaired to our cave and devoted ourselves to a deeper study of the Scriptures, seeking a higher and more intimate relationship with Him without distraction.

39

222

For more than eighteen years, both my wife and I have encountered the number 222 everywhere; on our bedroom digital clock, on a signboard advertising burgers for $2.22, a receipt showing total change received of $2.22, our assigned hotel room number was 222, reading a story about a found plane, lost during WWII, whose call number included 222. While waiting in the dentist's office I picked up a magazine and was drawn to an article regarding a PT boat. Included in its identifying markings was the number 222. This is just a few of the 222 sightings.

Here is an interesting sighting of 222. In the movie, *National Treasure,* a one hundred dollar bill shows the time on the Independence Hall bell tower clock to read 2:22. Now, if you check out an older version of the hundred dollar bill, one could say the clock tower shows the time to be 2:22. Alas, the Federal government and the Bureau of Engraving and Printing claim it actually reads 4:10.

Being the Lord communicated with me via numbers before, paying close attention was paramount.

I know there are those who consider numbers, numerology or gematria a sin. However, just as the dark human heart taints music, so it goes with those who see only evil in numbers, numerology or gematria. The regenerated heart sees God's hand and message in all of creation.

That's not to say that fortune-telling, for example, where numerical cards may be used to tell the future, is included in what I am saying. It, of course, is not. Many a Scripture verse advises us what God instructs about fortune tellers, mediums and the like.

Stay with me because I'm not talking about fortune-telling or anything of the sort here. I'm talking about the Creator of the Universe, the Creator of the earth and everything in it. As the Lord instructed me so many years before, He created the universe on mathematical laws and numbers and those mathematical laws and numbers govern all of creation. And so, once again, He rebuked me to *"Pay attention! Use your spiritual eyes!"*

Listen, God is the Creator of infinite mathematics and all languages. Our heavenly Father will communicate with us by using numbers as a language. He is a God of perfect order ("For God is not a God of disorder..." 1 Corinthians 14:33 NIV). Mathematics affords us an orderly life and prevents chaos.

If our earth were to tilt more than a degree one way or the other, we would be sure to feel the effects via climate, length of days and length of seasons, just to name a few. In the extreme, it would mean the difference between life and death on the earth. God's design put this earth right where it needed to be, in order to sustain life on this planet.

For those with ears to hear, who seek Him wholeheartedly and study His ways, then and only then, will one comprehend what He is saying. It is a seeking of an intimate relationship with our Father through Jesus Christ ("...No one comes to the Father except through Me." John 14:6), not always looking for a hand out, but a true seeking of Him to hear His voice. Jesus is speaking when "He said, "The knowledge of the secrets of the kingdom of God has been given to you, but to others I speak in parables, so that, 'though seeing, they may not see; though hearing, they may not understand'." (Luke 8:10 NIV)

In the chapter of this book entitled "Pocket Full of Change" God allowed a deeper understanding of how He reveals Himself to me. Now, my wife and I had to listen closely as He spoke to us through the multiple of the number two. What we learned along the way was that we were not the only ones seeing the number 222 or variations thereof, each one receiving a different part of His message.

One woman received the revelation of "open doors of favor, authority to decree God's purpose, the absolute guarantee of His promises and the keys to the kingdom" in relation to multiples of the number two. Isaiah 22:22 "I will place on his shoulder the key to the house of David; what he opens no one can shut, and what he shuts no one can open" is the Scripture she quoted.

To another 222 is indicative of a major outpouring of God on His chosen few and how God will deal with those who are against Him. He believes God will bestow a certain grace that will spare those, who cry out and pray, from the judgment coming upon the land. Daniel 2:22, "He reveals deep and secret things; He knows what is in the darkness, And light dwells with Him" is God's Word revealed to him.

These are just two of the many people who received revelation via the number 222.

Delving further into the mystery of the ever present occurrences of 222, a reading of the Hebrew word attached to the number, in Strong's Concordance, means "flame of God".

The Greek word attached to 222, listed in Strong's Concordance, renders the meaning as an Alexandrian; belonging to Alexandria in Egypt.

It goes without saying, the "flame of God" is going to "burn up" (that is destroy) all that belongs to Egypt ("For our God is a consuming fire" Hebrews 12:29 NIV). Alexandria is in Egypt and Egypt is symbolic for worldly pursuits and desires.

It is not wrong to be ambitious. But, Jesus admonishes us saying, "So do not worry, saying, 'What shall we eat?' or 'What shall we drink?' or 'What shall we wear?' For the pagans run after all these things, and your heavenly Father knows that you need them. But seek first his kingdom and his righteousness, and all these things will be given to you as well" (Matthew 6:31-33).

What remains is the remnant, those who have come out of Egypt, (the few chosen from the many called Matthew 22:14), who will rule and reign with Christ upon His return. It is the remnant who will teach those who remain the Truth of Jesus Christ.

To reiterate, the Scriptures make it plain that when Jesus repeats a thing, like verily, verily, for example, He wants you to pay attention because what He says next is very important. So, the number 222 was not just two or twenty two, it was the triplicate of the single digit.

In December, 2000, the Lord revealed just what 222 meant for us. For months, we had been petitioning the Lord to make plain the elusive meaning behind 222. The answer had evaded us for so long.

One particular evening after dinner was no different from other evenings whereby we sought the Lord. Without preamble, Marianne opened her bible to Isaiah 2:22 and read "Stop trusting in man, who has but a breath in his nostrils. Of what account is he?"

Each and every time our Creator speaks to us is an exciting and awesome encounter. However, sometimes....sometimes His revelation just blows you away. And this revelation was a giant gob smacker. "Stop trusting in men!"

Enthusiastically and gleefully we were thrilled to finally have our answer.

Wait....what? This one answer brought about more questions. "How does this apply to us? What does this mean....exactly?"

God's revelation of 222 did not come with complete clarity. So often with human impatience, we want all of our questions answered and we want the answers now! For years it appeared we were rendered deaf and could not hear His voice. Be that as it may, the number kept showing up, here, there and everywhere!

But then, finally, finally, I had ears to hear.

It goes without saying shutting down the ministry was a nasty blow to my ego. I looked to men as the standard of measure for approval and their definition of success.

One day, while wallowing in carnal self-pity, my heavenly Father brought to my remembrance the extraordinary God moment I witnessed on a street within the Old City of Jerusalem; that being the street where Jesus walked on the way to His crucifixion. As tears spilled from my eyes, I embraced the pain and sorrow of my first-hand witness. As the swirling sand and grit, the blood, sweat and tears, the crown of thorns, the jeers, the mocking and the derisive laughter fell away I gazed upon the battered and bruised Face of ultimate Love, Compassion and Sacrifice. As I looked into His eyes of loving kindness, the eyes belonging to my Lord and Savior, Yeshua Hamashiach, my Father said, *"He is worthy of your praise!"*

Continuing, Father said, *"I see your heart when you minister to Me. You are my son, not my stepson."*

Being not yet finished Father continued with His comforting chastisement. *"A prophet is without honor only in his hometown, among his relatives, and in his own household.*

"And furthermore, if you were ever recognized with that title, one day people will praise you and the next day they will want to crucify you. The people accused My Son, Jesus, of casting out demons by Beezebul, as it is with you. Stop putting your trust in men! If they hated Him, they will hate you! But, you, Tom, must continue to learn to love, in spite of the persecution!

"Keep your eyes on your Brother (Jesus). He will lead you. He will guide you. He will tell you great and hidden things that you have not known."

Humbled and convicted beyond measure and with no words to express my unfathomable thankfulness and gratefulness for my Father's love and discipline, a contrite, "Yes Father", was all I could reply.

****

God's revelation of the meaning of 222 was far reaching.

The Lord rebuked me for trusting in and looking to men for the success and failure of my endeavors. However, stop trusting in men did not just mean stop trusting in all the "men" out there somewhere, but to stop trusting in my own carnal suppositions and abilities.

The Lord showed me the reasons we believed we were sent to Lackawanna for ministry were not at all what we arrogantly assumed. We were not in Lackawanna to take down a principality or change the culture.

The commencing of our writing brought to bear the recollecting of our many experiences. The Yemeni family episode was no exception. Some fifteen years after the fact, along with the subsequent arrest and prosecution of the Lackawanna Six, our purpose in Lackawanna was made clear.

As only He can, the Lord had a far greater plan for us there in Lackawanna than we could ever ask or imagine. In His Sovereign omniscient wisdom, the profound design the Lord had for placing our ministry in Lackawanna was for intercessory light to expose the diabolical plot of the enemy's encampment from inflicting atrocious devastation.

And to that end, the commission the Lord put before us was accomplished-not by our might, but by His.

40

THE POLITICAL PARRALLEL

For many years, Marianne and I had little interest in the political scene. We simply voted the party line trusting the confidence we put in party leaders was sufficient.

That is until Donald J. Trump made his way down the escalator in June of 2015.

As most of the people we know in this Democrat controlled city considered Mr. Trump a joke and a fool, we held our counsel. As he took on the establishment however, we sat up and listened. As a matter of fact, we listened to all the hopeful candidates jockeying for position-a new experience for us.

What emerged from the cacophony of voices was a trump that rang clear and true. "...for there is no authority except from God, and those that exist are appointed by God." (Romans 13:1)

Appointed by God, Trump is a light shining in the dark and murky waters of the swamp, exposing the ugly underbelly known as Washington, D.C; a billionaire with a trumpet sound for America and Americans; a clarion sound for the forgotten people who built this country upon their backs.

A Trump shall become a trumpet as Kim Clement, a prophet and psalmist, prophesied in 2007.

From the website of Kim Clement, here is what he said on April 4, 2007. *"I am God and you have called to Me, and many from this Nation have said enough, enough of religion, enough, enough of dead speech. The Spirit of God said this is a moment of resurrection. For the Spirit of God says, honor Me with your praise and acceptance of this that I say to you. This that shall take place shall be the most unusual thing, a transfiguration, a going into the marketplace if you wish, into the news media. Where Time Magazine will have no choice but to say what I want them to say. Newsweek, what I want to say. The View, what I want to say. Trump shall become a trumpet, says the Lord! I will raise up the Trump to become a trumpet and Bill Gates to open up the gate of a financial realm for the Church, says the Spirit of the Living God!*

"The Spirit of the Lord says hear the Word of the Lord tonight: this Nation has waited and waited and they have said revival, revival, revival. God said, there is more than revival. We have revived and brought back but a spirit of resurrection is upon you. For God said, I am breathing, I am breathing upon the people of this Nation. I am breathing upon the churches that are going down and I am bringing them up, says the Spirit of God. I am breathing upon the political powers that be. For God

said, I will not forget 911. I will not forget what took place that day and I will not forget the gatekeeper that watched over New York who will once again stand and watch over this Nation, says the Spirit of God. It shall come to pass that the man that I place in the highest office shall go in whispering My name. But God said, when he enters into the office he will be shouting out by the power of the Spirit for I shall fill him with My Spirit when he goes into office and there will be a praying man in the highest seat in your land. And God says, even a greater move of the Spirit shall take place and your enemies will finally be subdued by the year 2009."

Then, again, on April 20, 2013, Kim Clement prophesied this: *"There is a man by the name of Mr. Clark and there is also another man by the name of Donald. You are both watching me, saying could it be that God is speaking to me? Yes, He is! Somebody, just a few minutes before you came on the show, you went out and you took the American flag and you said, "I'm proud of my nation." You raised it up, and God said, "You have been determined through your prayers to influence this nation." You're watching me; you're an influential person. The Spirit of God says, "Hear the word of the prophet to you as a king, I will open that door that you prayed about and when it comes time for the election, you will be elected."*

Kim Clement's prophecy of 2007 was fulfilled in 2016 when Donald Trump won the presidential election.

****

Lance Wallnau, a business consultant, an evangelical with a doctorate in ministry, also prophesied Donald Trump's presidency. Mr. Wallnau said the Lord spoke to him in 2016 saying Trump is a *"wrecking ball to the spirit of political correctness"*. A few months later, Wallnau saw an image of Trump as the 45th president and was led to read Isaiah 45 which speaks of Cyrus the Great, the pagan king of Persia. In 539 BC, Cyrus conquered Babylon, freed and returned the Jews to Jerusalem where they rebuilt the temple. (Lance Wallnau's website)

Isaiah chapter 45:1, "This is what the LORD says to his anointed, to Cyrus, whose right hand I take hold of to subdue nations before him and to strip kings of their armor, to open doors before him so that gates will not be shut:"

Lance Wallnau states that as he read further back in Isaiah 44:28, he saw that the Lord said of Cyrus, "When I say of Cyrus, 'He is my shepherd,' he will certainly do as I say. He will command, 'Rebuild Jerusalem'; he will say, 'Restore the Temple.'"

It was a certainty for Wallnau that Donald Trump would be elected President of the United States to fulfill the prophecy. A warrior against the global "demonic agenda", he is "raising the warning cry about the unraveling of America," Mr. Wallnau proclaimed. (Lance Wallnau's website)

Even though Cyrus the Great was not one of God's people, he was in God's plan.

****

Not only did Kim Clement and Lance Wallnau prophesy the coming of Donald Trump as president but a retired firefighter by the name of Mark Taylor did, as well. While Donald Trump was being interviewed in 2011, Mark Taylor states the following prophetic came to him as told to a conservative radio host in 2016.

"The Spirit of God says, I have chosen this man, Donald Trump, for such a time as this. For as Benjamin Netanyahu is to Israel, so shall this man be to the United States of America! For I will use this man to bring honor, respect and restoration to America. America will be respected once again as the most powerful and prosperous nation on earth, (other than Israel). The dollar will be the strongest it has ever been in the history of the United States, and will once again be the currency by which all others are judged." (Mark Taylor)

Taylor's prophetic word continues: *"The Spirit of God says, I will protect America and Israel, for this next president will be a man of his word, when he speaks the world will listen and know that there is something greater in him than all the others before him. This man's word is his bond and the world and America will know this and the enemy will fear this, for this man will be fearless. The Spirit says, when the financial harvest begins so shall it parallel in the spiritual for America."*

****

God directed our steps to the political arena and to political prophecies declaring Donald Trump the next president; yet, for what purpose? In order for us to plainly witness the incredible depth of deception in the institutions that had our trust and the length those involved will go to protect their interests.

Politics embody the height of corruption and deception. In recent years, we have been subjected to the IRS scandal, the Clinton Foundation scandal, the Uranium One deal, the Fast and Furious scheme, the FBI, CIA and DOJ scandals, Global Warming changed to Climate Change scheme, the One World Order scheme and last but not least the Trump-Russian Collusion non-scandal, just to name a few. Garnering our trust and hoping in our stupidity, most of the elite care not a whit about those who elected them into office. Power and enriching themselves is the end game.

With all the proffered on-going evidence that has and is still exposing the scandals, the schemes and deception, many continue to advocate for the righteousness of the corrupt. Right will be wrong and wrong will be right.

"What sorrow for those who say that evil is good and good is evil that dark is light and light is dark, that bitter is sweet and sweet is bitter." (Isaiah 5:20 NLT)

"Doom to you who think you're so smart, who hold such a high opinion of yourselves... And then line your pockets with bribes from the guilty while you violate the rights of the innocent. (Isaiah 5:21-23 The Message). As more and more corruption is exposed in the highest echelon of government and minds are blinded by delusion, the Leviathan spirit works its way throughout not only government, but, also, our schools, the church and society in general.

A Leviathan spirit will take statements and actions of a person out of context to suit its own agenda. And when that doesn't work, the Leviathan spirt, which is a demonic spirit, will spew forth out and out lies; not outlandish lies, mind you, but a lie with just enough truth to ensure believability. This tactic encourages division, suspicion and conflict. The thrust of a Leviathan spirit is to assail and disparage the righteousness of a person. Once the incredible damage is done, perceptions and judgments are not easily changed for the vulnerable.

****

"Lord", I entreated, "You've blessed this country beyond measure. And yet, our government has taken You out of our schools by eliminating prayer, by corrupting our children with the encouraging of promiscuity by handing out condoms, educating babes in the ways of deviant sexual practices, the girl's bathroom is not off limits to the boys and vice versa, and promoting LGBTQIA (Lesbian, Gay, Bisexual, Trans, Queer, Intersex, Asexual) gender identities. Our government funds organizations that murder hundreds of thousands of babies each year by abortion, promoting themselves as women's health guardians.

Lord, where will it end? "

"The land is mine", He replied. *"All who reside here are temporary. They return to Egypt to gratify the desires of their flesh denying My laws. To begin, man's deception has reigned here from its founding; from the Native Americans, whose territories were invaded and men, women and children slaughtered and whose lands were stolen to the founding fathers' deism, denying the divinity of My Son, to the enslavement of men, to the pagan goddess Ishtar taking the form of the Statue of Liberty and so on.*

"I have appointed one whose trumpet sound will blast the darkness into light. And I will judge the people of this land by stripping away their power. They love darkness instead of light because their deeds are evil.

"My message to My church is sure. But, first know, just as you have witnessed the resistance of the powerful deceptive men in government to relinquish their darkness, you will confront the same impediment from within the church. It is to My household that I bring judgment first, exposing the deceptive doctrines of men.

"I have sent to you a teacher to prepare you for this time. I have kept you from prosperity and power by the world's standard. I have kept you from the favor of men which breeds pride and a haughty spirit. I have guarded you from destruction. By experiencing the rejection of men and the sorrow that followed, you matured and grew in Love. For these reasons, I called you out of the institutions of men. Otherwise, you would not hear Me for all the clanging cymbals.

"I have saved you from the clutches of death more than once. I loved you as I chastened you and nurtured you in spite of your ungrateful self. I comforted you when you found no comfort.

"And My Son chose you for My purpose when He revealed Himself to you.

"Take heed lest your heart be hardened. Do not hate your enemies as David did. Yes, David sought me but, he hated his enemies. David ordered his son, Solomon, to kill his enemies and show no mercy. David died as a murderer and unforgiven.

"But, to you, I say love your enemies. Bless those who curse you and pray for those who persecute you."

****

Killing one's enemies, when ordered by God, was a way of obedient life in the Old Testament.

Yahweh smote the evil and wicked men with much war and violence who were corrupting His people. "You must completely destroy the Hittites, Amorites, Canaanites, Perizzites, Hivites, and Jebusites, just as the Lord your God has commanded you. This will prevent the people of the land from teaching you to imitate their detestable customs in the worship of their gods, which would cause you to sin deeply against the Lord your God." (Deuteronomy 20:17-18 NLT)

In verse 13, God provides direction on just how to put down all who will not accept Israel's offer of peace. "When the Lord your God hands the town over to you, use your swords to kill every man in the town." In verse 16, Yahweh commands, "In those towns that the Lord your God is giving you as a special possession, destroy every living thing."

Joshua 11:20, "For the Lord hardened their hearts and caused them to fight the Israelites. So they were completely destroyed without mercy, as the Lord had commanded Moses." (NLT)

However, modern day New Testament believers do not fall short of their fair share of murdering those who challenged their authority, which was not God ordained.

One of those who did not care to have his authority challenged was Martin Luther. He is well-known for his "95 Theses", opposing the Catholic Church practice of indulgences. Martin Luther was a theology professor, priest, monk and influential in the Protestant Reformation.

Martin Luther not only had issues with the Catholic Church, but also with the radical movement of the Protestant Reformation known, much to their chagrin, as the Anabaptists. The Anabaptists held infant baptism to have no spiritual benefit; it was just for show. They believed adult baptism to be the only proper baptism.

Disagreeing with the Anabaptists on this held belief, including additional doctrinal differences Martin Luther charged them with subverting respect for authority of the Protestant church. Consequently, Martin Luther and his friends put to death some 150,000 Anabaptists, including men, women and children.

Another beloved theologian, pastor and one of the reformers of the Roman Catholic Church was John Calvin. John Calvin, dedicated Christian that he was, promoted predestination.

 He was also a murderer. Selectively ignoring New Testament Scripture, John Calvin justified killing opposing theologians with discriminatory Old Testament Scriptures.

Disagreeing with Michael Servetus regarding the Trinity, and angered when the physician was critical of him on other matters, John Calvin had his long-time friend slowly burned at the stake in 1553.

Church leaders to whom followers give their implicit trust, ruled by intimidation, fear mongering, death and man's authority based on their own faulty Biblical interpretation and religious doctrines.

"But cowards, unbelievers, the corrupt, **murderers,** the immoral, those who practice witchcraft, idol worshipers, and all liars--their fate is in the fiery lake of burning sulfur. This is the second death." (Rev 21:8 NLT)

"Anyone who hates another brother or sister is really a **murderer** at heart. And you know that **murderers** don't have eternal life within them." (1 John 3:15 NLT)

The Islamic terrorist group, Isis, has nothing on tyrannical church leaders, the Crusaders, the Inquisition or the murderers of the Templars, just to name a few, who in the name of God slaughtered those who threatened their doctrinal beliefs or questioned their authority and power.

How does one put trust in murderous hearts who say they stand in God's name?

Did Jesus say anyone who isn't with me...kill them? No, of course not. What Jesus did say was "Anyone who isn't with me opposes me, and anyone who isn't working with me is actually working against me." (Luke 11:23 NLT)

Evil and wickedness occupied every aspect of life in the Old Testament; from sacrificing children to pagan gods, prostitution in the Temple as a religious rite and idol worship. Pervasive evil was polluting God's people. Yahweh had had enough and let loose His terrible judgment against man and land.

Today, God's people are exploited by another kind of evil....the corruption of His Word. The doctrines of demons and the doctrines of men are infecting the multitudes in their seemingly innocuous innocence as they continue to tout the party line. Here's what the apostle Paul has to say to his followers of the early church that Jesus built.

"I am shocked that you are turning away so soon from God, who called you to himself through the loving mercy of Christ. You are following a different way that pretends to be the **Good News** (emphasis mine) but is not the **Good News** (emphasis mine) at all. You are being fooled by those who deliberately twist the truth concerning Christ." (Galatians 1:6 NLT)

Paul was not yet finished as he said, "Be not deceived, God is not to be sneered at, for whatsoever a man may be sowing, this shall he be reaping also, for he who is sowing for his own flesh, from the flesh shall be reaping **corruption**, yet he who is sowing for the spirit, from the spirit shall be reaping life eonian." (Galatians 6:7-8 CLT)

****

A mere fifteen years, give or take, after the crucifixion of Jesus, Paul the apostle, soundly rebuked the church of Galatia for believing those who "deliberately twist the truth concerning Christ".

Before Paul, the apostle Peter, at Pentecost, speaking to the gathered group quoted Joel, a minor prophet of the Old Testament, when he said, "The sun shall be turned into darkness, and the moon into blood, before that great and notable day of the Lord come:" (Act 2:20 KJV)

As ominous as the Scripture sounds is as ominous as it is.

The sun gives light and warmth to those living on this planet in order to sustain life. Jesus Christ is the Son Who is God's light come into the world. John 3:10 "...God's light came into the world..." continuing "but the people loved the darkness more than the light, for their actions were evil."

The moon, on the other hand, reflects the light from the sun. It has no light of its own to give. If the sun were to be extinguished, the moon would also be no more.

As the moon is symbolic of the church it receives light, which is Truth, from the sun (Son) Who is Christ. Therefore, as the church receives the light which is Truth, it is then passed on to the congregation, and the sheep are fed.

However, on Pentecost, Peter proclaimed that the sun isn't going to give its light anymore; it shall be turned into darkness, "...because people loved the darkness more than light." (John 3:10) God is not going to give direct light to the people anymore. The light which should be coming from the church (that light which was already given to the moon by the sun to be reflected) is not going to give its light.

The church is going to run mad with murderous frenzy as apostasy sets in. And instead of receiving light from God and passing it on, the moon (i.e. church) is going to turn to blood.

How would the church turn to blood?

Way before the likes of Martin Luther and John Calvin, given elsewhere as examples of the murderous hearts of churchmen, those from the church (i.e. moon) who stoned

Stephen in Acts 7, forfeited the light they were to give to the world and turned to blood. They chose to become murderers both literally and metaphorically!

There are those who, in the name of God, literally murdered those who did not agree with them. Metaphorically, theologians and teachers have been annihilating (murdering) God's Word for centuries to fit their preferred agenda!

Even so, in these last days which began at Pentecost, and before Jesus returns, the apostle Peter again quoting Joel assures us that… "In the last days, God says, I will pour out my Spirit on all people. Your sons and daughters will prophesy, your young men will see visions, your old men will dream dreams. Even on my servants, both men and women, I will pour out my Spirit in those days, and they will prophesy. I will show wonders in the heavens above and signs on the earth below, blood and fire and billows of smoke." (Act 2:17-19)

Just as Joel said we will all prophesy as God pours out His Spirit on all people. Although "Now we see things imperfectly, like puzzling (*dim-other translations*) reflections in a mirror (*indirectly-other translations*), but then we will see everything with perfect clarity. All that I know now is partial and incomplete, but then I will know everything completely, just as God now knows me completely." (1 Corinthians 13:12 NLT)

The Message, a translation I enjoy, tells it like it is in modern lingo, and says it this way, "We don't yet see things clearly. We're squinting in a fog, peering through a mist. But it won't be long before the weather clears and the sun shines bright! We'll see it all then, see it all as clearly as God sees us, knowing him directly just as he knows us!"

41

RECLAIMING THE CHURCH THAT JESUS BUILT

Jesus said, "Don't imagine that I came to bring peace to the earth! I came not to bring peace, but a sword. I have come to set a man against his father, a daughter against her mother, and a daughter-in-law against her mother-in-law. Your enemies will be right in your own household!" (Matthew 10:34-36 NLT)

Whenever I read this Scripture, I always read it as pertaining to all those who reside in the same house-one's family. But is not the church family our household, as well? And isn't God bringing judgment to His household (family) first? Does it not follow that one's own enemies lurk within the church family?

Peter foresaw this exact situation unfolding in the church when he said, "But there were also false prophets in Israel, just as there will be false teachers among you. They will cleverly teach destructive heresies and even deny the Master who bought them. In this way, they will bring sudden destruction on themselves. Many will follow their evil teaching and shameful immorality. And because of these teachers, the way of truth will be slandered. In their greed they will make up clever lies to get hold of your money. But God condemned them long ago, and their destruction will not be delayed." (2 Peter 2:1-3 NLT)

Paul also recognized the coming condition. "For I know this that after my departing shall grievous wolves enter in among you, not sparing the flock. Also of your own selves shall men arise, speaking perverse things, to draw away disciples after them." (Acts 20:29-30)

Out of the asserted 20,000 some denominations and non-denominations do you suppose there are any heresies within accepted teachings? Well, yes, of course, there are! We just read from Paul and Peter this would be so. Even Jesus confronted the corruption in God's church which began in the desert with Moses. After Moses hiked up the mountain to meet with God, it didn't take long for the people down below to, once again, pander to their pagan ways.

From as early as the 2nd century onward church leaders ascribed to pagan heresies which originated in Egypt.

Thomas B. Thayer, a late nineteenth century leading theologian, in his "Doctrine of Eternal Punishment" wrote: *"Anyone at all familiar with the writings of the ancient Greeks or Romans cannot fail to not see how often it is admitted by them that the national religions were the inventions of the legislator and the priest, for the purpose of governing and restraining the common people.*

"The object of this sacred fraud was to impress the minds of the multitude with religious awe and command a more ready obedience on their part."

In turn, Augustine, an early Christian theologian, wrote in his "City of God": *"This seems to have been done on no other account, but as it was the business of princes, out of their wisdom and civil prudence, to deceive the people in their religion; princes, under the name of religion, persuaded the people to believe those things true, which they themselves knew to be idle fables; by this means, for their own ease in government, tying them the more closely to civil society."*

So, the heresies continue on down through the generations. Once a false doctrine is taught over and over it becomes an accepted truth and a denominational dogma.

And since Satan "deceives the whole world (Revelation 12:9), there are not many, except the chosen elect of God, who are not hoodwinked.

But, "God does not lie." (Titus 1:2 NLT)

"God is not a man, so he does not lie. He is not human, so he does not change his mind. Has he ever spoken and failed to act? Has he ever promised and not carried it through?" (Numbers 23:19 NLT)

"All Scripture is inspired by God and is useful to teach us what is true and to make us realize what is wrong in our lives. It corrects us when we are wrong and teaches us to do what is right" (2 Timothy 3:16 NLT).

"....Scripture cannot be broken" (John 10:35 KJV).

"Make them holy by your truth; teach them your word, which is truth." (John 17:17 NLT)

****

God does not lie, all Scripture is inspired of God, Scripture cannot be broken, teach them your word, which is truth.

It is God's Truth which released us from the doctrines of men and spurious passages. The conflict within to accept it was another matter, however. It was intense. The struggle within to accept His Truth was real. What is truth? We already had the truth, we so believed. How is it even remotely possible most of Christianity would or could reject the truths of God, we asked ourselves?

For years, being so indoctrinated into the teachings of mainstream Christianity, we continued to revert back to those teachings in order to deny God's Truth. We clung to the lifeboat of our learned doctrines, even at the risk of drowning in abject denial of God's written Word. The spiritual warfare against Satan's head games of havoc was harrowing!

Meanwhile, the number 222 dogged our every step; waking or sleeping, there was no escaping the constant reminder.

"Don't put your trust in men!" Father admonished, keeping us focused on Him and on track.

Once the scales fell from our eyes, God's Truth could not and would not be denied. Anger and shame and humiliation gained a foothold. To think men led us to believe that they, through their false doctrines, not God, were in control of our ultimate destiny.

The Truth I am about to share, here and now, is unequivocally and conclusively the **Good News**! A Good News Truth that will cut to the heart.

Set aside the arguments you've been taught that "well...of course, God desires it, wishes it or wants it but...man has free will", or "all does not mean all, all the time".

This is the Good News the Lord imparted deep within my spirit almost fifteen years ago at a Black Mountain ministry retreat in North Carolina; The Good News certainty and magnitude of the coming great harvest.

And that Good News is...... (Open your spiritual ears and hear the Word of the Lord).

"For this *is* good and acceptable in the sight of God our Saviour; Who **will** (*Strong's #2309 will, desires, wish (bold letters and italics mine)*) have **all men to be saved**, and to come unto the knowledge of the truth." (1Timothy 2:3-4 KJV)

"He is the atoning sacrifice for our sins, and not only for ours but also for the sins of the **whole world.**" (1 John 2:2 NIV)

"And we have gazed upon Him, and are testifying that the Father has dispatched the Son, the **Saviour of the world.**" (1 John 4:14 Concordant Literal)

In this Jesus has been denied and declared a failure. Mainstream Christianity truly believes, as they have been taught by scheming men for centuries that Jesus Christ has failed as Savior of the world as His Father commissioned Him! Yes, most Christians believe Jesus Christ, the Son of God, has failed because puny man's free will, in his own mind, is superior to God's sovereign will!

"For it is God (*not puny man or his free will*-italics mine) which works in you both to will and to do of his good pleasure." (Philippians 2:13 American King James)

God does not lie! God wills that all men be saved! God proclaims, "...My counsel shall stand and I **will do all my pleasure**...Yes, I have spoken it, **I will also bring it to pass: I** have purposed it, **I will also do it.**" (Isaiah 46:10-11 KJV) (emphasis mine)

In the unlikely event you missed it, God says, **I will do all my pleasure, I will also bring it pass, I will also do it.** Read it. Re-read it. Believe it.

Jesus affirms, "And He Who sends Me is with Me. He does not leave Me alone, for what is **pleasing** (emphasis mine) **to Him am I doing always."** (John 8:29 CLT)

"The Lord is not slack concerning his promise, as some men count slackness; but is longsuffering to us-ward, **not willing** (emphasis mine) **that any should perish**, but that all should come to repentance." (2 Peter 3:9 KJV)

There are those who say, "but, but...Mark 16:16 says, 'Whoever believes and is baptized will be saved, but whoever does not believe will be **condemned"** (emphasis mine), as though this Scripture contradicts the rest of the Word of God. God does not lie or contradict Himself!

Can you guess Who else was condemned? "And they all **condemned** Him (*Jesus*) to be deserving of death." (Mark 14:64 NASB)

Jesus, Himself, said "We are going up to Jerusalem, and the Son of Man will be delivered over to the chief priests and the teachers of the law. They will **condemn** him (*Jesus*) to death..." (Mathew 20:18 NIV)

Jesus was **condemned** to death. Is He still dead in the grave? No, of course not! The resurrected Christ Who was condemned, is the only Hope of the condemned world because He is the Savior of the whole world!

"For only when you come to judge the earth will people **learn** what is right." (Isaiah 26:9 NLT) When God's judgments come on the earth (future), then the world will learn that Jesus Christ is the Savior of all men!

Only then "…As I live saith the Lord, **every** knee shall bow to me, and **every** tongue shall confess to God." (Romans 14:11 KJV)

The definition of "every" is "without exception" and the definition of "all" is "every". Hence, without exception all knees shall bow, all tongues shall confess and Jesus Christ shall save every man, woman and child by virtue of Him being the Savior of the whole world.

Until that time, most of the world, including Christianity, is anti- (Strong's Concordance #473-against, opposite, in place of, instead of) Christ.

Reprimanding, Jesus makes known, "Anyone who isn't with me opposes me, and anyone who isn't working with me is actually working against me." (Matthew 12:30)

****

A hidden pearl of great price excavated from the rocky, pebble-strewn ground of learning regarding the number 666 of Revelation 13:18 is this: "Here is wisdom let him that has understanding count the number of the beast: for it is the number of **a man** (emphasis mine); and his number is six hundred threescore and six." (KJV)

Everyone I know has been taught 666 represents a man, the anti-Christ.

However, the Greek word used in Revelation 13:18 is *anthropos* meaning a human being, man and woman, not *aner*, which designates male apart from female.

Moreover, the beast of Revelation 13:18, number 666, is not **a man**; it is mankind. Meaning 666 is symbolic of mankind's attempt to sit on God's throne, usurping His power and wisdom. 666 is representative of whatever or whoever is anti-God.

There will always be those who desire to sit on God's throne. But they, my friends, are not the chosen few, but rather, those whose numbers are likened to the sand of the sea from the beginning of mankind 'til now.

A more accurate translation of Revelation 13:18 is, "In this case wisdom is needed: Let the person who has understanding calculate the total number of the beast, because it is a human total number, and the sum of the number is 666." (International Standard Version)

Open the eyes of your heart as you read the Word of God from Philippians 2:6-11:
"Who, being in very nature God, did not consider equality with God something to be used to his own advantage; rather, he made himself nothing by taking the very nature of a

servant, being made in human likeness. And being found in appearance as a man, he humbled himself by becoming obedient to death—even death on a cross! Therefore God exalted him to the highest place and gave him the name that is above every name, that at the name of Jesus every knee should bow, in heaven and on earth and under the earth, and every tongue acknowledge that Jesus Christ is Lord, to the glory of God the Father." (NIV)

42

WHAT DO YOU SAY? WHERE DO YOU STAND?

As you brood over the Good News presented within the pages of this book, consider how the people reacted to Peter when he proclaimed with certainty that "...God made Jesus, whom you crucified, both Lord and Christ" in Acts 2:37. "When the people heard this, **they were cut to the heart** and said to Peter and the other apostles, Brothers, what shall we do?" (Berean Study Bible)

When receiving the gospel at Pentecost the brothers repented of their sins.

On the other hand, when Stephen, who was one of the Lord's disciples, accused the high priest and the council of religious leaders of Israel of being the blasphemers of God, they reacted with brutal contradiction. Stephen spoke boldly against their stiff-necked, uncircumcised hearts and ears always resisting the Holy Spirit. When he fearlessly proclaimed seeing the Son of Man standing at the right side of God, the Jews were cut to the heart and gnashed their teeth at him. Stephen was then summarily cast out of the city and stoned to death. "Now hearing these things, they were **cut to their hearts** and began gnashing teeth at him" (Acts 7:54 Berean Literal Bible).

The Sanhedrin, including the high priest, would hear none of Stephen's message. Instead, they chose to murder him.

Two groups of people were **cut to the heart** upon hearing the Gospel of Christ.

The first group whose softened hearts readily repented and accepted the gospel; and those with hardened hearts whose blaspheming and murderous ways borne more out of fear of losing their political power positions and luxurious lifestyles, manifested in the death of an innocent man.

What do you say? Where do you stand?

Do you believe Jesus Christ is a failure? Or do you believe He accomplished what His Father sent Him to do?

Do you stand with the religious order of today? Or do you stand with Peter?

If you stand with Peter and the words he spoke almost two thousand years ago cut to your heart, do just as Peter instructed those gathered. "Peter replied, 'Repent...., every one of you, in the name of Jesus Christ for the forgiveness of your sins'..." (Acts 2:38 NIV)

Moreover, heed Peter's words of warning as he pleaded, "Save yourselves from this corrupt generation." (Acts 2:40 NIV)

****

"For therefore we both labor and suffer reproach, because we trust in the living God, who **is** the Saviour of **all men**, specially (i.e. not only or limited to) of those that believe." (I Tim. 4:10 KJV)

****

43

THE YEAR OF THE EARTHQUAKES

On January 14, 2018, the Lord revealed to me this is **the** year of earthquakes and the whole earth will be shaken. For the sake of authenticity I posted the same to my Facebook page. As we are now in the second half of the year, this is certainly coming to pass, as illustrated with just two extraordinary examples given to date as of July 2018.

CNN reported that on June 5, 2018, there were at least 12,000 reported earthquakes on Hawaii's big island alone, in a thirty day period, as described by the United States Geological Survey (USGS). The monthly average is one thousand earthquakes.

Upon reading my post, a friend of mine suggested I check out an earthquake forecaster by the name of Dutch Sinse. On June 7, 2018, he reported an awakening of a 5000 year old ancient volcano on the southeast coast of Africa on Mayotte Island.

Not only have there been increases in earthquakes and volcanos throughout the globe, but, fissures and sink holes continue to open up in number, as well.

On March 19, 2018, in southwestern Kenya, a 50 foot wide and several miles long crack appeared and is growing, as reported by the Washington Post. These rifts emerge due to a rupture process that is generally in conjunction with seismic activity and volcanism.

On July 20, 2018, it was reported by Daniel Nelson, Science Trends, an immense fissure opened up within the Grand Teton National Park. It is about 60 miles from the Yellowstone Volcano. The volcano has not had a major eruption in 600,000 years, but the area is being closely watched for additional fissures and patterns to predict its next eruption.

With just a very minute illustrative sampling, that's a whole lotta shakin' goin' on!

"He shakes the earth from its place, and its foundations tremble" (Job 9:6 NLT)

What is occurring in the physical world is a precursor to coming events in the spirit.

Christ is returning to a bride that is without spot or wrinkle. "… Christ loved the church and gave himself up for her to make her holy, cleansing her by the washing with water through the word, and to present her to himself as a radiant church, without stain or wrinkle or any other blemish, but holy and blameless." (Ephesians 5:25-27 NIV)

The Lord, as Head of the Church, is returning to an awakened bride where His Truth will prevail. A family divided and fractured by the many denominational pet doctrines of men will no longer be tolerated. "I appeal to you, brothers, in the name of our Lord Jesus Christ, that all of you agree together, so that there may be no divisions among you and that you may be united in mind and conviction." (1 Corinthians 1:9-10 Berean Study Bible)

As it is written first the natural, then the spiritual come (1 Corinthians 15:46 paraphrased). Not only is the physical earth being shaken, but our earthly vessels (that's us) are being shaken, also. Are we not formed from the very earth? Yes, we are of the earth; we are earthy.

"At that time his voice shook the earth, but now he has promised, 'Once more I will shake not only the earth but also the heavens." The words 'once more' indicate the removing of what can be shaken (*created things*-italics mine) so that what cannot be shaken may remain. Therefore, since we are receiving a kingdom that cannot be shaken, let us be thankful, and so worship God acceptably with reverence and awe, for our "God is a consuming fire." (Hebrews 12:26-29 NIV)

It is not enough for our earthy vessels, which rely upon the doctrines of men for the building blocks used upon our foundation, to be shaken. Our heavens need to be shaken; the heaven of own making where our thoughts dwell. This heaven is not God's heaven, it belongs to man. And man requires a renewing of his mind.

"Don't copy the behavior and customs of this world, but let God transform you into a new person by changing the way you think. Then you will learn to know God's will for you, which is good and pleasing and perfect." (Romans 12:2 NLT)

Do you not know that judgment comes first to the house of God? Although the institutional church has its place, in the natural, and satisfies the carnal expectations of those in need, pastor/teachers who pervert God's Word by teaching the "doctrines of men", which include the fear mongering of God's people for means of profit and control, will not escape His cleansing. "In fact, teachers will be judged more strictly than others." (James 3:1 Contemporary English Version)

The church system of today is straight out of the "synagogue of Satan". Satan attacks the institutional church from within its four walls.

In a previous chapter it was illustrated that when Jesus rebuked each one of the seven churches of Asia for their sins, He was addressing ALL the churches, then and now, down through the generations to today.

Keeping Jesus' admonitions in mind, where do we find those "who say they are apostles, but are not"? Similarly, where do we find those who "left their first love" (Rev 2:4), "say they are Jews (*spiritual*) and are not, but are the synagogue of Satan" (Rev 2:9, 3:9), "Satan's seat" (Rev 2:13), "where Satan dwells" (Rev 2:13), "the doctrine of Balaam" (Rev 2:14), "them that hold the doctrine of the Nicolaitans, which thing I (*Jesus*) hate" (Rev 2:15), "that woman Jezebel, which calls herself a prophetess, to teach and to seduce my servants to commit fornication and to eat things sacrificed unto idols" (Rev 2:19), "have a name that you live, and are dead", "are wretched, and miserable, and poor, and blind, and naked" (Rev 3:17), and "the depths of Satan" (Rev 2:24)? Where do we find all these things?

Ok...wait for it.....we find them ALL in the institutional CHURCH!

The year of earthquakes centers us upon the precipice of Christ's return, as the earth groans and travails in anticipation.

According to The National Earthquake Information Center (NEIC) there is an average of about 50 earthquakes a day around the world. Be that as it may, there are millions more that occur every year that are too small or weak, called tremors, to be recorded.

Now, consistent with what EarthSky.org reports, earthquakes greater than 8.0 have struck the earth at a record rate since 2004. Scientists, however, claim this seismic increase in number and scope is merely by chance.

Not only are some scientists blowing off earthquake increases, they are not recording all those of considerable size, if reporting at all. The biggest culprits for example, says Dutch Sinse, are China and Russia. Even the state of Oregon is not forthcoming in reporting the scope and size of earthquakes in that region, he declares.

Lucrative oil and gas fracking, along with geothermal pumping operations in the west, could have a lot to do with their reluctance to report activity. In fact, some will go so far as to downgrade the strength of an earthquake as measured on the Richter magnitude scale, he reported.

Dutch Sinse is often ridiculed and censored for his unorthodoxy in earthquake forecasting. Yet, he retains a 95% rate of accuracy!

To be sure, scientists have their place in God's scheme of things. After all, God and science are not mutually exclusive.

Nevertheless, commensurate with God's Word earthquakes of significance, which are symbolic of God's power, often precede His divine presence for His monumental purpose.

Take Moses on Mt. Sinai, for example.

"Mount Sinai was completely enveloped in smoke, because the LORD had descended on it in fire. And smoke rose like the smoke of a furnace, and the **whole mountain quaked violently** (*emphasis mine*)." (Numbers 19:18 Berean Study Bible).

God spoke to Moses in the thunder to warn the priests and people not to ascend the mountain. Not too long afterward God spoke the Ten Commandments for all to hear.

Let's not forget His divine presence and monumental purpose when the earth quaked as Jesus gave up His Spirit.

"Now Jesus, again crying with a loud voice, lets out the spirit. And lo! the curtain of the temple is rent in two from above to the bottom, and the **earth quaked** *(emphasis mine)*, and the rocks are rent, and the tombs were opened. And many bodies of the reposing saints were roused, and, coming out of the tombs after His rousing, they entered into the holy city and are disclosed to many." (Matthew 27:50-53 Concordant Literal Translation)

OK, one more scripture for the road so as to drive home the symbolic magnitude of earthquakes.

"After the Sabbath, at dawn on the first day of the week, Mary Magdalene and the other Mary went to see the tomb. Suddenly there was a **great earthquake** (*emphasis* *mine*), for the angel of the Lord, descended from heaven, rolled away the stone and sat on it (Matthew 28:1-2 Berean Study Bible).

God implemented earthquake fissures for punishment as explained in Numbers 16 known as Korah's rebellion. Korah and his two cohorts, Dathan and Abiram, along with the 250 leaders of the congregation and representatives in the assembly came against Moses. As a result, the ground beneath them split open, and the earth opened its mouth and swallowed them and their households; all Korah's men and all their possessions. They went down alive into Sheol with all they owned. The earth closed over them, and they vanished from the assembly.

"At their cries, all the people of Israel who were around them fled, saying, 'The earth may swallow us too!' And fire came forth from the LORD and consumed the 250 men who were offering the incense." (Berean Study Bible)

In order for Christ's church to be without blemish, He is shaking the very building blocks of His beloved bride bringing an awakening to His Truth. Not just for revival, which is fleeting, but for an unforeseen reformation of prodigious proportions, which will endure upon the earth, culminating in the great harvest at the end of the age.

*This chapter opened with "On January 14, 2018, the Lord revealed to me this is **the** year of earthquakes **and the whole earth will be shaken**. (*emphasis added*)

National Geographic dot com reported that on November 11, 2018, "Strange earthquake waves rippled around Earth".

Volcano Discovery dot com reported, "Earthquake report world-wide for Sunday, 11 Nov 2018. Big Think dot com reported, "An unexplained November seismic event 'rang' the Earth. Finally, RT dot com reported "Weird seismic event which shook the world for 20 minutes baffles experts."

Now, I did not read these reports until November 28, 2018. However, on November 11, 2018, I felt strongly led to re-post my earlier Facebook post, dated January 14, 2018, regarding the year of earthquakes.

Being the proverbial 'doubting Thomas', the Lord confirmed to me that what He says He will do, He most assuredly will do!

The shaking and purging of the institutional church and its corrupt system has commenced, and will clamber dramatically to a crescendo according to God's divine purpose, I believe, in 2022.

Agreeing with the political party of "obstruct and resist" who claw, fight, lie, and steal to achieve their goal, so do those in the institutional church in order to retain and maintain their corrupt power. However, the carnality of man, clothed in a deceptive Christian mask and deluded by an illusion of power cannot survive a foolish and ill-gained battle with the Great I Am as He brings the darkness to light.

"For everything hidden is meant to be revealed, and everything concealed is meant to be brought to light." (Mark 4:22 Berean Study Bible).   Nonetheless, puny man will continue to attempt to thwart the will of God.

"Son of man, you are living in a rebellious house. They have eyes to see but do not see, and ears to hear but do not hear, for they are a rebellious house." (Ezekiel 12:2 Berean Study Bible)

"And they will know that I am the LORD; I did not declare in vain that I would bring this calamity upon them." (Ezekiel 6:10 Berean Study Bible)

EPILOGUE

Our road has been long and bumpy with many a winding turn but, it ain't over 'til it's over!

Many questions arose as to certain biblical teachings we received over the years, that just could not be assuaged with the half answers or no answers or, quite frankly, the ridiculous answers offered. Questions from a very young age, such as, "Why do I have to go to confession? The priest is just a man. Why is he so special? Does he go to confession? How does this piece of flat white stuff that sticks to the roof of your mouth become Jesus? Why do we pray to saints, aren't they dead people? How can they hear us?" And so on.

Correspondingly, venturing onto the Protestant side of the aisle, the questions became deeper and tougher. "How can we have an immortal soul if only Jesus is immortal? God said Adam and Eve would surely die. Satan said they would not surely die. Why do we believe Satan? How can we die and be in heaven, when no man has ascended to heaven except the One who descended from heaven? What's the purpose of the White Throne Judgment if we go to either heaven or hell upon death, seemingly already judged? Doesn't all mean all? How can God send people to hell for eternity, when He tells us to love our enemies? How can one keep burning in hell for eternity? I mean, once something is turned to ash, it's done…right? Doesn't mercy triumph over judgment? And so on.

As important and searching as those questions might be, our quest for the answer to the Scripture that started it all for us is in 1 Corinthians 3:15 …. "If it is burned up, the builder will suffer loss **but yet will be saved--even though only as one escaping through the flames.**

One day, Lord willing, you too will put your trust in God and stop trusting in men.

To be continued.

CPSIA information can be obtained
at www.ICGtesting.com
Printed in the USA
LVHW011343010819
626156LV00003B/336